WAR LETTERS OF
FALLEN ENGLISHMEN

WAR LETTERS OF
FALLEN ENGLISHMEN

Edited by
Laurence Housman

FOREWORD BY JAY WINTER

Pine St Books

Originally published 1930 by E.P. Dutton & Co., Inc.

First Pine Street Books paperback edition published 2002
Foreword copyright © 2002 University of Pennsylvania Press
All rights reserved
Printed in the United States of America on acid-free paper

10   9   8   7   6   5   4   3   2   1

Pine Street Books is an imprint of
University of Pennsylvania Press
Philadelphia, Pennsylvania 19104-4011

Library of Congress Cataloging-in-Publication Data

War letters of fallen Englishmen / edited by Laurence Housman ; foreword by
    Jay Winter.— 1st Pine Street ed.
        p.   cm.
    Originally published: London : E.P. Dutton, 1930.
    ISBN 0-8122-1815-9 (pbk: alk. paper)
    1. World War, 1914–1918—Personal narratives, English. 2. Soldiers' writings,
English. 3. English letters. I. Housman, Laurence, 1865–1959.
D640 .W3158   2002
940.54'8141—dc21   2002025271

FOREWORD

Jay Winter

THE LEGEND OF THE "LOST GENERATION"

Three quarters of a million British servicemen died in the First World War. Another 250,000 men from the British empire and dominions lost their lives in military service—one out of eight of all who served. Officers suffered the highest casualty rates; junior officers in particular suffered disproportionately heavy losses. Perhaps one in four second lieutenants in the British army died in active service.

Social class position determined military rank in the early days of the war. Men from the upper and upper middle classes were likely to enlist earlier than men of more modest means; elites passed the rudimentary medical examinations at greater rates and joined the officer corps largely because they were deemed the right sort of people to do so. Since officer casualty rates as a whole were about twice as high as those of men in the ranks, it follows that the higher a man was in the social scale in 1914 Britain, the greater his chances of joining the "Lost Generation."[1]

Women nurses died in the war as well, but their place in the narrative of war was secured through contact with male bodies. Most such women were also from privileged families.

A cross section of this social formation wrote the letters collected in this volume. Of the 95 people whose letters are included, 82 were officers. Ten were men who served in the ranks and three were women. Most of these people were educated at the public schools and ancient universities of England. They did not speak for the nation as a whole or for the army as a whole; they spoke for their social class and used the cadences of its vocabulary and its outlook.

The Lost Generation as a whole extended well beyond this relatively privileged population. Roughly 96 percent of the ration strength of the British army in the war was composed of men who were not officers—sergeants, corporals, and tens of thousands of private soldiers. And by 1917 the supply of officers from the upper and the upper middle class had run dry and recruits had to be taken from the commercial classes. Recruitment of officers from working-class populations was a rarity.

Discursive forms do not emerge through democratic processes. By the interwar years, the language associated with the men who died in the war was that of the officers, which is to say, that of a social elite. Their prominence in prose and poetry was partly because they wrote more than did men in the ranks, but partly because what the officers had to say commanded attention, just as did their orders in the army.

There are enduring accounts of the war written by men in the ranks. R. H. Tawney, a Balliol man, refused a commission and served as a sergeant with the Manchester Regiment; his account of being wounded on the first day of the Somme is a classic.[2] George Coppard worked at a London taxidermist's office before joining up as a private in the Machine Gun Corps. His diary was published in 1969.[3] Isaac Rosenberg enlisted in the Suffolk Regiment in 1915; he was killed three years later, but left some of the finest poetry to come out of the war. His letters are among the few written by private soldiers and which are preserved in Laurence Housman's collection, *War Letters of Fallen Englishmen*.

Housman's edition tells the story of the war the officers knew, and this is not at all surprising. The men and women whose letters are collected here were the natural successors to positions of power, influence, and creativity in British society. They were the apprentices, used to taking for granted that in time they would command positions of authority and wealth. That was not to be. The war violated the natural succession of generations; the young would not grow into their fathers' shoes. Consequently, in the interwar years there was a sense of absence, of gaps in the ranks of the social classes who ran the country and the Empire. Second-rate men, it was said, had to do what their betters would have done had they not fallen in Flanders or France.

Here was a demographic explanation for Britain's dismal economic and political record between the wars. The people who could have done better were dead. Certainly, this argument was self-serving; any failure could be accounted for in this way. The vast majority of men who fought came back and took up the threads of their lives again. But legends do not respect statistical realities; they have a life of their own.

WAR BOOKS

This sense of absence, of a future truncated, accounts for the power and appeal of works like Housman's *War Letters of Fallen Englishmen*. But its publication in 1930 took on significance in part because it appeared in the midst of a wave of renewed interest in the war. Between 1928 and 1934 a flood of books about the Great War appearred throughout Western Europe. Some were memoirs, others fiction, still others autobiography faintly disguised as fiction. Many were collections of letters.

Echoing this publishing phenomenon was film. In 1930, the blockbuster of the German publishing industry, and an international best-seller, *All Quiet on the Western Front* by Erich Maria Remarque, was turned into an American film, directed by Lewis Milestone and starring Lew Ayres. It too was a blockbuster, a major commercial success. Featuring American actors speaking in palpably American accents as German soldiers caught up in the war, the film was a pacifist melodrama. Within the genre of war films it was highly unusual. Most cinematic representations of the war were not pacifist. They touched on many themes, from the epic to the comic, but rarely configured the war as pointless butchery, symbolized by the last clip in *All Quiet*, when Paul Baumer in the German trenches reaches for a butterfly and is killed by a sniper. All we see is his outstretched hand, reaching for beauty, quivering and then falling still.

This burst of print and film activity about the Great War highlights many of the contradictions inherent in what historians increasingly term the "memory" of the war, meaning the narratives contemporaries constructed after 1914 to frame the story of their lives and those of their generation. Collections of letters were part of this "memory boom," this attempt to retrieve the voices of the Lost Generation. *War Letters of Fallen Englishmen*, published in 1930 with an introduction by Laurence Housman, is a pacifist document, and yet, like *All Quiet on the Western Front*, Housman's collection of letters shows the ambiguities and limitations of pacifist appeals in the interwar years.

Both Remarque's film and Housman's collection are elegiac, conjuring up a world of lost innocence and promise callously discarded. But they also show the fascination of war as almost irresistible. The market for such publications in the 1930s was not unlike the market for works about the Nazis half a century later: evil and destruction have their attractions, even when they are directly and emphatically denounced.

Here is a central dilemma for pacifists like Housman: how can one inform people about the hideousness of war without attracting them to its excitement and its drama? Guy Chapman put it this way in another of the war books of the period. To him war had a "fascination" and a "power" of an almost erotic kind.

> Once you have lain in her arms you can admit no other mistress. You may loathe, you may execrate, but you cannot deny her. . . . Every writer of imagination who has set down in honesty his experience has confessed it. Even those who hate her most are prisoners to her spell. They rise from her embraces, pillaged, soiled, it may be ashamed; but they are still hers.[4]

Another way of putting the same point is to say that war literature of the twentieth century—extending to poetry, prose, memoirs, letters, and so on—tended to harbor, perhaps unintentionally, some degree of enchantment and an identification with the men who wage it. Well before the Second World War and the death camps further complicated the issue, the curiously ambivalent language of catastrophe exposed this central problem of representation: how do you glorify those who die in war without glorifying war itself?

That perennial question simply refuses to go away. In the interwar years, it was framed in the language of ambivalence. There were positive and negative elements in these accounts of war. They formed odd amalgams, oxymorons like the "soldier pacifists" Siegfried Sassoon and Robert Graves, who both hated war and loved the action in it. This mixture of attitudes and reactions informs many of the letters Housman incorporated in his collection.

There are scores of such published volumes of letters of participants in the Great War. They form a genre of their own—a set of war memorials in cloth binding, frequently the work of relatives or friends. The compilation of these memory books constitutes an act of mourning of a very personal kind, a way of saying that something must be retained of truncated lives. Letter writing is celebrated as a kind of intrinsically personal act, a statement of the ties that bind. Collecting them reinforces those ties, in ways similar to the construction of statues or monuments, or, in Anglo-Saxon countries, the creation of useful sites of memory—hospital wards, scholarships, libraries, even water troughs and cricket pitches. All these are offerings to the dead as well as assistance to the living, and thereby they construct some sense that good can come out of evil, that death on the monumental scale can be transcended.[5]

Books like Housman's are exercises in aesthetic redemption, in their search for and retrieval of beauty from the carnage of war. They are anti-war literature, but they bring out facets of war that help explain its curious allure. The problem remains, though, that in the most fundamental sense these pacifist appeals all failed. The dead have been forgotten, and the war to end all wars didn't do so. Nine years after the publication of Housman's collection of letters, the Nazis invaded Poland and the killing began again in earnest.

The republication of these letters now, seven decades after they first appeared, serves a wider purpose. It enables us to appreciate first the ambiguities and complexities of war literature, and second, the frailties (and the dignities) of the pacifist effort in the first half of the twentieth century.

HOUSMAN

A word or two may be helpful about the man who edited this volume. Laurence Housman was a poet, playwright, and graphic artist, a Victorian figure who lived between 1865 and 1959. He was born a year before Benjamin Disraeli became prime minister and died under Harold Macmillan's very different Conservative government. The son of a prosperous Worcestershire solicitor, Laurence had six brothers and sisters, including his eldest brother Alfred, the classical scholar and poet A. E. Housman.

Laurence Housman's romantic outlook infused all his work. In 1929, the year before his edition of war letters appeared, he declared that "You can't shut out romance from the human heart; you can't shut out wonder. And the romance and wonder of life will always find in Art the instrument to hand. It may all be an illusion, but if it is, so is life."[6] His lifelong spiritual quest similarly described a path of wonder; while an unconventional Christian, he never gave up the idea of an immanent God acting in the world.

Early on he was attracted to Blake's watercolors, and was trained in London's City and Guilds Art School, first in South Lambeth and then in South Kensington. Here he began to experiment in both drawing and in writing, being drawn to fairy tales and other exotic Victorian corners of the fantastic. The impulse behind much of his early work remained in one way or another the quest for divinity, or for a new form in which to house the sacred. He blended classical myths, folk tales, and country yarns in his writing, and he flirted with Roman Catholicism's ritual and aesthetic appeal. Too restless to choose any one denomination, he remained engaged in the search for a spiritual home for the rest of his life.

His first commercial success was less as a writer than as a graphic and book designer. First for Bodley Head and then for Macmillan, Housman created lush, vivid pre-Raphaelite landscapes as book illustrations and covers. With a steady though modest income from these sources, he could turn to the fantasy world of stories. Here his medievalism ran riot, yet again testifying to his preference for what he saw as a vibrant romanticism alive in the Middle Ages and unfortunately superseded by modern society. His was no conventional medievalism, though, and in this romantic iconoclasm he was accompanied by his sister and London companion Clemence Housman. In 1905 she published *The Life of Sir Aglovale de Galis*, a reconfiguration of the Arthurian legend, in which she suggested that Arthur's court broke up "because of his incest and Lancelot's adultery."[7] Visually he was drawn to Dürer, as well as to the woodcut techniques of William Morris and his circle.

It is as a teller of fairy tales that Housman earned the affection of a wide public. Here, in books he illustrated himself, he found his metier and his audience. In works such as *A Farm in Fairyland* (1894) and *The House of Joy* (1895) he created a genre with appeal to many different age groups. The symbolic language of his illustrations attracted a market far beyond that for children's literature without alienating the younger generation and those who bought books to entrance them.

By the turn of the century, Housman had decided to shift his interest to poetry and prose, with an aim of exploring many of the religious and mythical themes addressed in his visual art. But by then he had to cope with the celebrity of his brother, whose collection of poems *A Shropshire Lad* effectively and permanently eclipsed Laurence's own efforts.

Laurence Housman's voice remained distinctive, though, as a critic. He was fortunate in 1895 to gain access as a columnist and reviewer for the *Manchester Guardian* during its great days under the aegis of its legendary editor C. P. Scott. Housman's articles about the arts and cognate subjects secured him a steady income over the next sixteen years. This position also introduced him to a world that brought him in contact with politics of a very unmedieval kind.

That political scene in Manchester was dominated by the Liberal party and its vision of the future. After the turn of the century, Liberals left behind the old notion that the best state is the smallest one possible and created something contemporaries called the "New Liberalism." It was a kind of New Deal before the American New Deal of the 1930s, in that it supported the creation of a safety net of social insurance to catch those who fell off the high wire act of the labor market. It also championed the extension of the franchise to the 50 percent of the male population and 100 percent of the female population without the vote.

Manchester liberalism of the crusading kind presented Housman with an entree into social politics in general and campaigns surrounding two central issues in particular: women's suffrage and peace. The issue of votes for women was a cause Housman came to champion around 1910, when—as he disarmingly put it—he suddenly discovered that he had "that most uncomfortable of things, a social conscience."[8] He was one of the founders of the Men's League for Women's Suffrage and a defender of militant protest, including symbolic violence of the kind associated with breaking windows in Whitehall. If that were the only way to let the air of freedom into these corridors, then so be it, was his point of view. Housman designed banners for the movement, spoke at public meetings, and tried hard to get himself thrown into prison as a protestor. He failed, though his sister Clemence succeeded.[9]

Similarly iconoclastic was his work for the British Society for the Study of Sex Psychology, founded on 8 July 1914 to promote the "unprejudiced and thorough investigation of sexual divergences from average habits and standards." Together with Edward Carpenter, Housman wanted to provide a home for people interested in the new science of psychoanalysis, as well as those working for reform on the subjects of divorce, prostitution, and venereal disease. His aim was social analysis rather than moral judgment, and he saw the recognition of the significance of sexual questions as one of the happy outcomes of the women's suffrage movement.[10]

The outbreak of war in 1914 set aside all these issues—including women's suffrage—and brought to the fore entirely different matters that became central to Housman's work and life. He claimed that he was not a pacifist at the outbreak of the war but took on a pacifist position as the war dragged on and on.[11] Here too he was following the tide of Manchester liberalism, which had the same insularity of perspective as did most of British society at the time. Foreign affairs just did not matter to a country with the strongest navy in the world. That privileged position came abruptly to an end in 1914, and so did the secure world in which Housman had been raised.

One task Housman took on early in the war was helping to manage a home for Belgian refugees in West London. Over one million such people had fled the fighting, and the position of those who reached London was far from easy. Housman learned that not all refugees are saints. He shared the gloom of the war years, and took heart only at the news that the Czar had been overthrown. Whatever good might have come out of the war, though, was thrown away, he believed, in the Paris peace conference of 1919.

This trajectory from innocence to bitterness about the war and its consequences is characteristic of British liberalism as a whole. In this respect Housman shared the same sense of catastrophe that afflicted liberals like Scott of the *Manchester Guardian* and two Cambridge figures, the humanist scholar G. Lowes Dickinson and the economist John Maynard Keynes. Dickinson formulated many arguments for a League of Nations, arguments Housman came to propound in later years. And Keynes's vitriolic lectures at Cambridge in 1919, after he had resigned from the British delegation to the Paris peace conference, said much that Housman took to be true about the disastrous nature of the peace settlement of 1919.

To be against a Carthaginian peace and for a League of Nations made sense to a romantic ecumenical Christian artist like Housman. The problem remained, though, that such a position became more and more precarious over time. It is as if prewar liberalism and converts like Housman had wandered into another, harsher world. It is no accident that the Labour party displaced the Liberals as the alternative party of government in the interwar years. It was not only that the Liberal party suffered the consequences of fratricide between the Lloyd George camp and the Asquith camp, but the very heart of liberalism—a preference for a small state and a pacific foreign policy—seemed to beat to the tempo of another age. The 1920s and 1930s were altogether darker than the world Housman had come to know when he worked as an artist in London at the end of the nineteenth century. Two decades later, in the period of the world war, just as he made international Liberalism his crusade, domestic Liberalism wandered into the political wilderness, from which it did not emerge in his lifetime (or ours).

In editing *War Letters of Fallen Englishmen* in 1930, Housman was striking an elegiac note not only for the individuals who had died in the war, and whose letters had been preserved, but also for the world they had died to defend. The crushing irony was that to win the war, much had to be sacrificed, to preserve which these men had joined the army in the first place. What else is meant by a pyrrhic victory?

By the time this edition of letters had appeared, Housman was fully installed as a major figure of English letters. This time his celebrity grew out of his stage plays, and in particular his series of plays about Victorian figures, *Angels and Ministers*, as well as his forty-five "little plays" on religious themes. If his politics had entered the twentieth century, his stagecraft was firmly and uncompromisingly prewar.

This ambivalence about how much of the prewar world was left marked much of interwar British cultural life. The commemorative moment that followed the war was inscribed in prewar formal language derived from the classical, romantic, or religious traditions. Looking backward was unavoidable for those who sought a language in which to express their sense of loss.[12] And in Housman's collection of letters of men and women who did not return from the war, looking backward had a distinctly spiritual tinge to it.

THE SEARCH FOR THE SACRED

Housman did not specify the process whereby he selected the letters in the collection. Clearly he consulted the families and friends of those who had died, but there is little indication as to what criteria he used for inclusion or exclusion. There is, though, a similarity between the tone of many of the letters and some of the aesthetic and spiritual interests that marked Housman's work and life.

The reader of this collection cannot miss the powerful religious current in the words of these men and women. Consider the words of John Hugh Allen, a lieutenant in the Worcestershire Regiment, who was killed at Gallipoli on 6 June 1915 at age twenty-eight. Nine days before he died, he wrote a letter to his family in New Zealand about the suffering of wounded men. A man he had hardly gotten to know was severely wounded, and Allen tried to comfort him:

"Shall I go to heaven or hell, sir?" I said with perfect confidence: "To heaven." He said: "No, tell me as man to man." I repeated what I had said. He said "At any rate I'll say my prayers," and I heard him murmuring the common meal grace. A little later he made up a quite beautiful prayer—"Oh, God, be good and ease my pain—if only a little." (27)

Major Sidney Harold Baker, killed in France in 1918, helped one of his wounded men get back from a slimy mud crater to the British lines. In November 1917 he wrote to his brother about the incident and remarked, "We both agreed out there that God would help us somehow, and why should He not?" (35). Why not indeed.

"I don't know what you feel about what is called—with a sort of semi-aversion—religion," Lieutenant Christian Cresell Carver asked his brother in November 1916:

I find, in this sort of job, that I have to pray, and pray good and hard, otherwise one could not keep going. One must look up, and the God one looks up to is a God of Hope, and the Kingdom, a Kingdom of Light and happiness. Consciously or unconsciously, one always pictures Heaven, and I always find myself apt to slip into an idea of a sanctified place, with harps and wings and things floating about, illuminated by a sort of incandescent white light. But when you are struggling along, through foot-deep sticky mud, and there are shells bursting on the path in front of you, and corpses lying about, then when you pray, you think of all the happiness and beauty you have ever known, and get a closer conception. (67)

Conventionally steadfast was Lieutenant John Sherwin Engall, killed on the first day of the Battle of the Somme at age twenty-eight, whose last letter to his parents spoke of his having taken Communion, and having accepted that "should it be God's holy will to call me away, I am quite prepared to go" (107). Private Roger Marshall Livingstone serving with the Canadian Expeditionary Force believed that the men who died for the cause were martyrs in the same "cause for which Christ laid down His life" (176). Lieutenant Charles Stiebel died in

Mesopotamia in February 1917. In his knapsack was a letter to his wife affirming that "the love of God and the pure love of one another are one and the same thing," and urging his wife, should he die, to remarry: "If there was some one good and true and strong to support you, I should be glad" (267).

Faith and compassion of this kind were rare enough, in or out of the army. Certainly, many men had their faith challenged more severely than Stiebel's, but even so it is the struggle to retain some belief in God that is most striking in the language of the letter writers in Housman's edition. Lieutenant Peter Clement Layard was killed in France in August 1918. He had survived three years of combat; his belief in God was sorely tried: "Any faith in religion I ever had is most frightfully shaken by things I've seen," he wrote to his parents in March 1916, "and it's incredible that if God could make a 17-inch shell not explode—it seems incredible that he lets them explode; and yet on the other hand" (171).

And yet, on the other hand—that is where Housman stands. Not as a true believer, but as someone admiring those struggling with these issues. Many of them describe how their daily encounter with death brought both a stoicism and to some even a degree of calm. It is a state of mind they hoped their loved ones would share should they not survive the war. Captain Thomas Michael Kettle, Professor of National Economics at the National University, Dublin, died in September 1916. A few weeks before his death on the Somme, he wrote to his wife that, if God did not spare him, "I know now in my heart that for anyone who is dead but has loved enough, there is provided some way of piercing the veils of death and abiding close to those whom he has loved till that end which is the beginning" (167). Lieutenant Denis Oliver Barnett, who never made it to Balliol College, Oxford, but died in Flanders at the age of twenty in 1915, wrote to his mother these words: "I've looked at death pretty closely and I know what it is. A man is called away in a moment and goes before God" (40).

We must bear in mind that these men are writing for a particular public—their own families or close friends—and few if any had the slightest idea that their letters would be published. These letters indicate, though, that the men who served were in no sense blind followers of the national cause. Dissent, too, is one of the central motifs of this collection, and it is dissent with the moral authority of those who had put their lives on the line and had died in the effort. What better backing could there be for interwar pacifism than the sentiments in many of these letters?

There is anger here at the stupidity of war, so shocking to those deeply marked by pity for the suffering they had seen. Lieutenant Christian Creswell Carver mused to his brother in 1916 that "I sometimes think that war is <u>all</u> criminal folly, and that the excuse that we were forced into it does not excuse us. That we ought to have foreseen and taken measures to prevent it" (65). Lieutenant Horace William Fletcher wrote to his mother of his hope that "the mind of the Church—that great intangible authority—may be led by the Holy Spirit and guided by His power, to stop war henceforward? We know God can do it, that He waits for our co-operation" (109).

Lieutenant Melville Hastings, a Canadian schoolmaster who died in 1918, had a more domestic view of divinity, when a year before his death he wrote to the headmaster of Wycliffe College and observed that heaven could be found "largely in thinking of mothers and wives and children and other things that are thus beautiful." "Hell," he wrote, "consists largely in thinking of our own nastiness." In this regard, he was emphatic about the ephemeral nature of national differences:

German food and British food, examine them closely, they are the same. The same in terms of stomach, of ears, of eyes or of the immortal soul. A week since I was lying out in no man's land. A little German dog trotted up and licked my British face. I pulled his German ears and stroked his German back. He wagged his German tail. My little friend abolished no man's land, and so in time can we. (123–24)

"It is the soldiers who will be the good Pacifists" after the war, Sergeant-Major Frederic Hillersdon Keeling wrote in 1915. "I will not hate Germans to the order of any bloody politician, and the first thing I shall do after I am free will be to go to Germany and create all the ties I can with German life" (161). He died in the

Battle of the Somme eight months later. Captain Kettle had a similar plan. "If I live I mean to spend the rest of my life working for perpetual peace. I have seen war and faced modern artillery, and know what an outrage it is against simple men" (168).

Many of the writers whose letters were collected by Housman dreamed of a world opposed to the landscape of war, one in which ugliness did not prevail. Some found in traces of pastoral beauty the evidence they needed that the world from which they had come had not completely vanished. Others found in small acts of kindness—to their own wounded or to enemy wounded—hints that the callousness needed to survive the hardships of the trenches was only surface-deep. Captain Arthur Innes Adam, killed in September 1916, wrote to his sister from an uncontaminated corner of northern France that "At times I almost wish this spot were not so good—it gives me a fierce feeling of hatred of the present bondage that is hardly to be borne." His hope was that in the fall or winter of 1916 Germany would crack and then he could come home "and the true business of life will begin—to teach men the beauty of the hill-sides and the loathliness of the body and the lusts thereof" (22)

Adam never made it home, nor did any of the other men and women whose letters are collected here. But in their letters they wrote their own epitaphs. To bring these images of decency home to the survivors was clearly one of Housman's aims in producing this volume.

In short, Housman looked for spirituality, for a sense of beauty, and for a kind of courtesy and kindness that embodied what he took to be the best of the men who had gone to war in 1914. Reading these letters today, nearly a century after they were written, brings home the shriveling of hope, the loss of talent the Great War brought in its wake.

THE USES OF MEMORY

This book's intent is unmistakably pacifist, and as a cri de coeur it resembles much pacifist sentiment in the interwar years. The emotional content of this body of opinion is both its strength and its weakness. But the problem remained and remains today that to mourn those who die in war has never been an effective way of preventing its recurrence. By the time this book was published, the Japanese were already embarked on their conquest of China, and the world economic crisis was tearing down the rickety supports that underpinned the Weimar Republic. Hitler too mourned the dead of the war, but he did so in the view that it was time to finish the job that they were unable to complete. By 1933 a different "memory" of war underlay the new Nazi regime.

I raise this issue not to criticize Housman and the men and women like him who affirmed their belief in a set of values that were incompatible with the harsh turn of world affairs in the 1930s. The point is rather that this volume describes a kind of pacifism that has mourning as its central pillar; these pacifists formulated what might be termed a politics of bereavement. And as such it had very little purchase, either in the 1930s or today.

In addition, their condemnation of war by reference to the language of the men who fought between 1914 and 1918 contained complex and ambivalent messages. Housman's edition shows that the men who fought saw war in both a positive and a negative light. Most of those whose letters appear here were volunteers: they chose to go to war, though the one they fought was remote from the one they had imagined in 1914.

In this volume of individual responses to the tragedy of the Great War, there is much of what Samuel Hynes has aptly called "the soldiers' tale."[13] There is in this kind of writing a sense of adventure and more than a hint of the uncanny. These men saw ordinary and extraordinary things side by side. They lived years in a few moments and saw things they never dreamed they would see. What they showed in these letters was a world attractive and repulsive at one and the same time. It is this deep ambiguity in the message they left behind that make these letters uncomfortable reading for pacifists and conventional patriots alike.

Housman was well aware that mourning alone could never be a moral equivalent, or rather a moral alternative, to war. Some political project had to be advanced as a way of regulating or containing political and social conflict. In the interwar years these projects focused on disarmament, by and large through the

League of Nations, of which Housman was an enthusiastic supporter. The British pacifist movement was another venue for his beliefs. He was a close friend of Dick Sheppard, who had served as a chaplain in the Great War and who later became Canon of St. Paul's. In 1934 Sheppard wrote a letter to the *Manchester Guardian*, inviting responses by postcard from those who were prepared to renounce war and never again to support another. In a few weeks, 30,000 people had responded to the call; the organization that grew out of these sentiments was the Peace Pledge Union. These voices echoed those which had carried the motion in the Oxford Union Society a year before that "they will in no circumstances fight for King and Country."[14]

Housman knew that this affirmation was unlikely to stand the test of time. On 6 February 1933 he wrote to Sheppard about a meeting at which he had spoken in the west of England. Many young people there were "quite enthusiastically sceptical about the good of war." But, he mused, "I wonder would they hold out if war came? I doubt it. 'Call of King and Country' would then once more atrophy conscience, and abolish common sense."[15]

Housman's was the kind of pacifism that saw war as unthinkable and yet just around the corner.[16] That sense of doom made the effort to rally public opinion all the more important, and all the more futile. This Quixotic stance helps us to understand what the politics of bereavement meant: it was a cry of anguish and anger rather than a blueprint for an alternative future. If it must be concluded that Housman did not find the answer to the question as to how to outlaw war, the same is true for his entire generation.

Lest we think this is a matter for the 1930s alone, it is useful to extend this set of reflections to our own days. Charles Maier has written of what he terms "a surfeit of memory" in recent years,[17] and he has a point. There is a kind of "memory boom" underway today, in part a response to the Holocaust, in part a more general phenomenon.[18] The republication of this volume of letters is in itself a contribution to the "memory boom." There is indeed an active market for writings about traumatic events, and the disaster of 11 September 2001 is unlikely to alter the trend. Memory, we are told, is a duty. It also sells. But in political terms it is important to note how unlikely it is that remembering the victims of war will help outlaw or civilize it. The veterans of the First World War also said "never again," and never lasted twenty years.

Memory can be seductive; it can serve to steel the resolve or to yield a kind of romantic displacement in which politics dissolves in an emotional haze. Housman's letters present a challenge to us, therefore, one of which he was aware. It is how to evoke memory or use memory without spiritualizing it.

In the introduction to the book, Housman wrote of the war memorial to the dead of the Great War, the Cenotaph in London, as made up of blocks of stone that can speak to us. This is of course a metaphor, but it is one used by many other commentators to locate memory in objects—letters, or bricks, or other physical objects. The ruins of the World Trade Center in Manhattan have been the focus of similar remarks. This position brings us to the central issue. Both Housman in the 1930s and many in our own time want to use "memory" to let the dead speak to us, and thereby to restore a sense of the sacred in those shaken by the harshness of the world in which they live.

Housman's *Letters*, therefore, bear rereading today for a host of reasons. They offer us a glimpse of what was lost in the Great War, a taste for the language of decency and romance that the men who fought used in their own letters, and a sense of the deep knowledge civilians had of what the soldiers were going through. Soldiers did not live in a world apart: they shared the same aspirations and cadences as did those who remained behind.

These letters also open up the world of interwar pacifism. We see here the urgency of the task they faced of making war unthinkable. The paradox is that these letters show war to be very "thinkable" indeed. In that sense, they expose the deep contradictions in what might be termed cultural pacifism—the use of the language and gestures of the fallen to describe the way war impoverishes us all. Letters are indeed a trigger of memory, but they are not the stuff out of which a moral equivalent to war has emerged.

1. For a full discussion, see J. M. Winter, *The Great War and the British People* (Cambridge, Mass.: Harvard University Press, 1985).

2. R. H. Tawney, *The Attack and Other Essays* (London: Allen and Unwin, 1929).

3. George Coppard, *With a Machine Gun to Cambrai: The Tale of a Young Tommy in Kitchener's Army, 1914–1918* (London: HMSO, 1969).

4. Guy Chapman, *A Passionate Prodigality* (London: Nicolson and Watson, 1933), cited in Winter, *The Great War and the British People*, 292.

5. See Jay Winter and Emmanuel Sivan, eds., *War and Remembrance in the Twentieth Century* (Cambridge: Cambridge University Press, 1999), chaps. 1, 2, 8.

6. Laurence Housman, "Pre-Raphaelitism in Art and Poetry," *Essays by Divers Hands* (1933): 29, as cited in Rodney Engen, *Laurence Housman* (Stroud: Catalpa Press, 1983).

7. Clemence Houseman, *The Life of Aglovale de Galis* (London: Methuen, 1905), cited in Engen, *Housman*, 59.

8. Laurence Housman, *The Unexpected Years* (Indianapolis: Bobbs-Merrill, 1936), 223.

9. Housman, *Unexpected Years*, 239.

10. F. W. Stella Browne, "A New Psychological Society," *International Journal of Ethics* 28 (1917/18): 6–9.

11. Housman, *Unexpected Years*, 250.

12. Jay Winter, *Sites of Memory, Sites of Mourning: The Great War in European Cultural History* (Cambridge: Cambridge University Press, 1995).

13. Samuel Lynn Hynes, *The Soldiers' Tale: Bearing Witness to Modern War* (New York: Penguin, 1995).

14. See Martin Ceadel, *Pacifism in Britain, 1914–1945: The Defining of a Faith* (Oxford: Clarendon Press, 1980).

15. Laurence Housman, ed., *What I Believe? Letters Exchanged Between Dick Sheppard and L.H.* (London: Religious Book Club, 1939), 203.

16. For French parallels, see Antoine Prost, *French Identities in War and Peace* (Oxford: Berg, 2002), chap. 4.

17. Charles S. Maier, "A Surfeit of Memory? Reflections on History, Melancholy and Denial," *History & Memory* (1993): 136–51.

18. Jay Winter, "The Generation of Memory: Reflections on the 'Memory Boom' in Contemporary Historical Studies," *Bulletin of the German Historical Institute* 27 (Fall 2000): 69–92.

INTRODUCTION

A block of stone, with hanging flags, stands in the centre of a London street—the very design suggestive of the silence which has fallen on the most continuously devastating conflict that the history of man has ever known. On it only a few words; but because of what it stands for, even now, twelve years after the event, thousands salute as they pass daily.

That memorial, composed of a few hundred stones, represents over a million dead. And could each stone have a voice proportionate to the whole, it would cry out for a thousand lives laid down, with the hope held, or with the hope lost, that war might be no more.

But even among those stones there would be a divergent minority : a few, just a few, would cry that war in itself is a fine thing and worth while. They, and they only who have been through it, have the right to say so, and to be heard—not with agreement, but with respect.

Here, in these war-letters, the Cenotaph finds its two voices : the voice of a majority, the voice of a minority. A large majority, though firmly convinced that what they do is right—or right in the sense that it is inevitable—show their detestation of war in its operation. Yet some of these express the keen satisfaction it gives them as an individual experience—mainly as a test of themselves, of their power to conquer fear, to live at the full push of their energies, mental and physical. To them, individually, active warfare gives life a fuller expression ; for it is a life lived daily in the power to face death.

Nobody can say that, for the individual, there is anything in that standpoint unworthy of noble minds. It led to great deeds of courage, tenderness, self-sacrifice. It produced some of the finest war-poems—the poems of Rupert Brooke and Julian Grenfell—the former a theoretical acceptance of war as a good thing; the latter a practical acceptance, after trial. At the back of both stands the conviction that, in this self-realisation, they are serving the cause of their country, which they believe also to be the cause of humanity.

But alongside of this standpoint there are others equally worthy of respect—representative of other types of mind and character, of men who are not born fighters, men who have had a hard struggle to conquer their individual fears, temperaments, and disgusts, and have not come through with elation, or even with conviction. In some of these letters is the cry of a violated conscience, or at least of poignant doubt. In many—in some of the best—is the record of a diminishing hope : of men who went into the war with ideals, from which the reality (military and political combined) slowly crushed out the life.

Many of us, looking at the world to-day, will hold that those lost hopes came nearer to the truth, as to the practical outcome of war, than the high elated expectation with which so many went into it.

But though the mind of the age is divided as to what war can or cannot do, few who read these letters will differ as to the high qualities of human nature, amazing in their beauty of staunchness, endurance, and tenderness, which the war tested and proved.

One of these letter-writers describes war as a thing of contradictions, full of beastliness, brutality, and many other things, a misery to mind and body, yet of fineness as well. But that fineness is not of war, but of the human nature whose strong quality it tries out and reveals. To attribute any nobility to war itself is as much a confusion of thought as to attribute nobility to cancer or leprosy, because of the skill, devotion, and self-sacrifice of those who give up their lives to its cure, or because of the patient endurance of the sufferers. And this confusion of thought will be found in some of the writers of these letters. One—pre-eminently of the fighting class—writes that he " adores war " ; yet in the same letter he speaks of the hopeless misery inflicted by war on non-combatants ; he writes that you never love your fellow-man so well as when you are out to kill him : yet tells later, when prisoners are taken, how " one felt hatred for them as one thought of our dead." But the story does not end there : human nature nobly contradicts itself, and reaches truth. He meets face to face a man as noble as himself, one of the enemy ; tries to hate him and fails. The man salutes him. " It made me feel terribly ashamed."

What such men find " adorable " in war is the tremendous test to which it puts all their powers, moral and physical ; and so long as they can believe that the instrument by which they are tested can produce good results, commensurate to the accompanying horrors, war does not violate their conscience. That is a matter for the individual alone : it does not make war " fine."

These letters contain darker records of what war and obedience to authority require, not merely of a man's hand, but of his soul. Some of the most horrible things are told almost without comment ; their reticence is eloquent. In one letter we read how a Winchester boy—almost a boy still—officer in a famous Highland regiment, goes out with a small bombing party to clear an enemy's trench. The bombs are gas-bombs ; and as the suffocating and helpless Germans emerge from the ground, they are all bayoneted —not on impulse, but on definite instructions from above, because men cannot be spared to take prisoners to the rear.

That was one of our " military necessities " which were kept from our knowledge during the war ; it was the sort of thing which was then supposed only to be done by Germans. It is well that we should be told of them now, for that truly is war. It is doubly well that the telling should be by men who died in war, accepting the dishonour it imposed on them as part of the sacrifice they must make while war remained the chosen instrument of their country's good.

But is that terrible acceptance still to be accepted by us

who have not to do the horrible thing ourselves, but only ask that it shall be done for us ? If such letters bring home to us the dishonour vicariously borne by men of noble character, who went into active service believing that war would call on them to do only honourable things, they will teach better wisdom to the race than those, of the more popular kind, which extol the " fineness " of war because of the appeal which, in certain of its aspects, it makes to the adventurous courage of youth. To insist upon the truth that war is a beastliness and a blunder is not to detract from the high heroism with which the beastliness and the blunder were faced. It is right that human nature should be able to feel a fearful sort of joy when—put to the hardest task—it finds it has not failed. But all that nobility of courage—of the will to face death—which war brings out, does not make war a noble thing, does not make it more tolerable as an accepted means to high ends, any more than the perfect death of Christ upon the cross made crucifixion itself anything but a wickedly invented device for the punishing of criminals.

People deceive their consciences who think that the heroism of the men who faced out the horrors of war makes war itself less horrible, less brutal, less of a blunder. But with the baseness of war firmly fixed in our minds, what worth, what unexpected qualities in average human nature we see revealed against the darker background, made more prominent by the ugliness of their surroundings. The things here seen are not all of one kind ; and often, in their abnormal setting, their values become changed. Kindness to a dog, for instance, is a small thing, and we think little of it ; but in the account here given of the great charge at Thiepval, does it not catch one by the throat, that incident of the dog running out from the German lines, and of the man who, with comrades falling round him, stooped down and fondled it, and ran on, to be himself perhaps in another moment one of the dead ? Or take that other incident of the two Irishmen, having a private quarrel of their own, who leapt out of their trench and fought in the open, with the

German enemy cheering them on. Under such circumstances that fight goes up into the Heavens, a deed of unrepentant sinners fit to make angels rejoice. Here too we read, from one who took part in it, the account at once so humorous and pathetic of the Christmas Truce, which—winked at and condoned, in its first occurrence—was adjudged too dangerous for repetition, and so in the second year was not allowed.

These touches from life on its lighter side have here a moving beauty, coming with a difference across that face of storm.

War is an emergency ; and in emergency human nature can be very wonderful—but also unexpected, not uniform. Amid the pressure of the emergency many phases arise, which all have their wonderfulness, yet may be almost contraries. For into this pit of destruction go all kinds, the clean and the unclean together, there to become more alike, or more different, as the case may be. None who has not been through it can know of the affinities between things honoured and despised which war reveals : and the charity toward human weakness of the fighting man, is often greater and of more understanding than the charity of the man who stays at home.

Courage itself is an enigma ; it is not a simple virtue, for it does not come to all alike. Men achieve it differently. The man who is afraid of being afraid, the man who feels fear and shows it, but carries on ; the man who feels fear and can hide it ; the man who does not feel fear : all alike have the gift or grace of courage in them ; but how differently it may act on their souls, coming to some easily as an instinct, to others as a hardly won escape from bitter temptation—sometimes only achieved at so great a strain that, in the end, they break. There is the further thought, unwelcome to some, that the man who falls to cowardice cannot always help himself : it may be a weakness lying beyond his nature to control.

Of the strengths and weaknesses of human nature, the war must have brought to many young minds a deeper experience and understanding than those outside can share or realise. Many must have had friends whose courage failed, and yet loved them, having a wiser pity for them than the contemptuous ignorant ones who sat in easy judgment at home.

A young man known to the present writer—utterly unfitted for war—of a temperament too highly strung, an artist, gifted with a wonderful voice—went into it, having no escape, war gave him no alternative. His muscles were sufficiently fit to pass the test ; psychology did not count. He went out to the war in anguish of mind, just managed not to run away—got shot. A letter of his exists which cannot be printed here ; it is too agonising a confession of weakness ; but he too is dead, and was not shot as a deserter. And he— or one like him—may be the " Unknown Warrior " lying in Westminster Abbey. That representative of all the dead need not be a man who was specially brave, or brave at all in the accepted sense, but just one who managed to die at his post.

The agnosticism imposed on us by that memorial is good medicine. The million of our own countrymen who died in the war were not all brave, nor were they all willing to make that sacrifice which war required of them. They were not all lovers of war, or believers in war. In the four years while it lasted, many of them learned to hate war, from having known it, as they could not have hated it before. And they—those who so tasted war, and in their souls turned from it with loathing, not believing in it any more— have as much right to be remembered, and to claim that the Cenotaph is *their* memorial also, as those who died more happily, accepting war as a means and believing that good might somehow come of it.

The Cenotaph is a silent memorial of those it stands for. These letters are a memorial that speaks, and that speaks truth. And though they speak of willingness and courage, and devotion, poured out with a generosity and a faith that put to shame the feeble efforts we have made since then for the restoration of world-peace, they speak also of disillusion and doubt, and a growing distrust of war as an instrument for bringing to pass any good commensurate with so huge a sacrifice of body and of soul. There is a notable difference between the earlier and the later letters. As the war went on, its quality changed, and the exceeding wastefulness came more and more home to those whose lives it was wasting. But though that is the note which more and more emerges, no preference has been given, in the selection of these letters, to any one standpoint. Quality, or some special circumstance, has been the deciding factor. A few letters, very simple in expression, left to be read after death, have been given for that special reason. But every one of these letters are letters which only come to be read now because the men and the women who wrote them died while on active service.

I wish here to record my very special thanks to all those friends and relatives of the fallen, whose generous contribution of letters has made this selection possible. Very many had to go back unused for lack of space ; and if, after their kindness, those who sent them feel disappointment that their letters were not included, I can only beg them to believe that their sending has helped to make this selection more varied, and more representative of that great generation of lives, full of the hope and promise of youth, which the wastefulness of war has carried away.

In the title of this volume, " Englishmen " is used in the widest sense, as applied to soldiers from all parts of the British Isles and the Overseas Dominions (and in at least one case from the United States) who fought under the British flag. Many of the letters, including some of the most notable, are by writers whom it is not strictly correct to describe as Englishmen. But all spoke the English language as their native tongue ; and if " Englishmen " has been loosely used, it is only for lack of a more comprehensive word.

LAURENCE HOUSMAN.

ACKNOWLEDGMENTS

In addition to the relatives and friends of the fallen, to whom I have already expressed my gratitude, I desire to acknowledge my indebtedness to the publishers, editors, literary executors, and others, by whose courtesy I am permitted to include the letters mentioned against their names in the Table of Contents. I desire also to acknowledge the valuable assistance I have received from many quarters in the selection of the unpublished or privately printed letters which form a large proportion of the whole. Among those to whom I am particularly indebted in this connection are the authorities of a large number of schools, colleges, and other institutions ; the Imperial War Graves Commission ; Mr. H. Foster and Mr. L. P. Y. Smith, of the Imperial War Museum Library ; the Master of Balliol, Mr. F. F. Urquhart of Balliol, the Headmaster of Wycliffe College, and the Headmaster of the Dragon School, Oxford. To all of them I tender my grateful thanks. I must also mention my very special indebtedness to Mr. Leonard Stein, without whose untiring help I should have found the work of selection and editing quite impossible.

L. H.

CAPTAIN ARTHUR INNES ADAM
Cambridgeshire Regiment

Educated Winchester and Balliol College, Oxford (scholar). Joined Army while an undergraduate. Wounded and missing, France, 16 September, 1916, at the age of 22.

[France]
[To His Sister] *July 9th [1916]*

To feel the wind blowing from the sea ; to be able to walk and run among real villages with decent folk to wish you good-morning ; to sit on the top of a hill and see for miles around the sea on one side and flourishing farmsteads and woodlands on the other—to find the old spring returning to my legs and the old joy of solitude and fast walking without any object save to see as much as possible of the beauty of God's world—these are what my good fortune brings me to-day ; and this rhapsodical balderdash is only the natural froth of a mind bubbling with the beauty of an extraordinary fine day whose happiness can be enjoyed unlimitedly.

It is Sunday ; and there is nothing to bother us—no ridiculous military precision to interfere—and France is a big country, wherein it is possible even for a soldier to get far enough away from his kind to be able to unbutton his coat and look untidy. . . . There are times when the deadening nature of the instruction . . . becomes quite appalling. . . . But Saturday and Sunday we have alone : yesterday afternoon I was in Boulogne, whence I walked back with a man called Pearson—a master at St. Paul's and a tremendous runner : so we walked as if the world depended thereon . . . partly on the cliff, partly on the wonderful sand, and this after a tea of patisserie, strawberries and ices.

Then this morning after a late breakfast I have wandered out alone, with Homer, a novel, a pair of bathing-drawers and a small amount of paper. I have wandered for an hour or two and find myself now not far off Etaples on the top of a rolling hill, whence you see countless other such hills and the sea opposite to them. It is a day when even the ugliest muck-heap would look splendid, and this is a gorgeous country ; I believe one would think so in times even of peace : inland there are woods and flowers, everywhere there is corn, and usually it is filled with the reddest of poppies ; and one can find villages too where the hand of the Englishman has not penetrated with its usually vulgar effect ; the military Englishman I mean. . . .

At times I almost wish this spot were not so good—it gives me a fierce feeling of hatred of the present bondage that is hardly to be borne—and there are times on parade when it seems impossible to do what one is told. So I probably shall be badly sat on before long, for general slackness, but . . . sometimes . . . you begin to sympathise with the socialist who wants to revolt against any and every thing. Then too England is so absurdly near, and I long to see and to bathe with more congenial company than one finds here.

But it isn't any good to enlarge on these things, and it is clear that a world so utterly awry as this is but a passing stage of existence ; so one can keep an interest in life ; and I still believe this is to last but for a season.

And in my case, while the Battle of the Somme is still going on it is selfish to talk like this at all. That show, as you may guess, has not gone entirely right. . . . None the less . . . one may still hope that Germany will crack before the winter. Then maybe I shall come home, and the true business of life will begin—to teach men the beauty of the hill-sides and the loathliness of the body and the lusts thereof.

Good-bye. . . . I do wish you were here.

―――――

LIEUTENANT JOHN HUGH ALLEN
Worcestershire Regiment

Educated Wanganui College, New Zealand, and Jesus College, Cambridge. Bar student. Associated with " *Round Table* " Group. Killed in action, Gallipoli, 6 June, 1915, at the age of 28.

Transport *Orsova*,
[To His Father] [en route for Gallipoli]
My Dear Father, *May 12th,* [*1915*]

A number of regiments sent out to South Africa to fight the Boers were insufficiently trained. They had four months or so in barracks, but many of them had never fought an outpost or advance action. In this war of course training has been much more thorough. For the men no doubt it has been sufficient, but six months is too short to make an officer. . . .

I thought it was impossible to make officers without years of training. But I found the Inns of Court proposed to do it, and I joined them and began training in London. . . .

I remember those autumn mornings so well. One came up out of the tube lift and stood about outside Stone Buildings in Lincoln's Inn, talking or reading the paper. Only a few months before, *The Times* had fallen to a penny, and we all read it. Occasionally one saw an officer who had been commissioned and who was going off to join his unit. What a wonderful creature we thought him !

On wet mornings we had an hour's lecture from the Adjutant in the old hall at Lincoln's Inn. It is in the place where, a few weeks before, I heard the results of the Bar exams announced. Rainsford Hannay of the Queen's lectured well. We drank in every word—so strange it all seemed then, so familiar now. Sometimes he talked of attractive things, such as what an officer does when he joins his unit. I hadn't the glimmer of a notion. As a consequence of his advice, I carried a dinner-jacket and a suit of mufti to the Point, but I never wore them there or at Looe. At other times he spoke about feet inspections, or orderly room, or things more military. He told us to keep on the lee-side of men's feet. I couldn't figure myself inspecting soldiers' feet. The last time I did it was a week or more before I left Looe. I looked upon it without emotion as pure routine. Then there was a Major whose lectures were dull, and who blew a whistle before he began. We took exception to his blowing a whistle and to his dullness. A young man called Lefroy, who had had to leave Woolwich with a bad knee, and who later on got a commission in the Inns of Court, lectured on musketry. I used to marvel at his knowledge and precocity : he knew all about a rifle. . . .

At that stage the parades were voluntary, but I don't think I missed any. There was always a chance that Warner might appear and tell you he had a commission for you. But in those days the prospect of that seemed most remote. We were dismissed at tea-time, and found our way into a convenient Lyons, after which I would go to the Colonial Institute and read Trevelyan's *Life of Bright*. I selected that because author, subject, and period were equally removed from the obsessions of war. And in the evening end I would mount a bus and ride through the Haymarket, Piccadilly Circus, Regent Street, and Oxford Street, to the Marble Arch. The newspaper placards, the recruiting notices, and an unwonted number of figures in khaki, were the only visible comments on the giant grapple of steel and souls less than a hundred miles away. In the light of that, one's successes at drill didn't seem much. But one was at least making a beginning. From the first it was a mental comfort and stimulation to be an insider and not an outsider. For the latter the more delightful or beautiful a play, a person, or a piece of music, the greater the reproach its splendour would convey. I couldn't have looked or listened if I had missed my chance. . . . I came to London in a Dick Whittington spirit, set upon learning above all things to speak. I spared no pains to learn how to do that. I routed out a little ex-actor, who gave me lessons at the Men's College at Mornington Crescent. I did in over-measure the exercises he set me. I made long, uncomfortable journeys about

London to hear great speakers ; and, I am afraid, chiefly for this reason, I went to church regularly on Sundays and even on week-days. Conscience-stricken, I played truant from chambers to sit in the gallery of the House of Commons. I was always tempted to ignore ——'s cases on the chance of hearing a great counsel. The theatre attracted me because speaking there was carried to its most elaborate—for my purpose too elaborate—art. . . . I wanted to know how it was done, and do it—how I wanted to do it ! You figure me on London pavements, in the bare country-side, on a rock on a Brittany beach, imitating, copying, and imitating again, those masters of the human voice—never for a moment was my discipleship anything but a pleasure. I wanted to be able to speak more than I wanted food and drink. . . . What was real was my keenness. Most of us have some secret and sustaining delights ; that was mine.

Only a convulsion could have ended my pre-occupation, and a convulsion did end it. The war did not hit me in pocket or position ; but it hit me there, and it hit me hard. The willing sacrifice of it is my little contribution to England.

And so though I feel a brightened interest in the emotional developments of a play, the old interest in the manners and methods of the actors is gone. The war ended that delight.

Your loving son,

JOHN

[TO HIS FAMILY]   [Gallipoli]
To All at Home and Wairewa.   *May 28th, 1915*

We have been worked ceaselessly since the day I wrote to you from a relatively comfortable trench now in our rear. Since then we have made two advances by night, and are consequently nearing the enemy. You advance by night from your trench and dig yourself in—that is, dig a trench—in your new position. The operation is done under machine-gun and rifle fire from the enemy—you crawl out of the security of your trench and the bullets play about you. We had an infernally perfect moon.

I don't remember ever vizualizing what trench-life was like except that speaking generally it could not be called pleasant. I now know it to be an unimaginable mixture of horror, strain, discomfort, and fineness. Sometimes in danger the strain leaves you. Before going out last night we waited for an hour, expecting orders every moment, our feet feeling for the stepping-holes we had made in the side of the trench. I had a feeling not unlike that I used to experience, especially in early days, before a speech at the Union. At last the word came, and we scrambled over. I had passed down a message to run at a steady double. Fire rattled on us on our left flank. We had a hundred yards to go before we reached the cover of an evacuated enemy trench. I believe all thought we should never get there. And at fifty yards a glimmer of hope dawned, at twenty we quickened our pace, and at five with relief one thought— By Jove! I'm all right after all! The men arrived panting like animals with exhaustion and strain. Remember, they carry their whole wardrobe in their packs, sandbags for cover, a spade or a pick, a rifle, and one hundred and twenty rounds of ammunition, and that they run half-bent-up. It is also a grim and in a way grotesque running of the gauntlet—it makes one laugh—afterwards. When we arrived in the enemy's trench, a terrific fusillade between the ———, who were covering our advance with fire, and the Turks, broke out. We had cover and were all right. What a row! We thought the Turks were drawing nearer. Some-one came to me and said he thought the Captain was wounded. They put me in command. Turk fire grew louder and louder. I gave the order " Fix bayonets," and we lined the trench facing the Turks. The Manchesters had not come up on our right as arranged, nor had our fourth platoon. Our left rested on the trench we had left. It seemed obvious our plan was to await the Turkish charge and pray for the Manchesters.

Suddenly this critical phase evaporated. The Captain

reappeared and the Turks didn't come. We pushed into the open and dug our trenches.

While the trench was being sited, an incident occurred that drove strain out of one's mind to make room for horror. Before I came here and fought in a war, I read casualty lists with sympathy but without intense emotion. But nothing can convey to you how dreadful is the sight of the suffering, badly wounded man—nothing can convey it to you. I heard two short surprised coughs, and saw a man bend and fall. A friend darted to him, opened his tunic, and said to him : " You're done, Ginger, you're done ; they've got you." This frankness really seemed the most appropriate and sincere thing. They bandaged him up, with the lint every soldier carries inside his tunic ; then, knowing evidently that I had a medicine chest with sedatives, he asked for me. By a stroke of providence I was given a beautiful pocket-case with gelatine lamels of a number of drugs. It cost twenty-seven shillings—and under present circumstances worth ten times the money. By the light of the moon—useful for once—I read and tore off the perforated strip. While I was with him he said some remarkable things. I had only known him a day or so, but spotted him at once as a first-rate soldier. He said : " Shall I go to heaven or hell, sir ? " I said with perfect confidence : " To heaven." He said : " No, tell me as man to man." I repeated what I had said. He said : " At any rate I'll say my prayers," and I heard him murmuring the common meal grace. A little later he made up a quite beautiful prayer—" Oh, God, be good and ease my pain— if only a little " ; and then : " I thought I knew what pain was." All the while it was unbearable to see what he suffered. Someone digging in the trench hard by said : " He's sinking." He said : " What's that ? " I said : " He means the trench." And then, slowly drawn out : " I didn't mean to groan, but "—in a long-drawn-out groan—" I must." It was intolerable. They carried him back to this trench on a blanket. He remains here twenty-four hours, till a stretcher can be brought up in the dark to convey him through the communication trench to the supports, and finally to the base. That's war. And everyone around, as they went on with the digging that alone would save them when the light came, bent over their life-and-death work. I went to see him this morning. He was in a trench just wide enough to take him, a piece of newspaper over his face, the sun beating down upon him. Passers-by stepped over his body as they went on their way. I pray that he will live—his endless courage may pull him through.

Ruskin was right when he talked about war bringing out fine moral qualities, but I don't think he ever was present at such a scene as this morning's. As I write, the word comes down the trench, " Somebody hit." So the thing goes on.

JOHN

[TO HIS FAMILY. *He was killed six days later.*]

A Base [Gallipoli]

To All at Arana and Wairewa.   *May 31st, 1915*

This is happiness ! We reached this base between 2 and 4 this morning. All yesterday we were in a second-line trench. Our relief was to come at 9 p.m. We took our places shortly before, and were under heavy rifle fire, and the trench was in parts enfiladable. The regiment before us lost several men in the trench for this reason. 9, 10, 11, 12 passed, and no relief came—our hearts sank. We had posted double sentries. Then a messenger passed through the trench saying : " You'll get no relief to-night." Immediately after the relief came.

We filed away through trench after trench, and occasionally doubled over open country. Soldiers asleep in every imaginable position—below their overcoats one saw mud-stained putties and boots. The young sentry said : " This shrapnel is awful," as though it could be prevented, and in the name of reason it should be stopped. Then we got into a deep nullah, and gradually the sound of rifle fire took softer and softer tones. We left horses picqueted, Indian sentries, waggons, and stores, behind us. It is all country the Turks had to retire through. The perfect moon is still with us, and the temperature of the night was delightful.

I felt an extraordinary elation. It was not so much that one had left the firing-line as that one had been in it. I often think of H. Benson's story of the man who knew he was to be tortured and of the agony of his dread. When he was put on the wheel they saw he smiled. His suffering was less than his suspense. Full of wretchedness and suspense as the last few days have been, I have enjoyed them. They have been intensely interesting. They have been wonderfully inspiring.

That they have been so is due to the men with whom I have been. I always was an optimist, I have never lost faith in human nature. Now I know, now I know I was right. I was looking through the reports of the characters of the men in my platoon. They were prepared in Mauritius, where the regiment was in August. The characters of the men are marked D., F., G., VG., E. There was no B. A soldier called Saunders is marked " D "—I know better. I have seen him tending a wounded friend under fire. Let his character be judged by that.

It has been heart-breaking seeing men one had got to like only in a day or so killed—or worse, receive wounds of which they died. It has been bad enough for me. It is unspeakably worse for those who have been their soldier friends, who have drilled, slept, eaten, worked, and now died together. The men have been twelve days in the trenches and are shaken in morale. A groaning, tortured man lying below you in a trench is not pleasant company. Three days and nights we have been at work almost continuously. Yesterday we had a quiet day after we left the fire trench. The men talked about wounds and dead men all day. It was getting on their nerves—remember Wellington's observation that every man in uniform is not a hero. When a man is hit, their way of putting it is that he has ceased to reign—so many kingdoms of this sort have been shattered lately. . . .

MAJOR FRANCIS SAINTHILL
ANDERSON, M.C., R.H.A., R.F.A.

Educated Haileybury and Woolwich. Regular Army. Served in France
in " Eagle Troop," R.H.A. Commanded A/15 Battery, R.F.A., in
Italy and France, November, 1917, till killed in action, France, 25
August, 1918, at the age of 23.

N. Battery R.H.A. (The Eagle Troop)
[France]

[To His Mother]   *Late evening of November 6th [1916]*

... I now go farther still in my opinion of the War—I won't
express it on paper, because being a soldier by profession it
would not be considered suitable—Your attitude is *wrong*
like everyone else's at home, who doesn't realise it. If people
would cease to be stupidly casual and untruthful when on
leave, and let people know the truth—you for one would
very soon alter your opinion—Europe is mad and no one
realises it.

Don't you realise that Socialists will rule the world after
this War, and who are greater pacifists than the Socialists ?
—Then consider the power of Socialism in Germany and
remember that *all* the manhood of Germany has seen this
War—it is foolish to prate about another War in the next
generation, but I can't express myself forcibly and con-
vincingly when my strongest arguments are not put forward.

This isn't War as the world understands the word at all.
The truth of the matter is everyone out here considers it
only fair to one's womenkind to hush up the worst side of
war, and make light of it—vide Bruce Bairnsfather—I don't
find him nearly as funny as I used to.—No one can accuse
me of having a dull sense of humour, but there are subjects
one simply can't joke about.—Mind you I am not under-
going any horrors myself, which makes my arguments all
the more unbiassed and valid ! I have now got my own con-
victions, and I am not ashamed of them to anyone, though
it may be unwise to express them—I think you will realise
that up to now when on leave most of my statements about

30

the war were sound, and my prophecies pretty accurate, though considered pessimistic by the " Germany is on her last legs and will be brought to her knees next week " party.

You may remember I gave you a pretty shrewd idea about the Somme battle then, long before it started.—I won't burble on, as you probably think it's nonsense, besides there is no night shooting to-night, so I am going to have a damned good night.

Much love,
SAINT.

[Italy]

12/12/17

I don't think I told you the amusing incident of my Italian welcome.—

One night on the train journey, just about 12 midnight, we stopped at a station—I was naturally in my flea-bag etc.—the R.T.O. woke me up and told me that n Italian Colonel was on the platform, waiting to welcome me and any of my Officers who cared to come. He said it was a thing not to be avoided, as it would cause offence, but I could come " just as I was " ! Thank the Lord I didn't take him too literally ; I hopped out, pulled on a pair of slacks, muffler and coat, slipped my feet into unlaced shoes, and prepared to Entente.—Met the Colonel who was most effusive and took me off as I thought to his private room to drink to the Allies :—not a bit of it—he led me into a brightly lit up and crowded waiting room, with the remains of what looked like an Alderman's banquet on the table.— Crowds of ladies, soldiers of all nationalities and civilians, who all stood up at once.

I have no recollection of ever having been so badly frightened before, during the whole War.—I was led round and solemnly introduced to all these ladies, frightfully conscious of the disgusting condition of my nails, hair, etc.—

(we had been in the train six days, with poorish facilities for washing, and one is never at the top of one's form having been woken up at 12 mid-night !) I was then given the chair of honour and my embarrassing Ally filled glasses, rose, and made a flowery speech in French for my benefit ! I was immensely relieved for a moment at getting out of the limelight, except that my embarrassment was increased by a constant flow of beauteous damsels, who gave me various flowers and flags symbolical of the Entente.—Then it suddenly dawned on me that I should have to answer that speech, and I felt very like seizing my hat and bolting— however I duly rose, started in French, decided it wasn't worth the extra labour entailed, as only the Colonel spoke French, and carried on in English.—As I rose, everyone else stood up too, which made things worse.—They tell me since that there was a Press representative there at this critical moment taking photographs—if I'd spotted him I should have intercepted my speech to throttle him ! Having got off all the flowery stuff I could think of, I wound up by proposing " le Roi d'Italie," had a frightful spasm for one moment that Italy was a Republic after the recent troubles—recovered my composure and sat down exhausted.

We all trooped out to the train, taking individual farewells to everyone as we went out—I am convinced I shook hands cordially with the waitress, but I didn't mind by that time—I might as well go the whole hog and be the eccentric foreigner.—I entertained thoughts at one time of kissing the Colonel on both cheeks, but realised the consequences would be too embarrassing for the subalterns and everyone, so stamped stolidly out, and nearly died of hysteria when I got back to the train.—I laughed the whole rest of the night without control—Lord I have never seen anything so funny in my life.

Much love,

SAINT.

———

[To His Mother]   *July 1918*

    . . . The war goes on monotonously, and everything that happens is just rather less than an event, and forgotten very soon. I must confess I'm rather tired of it, but I wouldn't be out of it for anything—which is again an inexplicable paradox.

    Yes, the French news is very good indeed—quite wonderful when one considers the circumstances of it all—we have still however to await the main German Offensive, which must be rather overdue. . . .

———

MAJOR SIDNEY HAROLD BAKER
Gloucestershire Regiment

Educated Bristol Grammar School and Jesus College, Oxford. Schoolmaster. Killed in action, France, 23 March, 1918, at the age of 38.

                                                   [Macedonia,
[To His Brother]   *Early 1916*]

    . . . It is sad enough if in these days, when one might have hoped to see paltry minds merge strong, that one should learn more than ever before, that the measure of man's mind may be infinitesimally small ; that when each might try to bear the other's burdens, difficulties and disparagement instead are strewn in the path. Perhaps there is some strange purpose in it all, and maybe those who are young and inexperienced may gain more than we can tell. Yes, a whole year toiling uphill amongst unseen pitfalls should try heart, and nerve, and muscle too ; for how can one be forearmed ? The drum that beat Reveille sounded an ever-insistent note, " Shall I of my heart take counsel ? " but the drum answered " Come ", and its terse insistent summons promised that the path should be clear and straight. What, then, of those who spread the snares ? Have the anxieties at home strengthened our national character ? Are we all different from what we were before ? Is there

CE   33

more sympathy amongst our fellow creatures ? As for me, my fault seemed that I had too much, and in the Army it would seem that there should be none. Yet I am not repentant, and feel that I have been taught nothing, save that I would willingly forget. . . .

———

[TO HIS BROTHER]

. . . It was due to things going a wee bit awry that I found myself nearer the German line than our own. The Bosche had the full moon directly behind us, just myself and my servant, after the relief was reported completed, setting out to visit the " line." The Bosche sniped us from the wood, so we moved to the flank a bit, but still they went on ; then a dozen or fifteen rounds in quick succession, and we got into a crater ; and at that moment my servant was hit, and badly too, in the right breast. I wondered if they would come for us, and I got his rifle ready ; but I don't think the Bosche has much initiative. The crater was partly full of water, and still worse, it was a crater near or in a ditch. These craters are so many bogs, and you can imagine what happened. " Sir, give me a drink. Oh, Sir, do get my legs out ! " He was slowly sliding down the crater, with his legs buried and doubling underneath him ; but I got him out and pushed him further up, but seemed stuck for ever myself. At last I got one leg out, and by scooping with my hands and lying on one side (and it seemed after ages of pulling without a sign of movement), at last I was out. It was useless to creep back for help, for how could stretcher-bearers come out there and call for help ? The Bosche could be there first, and why should he know he had got one of us ? Yet how to get him back ? I shouldered his rifle—I didn't think a revolver alone good enough—and hauled the poor chap to the edge of the crater. He stuck it well, but it must have been horrible. Then a friendly gunner from somewhere put a few rounds of shrapnel bang on the very spot from which we had been sniped. I found I could not manage the rifle, but I got poor old Barnbrooke up and carried him a few yards ; more was impossible, the mud is so horrible. We had started off that afternoon at 3, and now it was past midnight, so you may imagine how hopeless one's strength seemed to be, just when it was wanted. Those few rounds of shrapnel gave us just the little chance ; but the snipers started again, and the edge of the wood was still 80 yards off. I thought the poor chap wanted me to leave him ; he was as plucky as could be all the time. I told him we would be alright in the wood ; couldn't he manage to walk a wee bit ? So I got him up, and with his arm round my shoulder, we pushed ahead a few more yards, then another rest, and I carried him again, and though you could scarcely believe it, he was game enough to walk another bit, when suddenly we heard a whispered call : " This way, Sir. Here you are, Sir," and at last we were in one of our own shell-holes. It was some time before we could get the stretcher-bearers down, and a hard time it is for those poor fellows, but thank God, we got him up to our own pill-box. They thought it was all up when they saw him, but I will not believe that. I feel somehow that his pluck will pull him through all right. We both agreed out there that God would help us somehow, and why should He not ?

It was dawn before I turned in, for this incident had prevented my going round the line, and so I had to get out again with another orderly, and dawn saw us still hunting in that unspeakable wood for the outer flank of our post. . . . It was not a night I should care to go through again, and yet the very next night I found myself trying to comfort a wretched wounded man till the stretcher-bearers should somehow scramble through the torn branches and cross the shell holes and get him back to the Aid Post. Poor fellow, I found him there by his cries ; he had been calling, calling, calling, hour after hour, ever since a shell had knocked him out in the darkness, long before the dawn, and now it was night again. He had crept into a hole for shelter, alongside a ruined pill-box, and was utterly helpless and numbed with cold. I could get no warmth into him at all, but a drink and a cigarette and yet another drink helped him a bit, till at last four stretcher-bearers stumbled and scrambled back with him. Poor chap, I doubt if he comes through. Perhaps he will not care if he does or not, when he knows ; yet his pluck and his gratitude, and his long struggle all through the day should earn the poor fellow something more than a horrible maimed existence.

'Tis a horrible business—enough to make a strong man weep. It seems to me just one long degradation ; it is the enemy who has " willed it," and we have to go through with it. How can anyone speak soft words to him, even if they know only a fraction of all the misery and horror ? This is hardly a letter to show mother ; I think she's worrying more this time than before. . . .

————

LIEUTENANT DENIS OLIVER BARNETT
Leinster Regiment

Educated St. Paul's. Scholar-Elect of Balliol College, Oxford. Joined Army on leaving school. Killed in action, Flanders, 15 August, 1915, at the age of 20.

[France]
[To His Mother]   *New Year's Eve [1914]*

. . . You probably don't know what a village looks like when it has caught it in the neck. It is a wonderful sight. Each house has chosen its own way of sitting down, and the whole place is all huge pits where the big high-explosive contact shells—Black Maria and her relatives—have burst. It's an extraordinary experience marching through a place like this for the first time, at night. Perhaps you don't know the two sorts of shells, which are absolutely different. There's the big brute, full of lyddite or melinite or some high explosive, which bursts when it hits the ground, and makes a big hole, blowing out in every direction, but chiefly upwards ; so that if you are lying down you are all right, unless the thing bursts on you. This chap does not have any bullets in him, but he does his business in big jaggy bits, which you hear flying round—bzzzz, and may kill you some hundreds of yards off, if you are exceptionally unlucky, by dropping on your top-crust. He is generally a heavy shell, fired from a howitzer, and goes dead slow. A Black Maria comes trundling along, whistling in a meditative sort of way, and you can hear her at least four seconds before she gets to you.

The other sort is really much more dangerous, as it is full of bullets, and is timed to burst in the air, when the bullets carry on forwards and downwards in a fan shape. He is almost always an express, and comes up not unlike an express train, only faster. The crescendo effect is rather terrifying, but if you are in a trench, and can keep your head down, he can't get at you seriously. The Germans have a little motor battery of 3-inch guns (they gave me my first taste of shrapnel) which is very unpleasant. The shells come in with a mad and ferocious squeal, and burst with a vehemence that is extraordinary for their small size. They have very small bullets in them, and lots of them.

Anyway, we're getting guns up here hard, all sorts. We've one big chap communing with a cross-road ten miles off ! There is not much doubt that we're getting superiority in artillery, and the German gunnery is going off, also their ammunition is often badly finished and doesn't burst. I hope you aren't bored with all this rubbish, which you must have heard heaps of times.

And then there's the Censor ! . . .

———

[France]

[To His Mother]   20th Jan. [1915]

I had my digging party out last night, and we had to carry all sorts of material for dug-outs up to the line. . . . When I was going along the road I heard a horrible crash in front, and a burst of profanity. I found, when I got up, that there had been a break between two gossoons who were carrying a big piece of corrugated iron. ' This fellow was afther callin' me names.' There they were, about 350 yards from the Germans, making a frightful noise, and quite ready for each other's blood ! I reproved them gently and passed on half dead with not laughing.

That reminds me of two lads in this regiment who got fed up with each other in the trenches. So in broad daylight they got up on the parapet and fought. After $\frac{1}{4}$ hour one was knocked out, but all the time the Germans were cheering and firing their rifles in the air to encourage the combatants ! Who says the Germans are not sportsmen ?

You can gather from these stories what sort of chaps I've got. They will only obey their own officers—they obey me all right so far—but they make magnificent fighters. They are much cheerier than English Tommies, and able to stand anything. The only way is to jump heavily on serious offenders, and condone little things. Of course drunkenness is the main crime, and that I suppose is a national failing, but beyond an occasional ' blind ' the men's discipline seems to me extremely fine. . . .

———

[France]

[TO HIS MOTHER]   *March 29th* [*1915*]

Thank you very much for your letter, which was a dear letter and made me think of you. It is nice to think of you thinking of me.

Everything goes very well here. The days are bright and warm, and the nights bright and cold, so everyone is satisfied. We are having a very peaceful time just now, as they have not shelled us, and the sniping is mostly done by us, though goodness knows there is never much to shoot at, except loopholes, tin chimneys, and an occasional flat cap, which disappears as soon as one sees it.

Trench warfare in the spring is really very nice—barring

the smells, which begin to get offensive. We've got lots of quicklime now, and are disposing of heaps of odd bodies ; so the smells are even now diminishing. It is lovely sitting in the sun and listening to the cock-chaffinches and yellow-hammers tuning up, and expanding in the *aura* which has come straight from Burnt Hill. There's nothing like spring air to take you away and back. Even in this hole in a turnip-field we are conscious of the *largior aether*, which is as broad as from here to England at least, and as deep as all past years, made warm with old happiness, and all alive with fancies that come in and laugh like the ghosts of little kiddies that keep on playing though no one takes any notice.

Then we go back to the trenches. We have a good line now. The parapet is high, perhaps five feet above the ground level, built of sandbags and banked up behind with earth, four feet thick at the top and anything over ten at the bottom. You see, they are pretty powerful earth-works really ; and sometimes a light shell bursting on the bottom of the slope does not get through. But of course direct hits high up blow a chunk right away. No parapet is ever meant to stand against shell fire ; the only thing is to throw up tons of earth in front and hope that it will not be a direct hit, which is a fairly rare thing, T.G. ! . . . .

———

[To His Mother]   [France]
                                        May 12th. [*1915*]

I've just heard Kenneth is dead. Kenneth was a good boy, and I'm sure he died just as he lived, and no one could better that. I've written to his people. This is the first time the war has hit me hard. Cheer up, my very dears. Kenneth's all right. He'll carry on. It would take more than that to stop him.

Of course I've got a bit gone, but I'm healed, and can carry on, and do better work. It is only the selfish part of us that goes on mourning. The soul in us says ' *sursum corda.*'

I've looked at death pretty closely and I know what it is. A man is called away in a moment and goes before God. Kenneth went as we know him, the boy we are proud of. Think of him as he is, and the grief slips off you.

———

[To His Father]   *May 19th [1915]*

You are one of God's own dears. Thank you very much for your photograph, which I like very much.

I've got a long account to settle out here, and Kenneth is at the top of it. I think they'll find that will cost them a lot. His death hits me harder than the death of all the valiant men I've grown to like and love out here.

The love that grows quickly and perhaps artificially when men are together up against life and death has a peculiar quality. Death that cuts it off does not touch the emotions at all, but works right in the soul of you ; this is so incomprehensible that you are only vaguely conscious of the change which you find there later, and shake hands with it. Regret is what you feel ; but there is something rather better than that really, which I think is what makes men. My love for Kenneth was not a war-baby, and so his loss is more painful to me than any other. But I know he's all right.

Don't be anxious about chlorine ; we've got it beaten by an extraordinary rapidity of organisation which is quite unlike the work of the Army I belong to.

I do hope you aren't having a θυμοφθόρος time at inspections. I'm always thinking about you and praying that you aren't unhappy about me or any other worry. If there is any soul εὐδαίμων in this world, it is me—real happiness of the whole being, the only sort there is, οὖσα ευδαιμονία. It makes me sing and grin to myself in the dark. And thank God, I believe I can do what is up to me.

———

40

LIEUTENANT EDWARD WILLIAM BELL

Machine-Gun Corps

Educated Cheltenham Grammar School. Optician. Killed in action,
Palestine, 8 December, 1917, at the age of 30.

[To His Family]   [*June, 1917*]

THE DIARY OF A SUB.

On his second attempt to cross the Mediterranean unsunk.

Sunday, June 3rd, 1917. Orders having been received—probably from the War Office, or some other Institution interested in the Great War—I am awakened at 5 ac emma by the noise of my batman cleaning the wrong boots, and rise to say once more good-bye to the old familiar scenes—and things can be most familiar in Marseilles—and the pretty " rest camp," where the shattered nerves of three thousand " survivors " have been slowly unshattered for a month. . . .

. . . The entire British Army having now embarked, and crowds of German spies having been kept back by the police on the quay, and the qui vive, sentries are posted at the gangways. . . .

THE SPEECH

7 p.m. The Captain, a fellow of infinite chest, a man whose yea is yea, speaks a few kind words, tells us what to do, when and if and how—with methinks, far too much emphasis on the " when "—informs us that the life-boat accommodation, including rafts, is enough for, well, dozens ; tells us what the Alarm will be, says we must not strike matches on the Steward, light our pipes at the funnel, nor let off fireworks on deck ; and mentions that we shall sail at 7 o'clock in the morning. Great amusement is caused in the meeting by the order that all " unattached officers," in the event of being torpedoed, would repair to the "lower bridge," and owing to scarcity of boats, take their chance with the Captain. I, being one of them, feel straightway more unattached than ever in my life, and join heartily in the laughter. O.C. Troops, a dear old Major of several summers and the north of Scotland, begs to thank the gentleman for so kindly coming to open the bazaar. . . .

Monday, June 4th. Contrary to all military etiquette, we sail at the appointed hour, and as I turn my head on the pillow—thereby bumping my ear on the ceiling, for I have the upper bed—I see through the port-hole that we are no longer attached to Europe by a rope. The engine throbs, or the engines throb, as the case may be. (I must inspect the engine-room later, for I understand all about machinery, having once had a magic-lantern.) Hastily dressing, and completing my toilet with my life-belt, I emerge on to the deck for a last look at Château d'If. . . .

THE ESCORT

They are here, Cuthbert and Charles—no one saw them arrive—such is the Navy way—two gallant little de-stroyers, neat and shapely, like two shining beetles, one each side of us, half a mile away, perhaps a quarter, now in front, now behind. We raise our hats to them. They are our comfort, our help in time of trouble, as everybody knows too well. And this time they wave the British Flag ! There being no nurses aboard, we hug the coast. Is it to be the old route ? Nice, Monte, Savona, where we all " survived " last month ? Come, let us ask the Captain—here he comes, white ducks, gold braid and all—party, 'shun !—wrong, it's the pantry-steward. Pah !

THAT PERISCOPIC FEELING

12 Noon. We are reckless, for we have left the coast, and make due South. So good-bye to land. Let us now zig-zag. We do nothing else, not zig to Corsica, and zag to

Malta, as I in my ignorance thought, but a positive wobble. Even the ship's cat, whose name is Legion, staggers in her morning stroll. All that I cherish most is in my pockets, and there it stops ! My belt is on—for we will save ourselves this time, if it kills us—and I join in the universal pastime of looking out to sea, watching, gazing and searching. Never has a tin can been so attractive to five thousand eyes, including rights and lefts, a mile or so away. Or perhaps an empty bottle will cause the ship to change her course.

2 p.m. After a heated argument, in my best Hindustani, with one Gama, my Lascar servant, (and may he be Omega !) about the cleanliness of my other collar, I proceed on duty. It is my four hours of " Military Watch " from under the bridge. My duties are arduous. I stand on my several feet alternately, I act as go-between in messages from Bridge to O.C. Troops, I amuse the Captain's puppy, I count periscopes, I see things that are not, I am sent to the sentries, hourly I inspect galleys, scrutinize scuttles, and peer into poops. Indeed I am an important fellow. . . .

THE NIGHT

A Natural Variety Entertainment

First a sunset, to describe which without coloured inks and slow music is impossible. All lights go out on board, and, after a polite interval, the Moon comes on. She is Top of the Bill. I look at her and make no complaints. Cuthbert shines silver, Charles a dead black silhouette. Troupes of performing porpoises are the next item. They are alarming at first, but what isn't ? The whole ship quivers with alarm ; hundreds of hearts jump at every door-slam. Curse that fellow whose cigarette-end drops with such a thud ! Brave men sleep. Others don't ; they admire the scene, and see thousands of periscopes shining silver by the moon. Suddenly the moon swings halfway round the heavens ! Cuthbert tarries, Charlie darts

43

ahead ! Keep your seats, gentlemen. We zig. The phenomenon is purely optical. In five minutes we zag, and East again is East, according to contract. But what corners ! Surely there must be a hinge in the boiler.

Tuesday, June 5th. 4.30 a.m. The Sun peeps over, sees all is safe, so leaps over the parapet. Some blood-orange ! This is the " dangerous hour." But all goes well.

8 a.m. We eat and enjoy—most, some only eat—a five-course breakfast, the oatmeal being specially so. We now read the day's news, wirelessed to us each morning, and see Haig has taken yet another prisoner, no one has abdicated since yesterday, and the Swiss Navy is out at last.

9 a.m. I get no letters this morning. Tut !

10 a.m. Great excitement on deck, as I am about to go two no-trumps. What is it ? Doesn't it ? Yes . . . no, it isn't. It's whales. No, not the geographical variety, but an oily green and black, and thoroughly enjoying themselves. They tumble and splash about in the violet waves just as if Peace had been declared.

3 p.m. Like several others on board, I have People at home, so I sit me down and write, telling them it leaves me at present, and that I have arrived safely in the middle of the ocean. Doubt arises in my mind as to when and where I can post these letters. Some say Malta, others don't, while again others do, whereas many think nothing of the sort. By the way, where are we now ? Hail, Columbus ! We see land, away on the port-bow. Out comes my atlas, for the hundredth time to-day. Now we know. It is *not* Newfoundland. It is Sardinia, and we have given the rudest go-by to Corsica. . . .

9.30 p.m. Lights again all out; the moon is not yet up. Twos and threes pace the decks, talking, joking, trying to seem at ease. Every plank and timber of the ship vibrates and throbs, the engines roar below, the night has started, and with it every ounce of speed. Sleep is obtained in any odd corner on the decks, but, like sugar at home, in small quantities and seldom.

10 p.m. I meet the two men, whose pyjamas (empty) share
with mine the cabin below, and in the subdued light of
the shuttered bar, with solemn faces, deep feelings,
shallow jokes, big hand-shakes, and small Benedictines,
we write notes about each other's next of kin. Each,
when we part, wonders how he will word it about the
other two, when the time comes.

LOST—A DESTROYER

Gradually we realize why the moon is late to-night—
a fog is creeping up. Thicker and thicker till the escorts
both grow dim. Then we see nothing, and feel our speed
gets less. Where are the 18 Knots? We simply lounge
along. And now the single blast, which wakens all the
ship. Now the reply, a shrill wail from a destroyer—
some signalling by lamp. We blast again—they wail;
and so for hours, the mother calling to her child throughout the night—always the deep loud call, always the
piercing wail. But only one who answers.

Wednesday, June 6th. 4 a.m. The dawn coming on and the fog
lifting. The signals and the sirens stopped an hour ago.
We gaze into the growing day, and still we see but one
follower. But a tiny speck of smoke appears on the
horizon. She comes at umpteen miles an hour, or in
nautical language, umpteen knots, ploughing up the sea,
smoking at three funnels, and calmly takes her place.
Our hearts are thankful. But " who were you with last
night?" . . .

1.30 p.m. I am told " a gentleman called to see you, sir."
I go on deck, and lo! My old friend Stromboli, miles away
on my left, with the same old cloud of smoke rising to the
heavens in a thin stream. He's an inveterate smoker, this
fellow.

3 p.m. The Straits at last, and friendly craft nose round
and stare at us. A view that charms. Between Scylla and

45

Charybdis we go, now reach the harbour of Messina, ring
the bell and enter. . . .

8.30 p.m. (Correctly, 20.30 o'clock Navy Time.) The
Concert on deck. All take part, even those who can
sing. Lanterns are lighted. A piano is discovered and un-
covered. O.C. takes the chair. The Naval officers are
unearthed, wines are uncorked and merriment is un-
restrained. The SONG that for us will live for ever—the
song of memories—is sung, shouted, roared, and roared
again :

> " *We're all together agen, we're here !*
> . *We're all together agen, we're here !*
> *Who knows when*
> *We'll be all together agen,*
> *Singing ' All together agen, we're here ' ? "*

12 Midnight. Sleep, in no uncertain voice. Everybody tired,
but the voyage is half over and for the night all is safe.

Thursday, June 7th. . . . A day on land, amongst the beautiful
buildings that once were, the shops that now are, and the
swindling little " cafés " that ought not to be. Miserable,
dirty little folk are the Sicilians. . . .

Friday, June 8th. . . . We watch the stately entry into port of
another ship—a mail-boat—that has followed us from
the same place, and is bound for the ends of the earth.
I must not say where that is, or I am giving away
information of value to the enemy. She has come without
escort—truly those men at the War Office are plucky
fellows—probably having nothing more valuable on
board than some letters for me. Every time I see coal-
barge or cruiser this thought occurs to me. . . .

Saturday, June 9th. A very short spell of moon last night ;
they forgot to call her till one. A cool, calm sea, with
only the dull throb of the ship and the swish of the waves

as music. Again land is lost. I must have slept, so make
a note of it. We are told a submarine was passed in the
night, but we turned our back on her, and did a two-
step, considerably more than many miles out of our
course, in order to save arguing the matter.

3 p.m. We again get reckless. We play riotous games of chess
and the like, utterly regardless of perils of the lurking
variety. Now news reaches us that we are entering the
biggest danger-zone of the voyage. This fact casts a
gloomy spell over the ship. I, personally, lose a pawn.

THE SMOKE SCREEN

4.30 p.m. As I offer a friend an expensive cigar, I feel something unusual is happening. Accompanied by field-
officers, field-glasses and waiters, I rush on deck, putting
the nineteenth knot in my life-belt string as I run. Yes,
Crow's Nest has seen a periscope three miles away as the
fly crows. He has megaphoned the fact to Lord Nelson
on the bridge. Horatio turns the ship, probably ramming
a minnow in so doing. But the destroyers—surely they
have gone mad ! They are dashing about, backwards,
forwards, round and round, rolling out onto the water
dense clouds of the filthiest and blackest smoke it has
been my pleasure ever to see or smell. This, then, is the
famous Smoke Screen one reads about in the " Daily
Mail," and other comics. We are hidden from Hun optics
—we are thus cut off from aim. We all stand watching,
thinking the last moment will be our next, and waiting
for something that does not come. We are too quick, we
are indeed a fast lot, for in half an hour all settles down
again. Cuthbert and John Willy resume their proper
places, for we have out-paced Fritz. Ours was the only
gun that saw him, and the smoke prevented our firing.
We *are* annoyed. So we carry on, leaving Germany still
to Rule the Waves ! And Crow's Nest gets his twenty
pounds. But another experience like that, and I shall
make a separate Peace.

Sunday, June 10th. The dawn, a sea like glass, a view : the same—nothing ; but what there is blue and beautiful. The glorious feeling fills our minds that there's only one night more, for we are due to-morrow. We converse with the junior wireless operator. The S.O.S. has been received this morning from a French ship a hundred miles North East. Fritz has been that way. We carry on, for it is war. An uneventful day. We *feel* we are nearing land. We eat heartily, the Lascars become more attentive, the Captain moderates his vocabulary, the men are more noisy, and a second lieutenant is heard to inquire of a senior officer if we are downhearted. Several services are held in as many parts of the ship.

THE VILLAGE IDIOT ON BOARD

Sunday night, and there is evidently a fool on board—a large one.

2 a.m. There is a smell of burning throughout the ship, and, incidentally it interests the Captain. He rises from his bed, thirteen to the dozen. We all do precisely the same, and we begin the search, which goes on for half an hour. Where is the fire ? I ask you. We parade our insinuating noses along each deck, inserting them into hatches, ports and things like that. Furious signalling with Cuthbert and John Willy. With that skill for which I am noted, I read a reply, flashed in Morse : " Slow down if necessary, but do not stop on any account." I notice we are slowing down if necessary. Now the discovery is made. The Fool has been messing with the electric light in his cabin, and, while he sleeps on deck, the woodwork burns. He is, of course, an officer. Everybody having expressed an opinion, and the flames having been dealt with gently but firmly, we carry on.

Monday, June 11th, 1 p.m. . . . A thin grey streak due south, resting on the surface of the sea. Some say it's Africa, so does everybody else. Alexandria it is ! The noise on board is deafening. But we've miles yet.

2 p.m. The houses are clearly seen, the docks, the streets, the well-known lighthouse.

3 p.m. We stop outside the harbour, and run little flags up and down a piece of string tied to a pole at the front end of the ship. A pilot comes out to us in a tiny steamer. He takes months to reach us, and we hope he is seasick with the tossing about. But he isn't. He wears a fez, therefore he must be a Turk. He guides us between the mines—at least we are told so—safely into dock. The inhabitants come out in thousands to greet us—I do *not* think. The Pilgrims no longer need their burdens, so life-belts are not only discarded, they are hurled across cabins, and at friends of long standing. Little motor boats run round us with staff officers in, and ladies in summer white. Pleasure-boats, nurses and parasols are abundant. Important Persons board the ship and examine the Papers.

4.30 p.m. With an effort, for it is very hot, we breathe again, we live, we are on land. We look back from the Quay where we stand surrounded by only too obliging Arabs, and bid a last, long Farewell to the old ship, and wish her many another safe arrival. We are sorry, in a way, to say good-bye. She is a dear old ship, the *Kashmir*.

Now we are safe—safe to settle down to peaceful fighting, after having risked the Horrors of War for eight days. In our different ways, we offer up thanks, for

" We're all together agen, we're here ! "

———

PRIVATE FRANK BRIGNALL
11th (British Columbia) Regiment,
Canadian Expeditionary Force

Educated Brighton Grammar School. Farmer in British Columbia.
Killed in action, Flanders, 24 April, 1915, at the age of 37.

[TO HIS FAMILY. *He was killed six days later.*]
[Flanders]

Dear People,   *Sunday, 18 April, 1915*

...My last letter spoke of a movement on our part to outside a certain town on Monday, April 5th. We were billeted in a most comfortable farm until Wednesday, April
14th. . . . The day before pulling out we marched to the
town and had a splendid hot shower bath and strolled back
by way of the fields and streams and hop fields in preparation. War was the last thing that was evident if one forgot
the khaki around.

Wednesday, April 14th, reveille 4.30, get up from the
straw and slide down the ladder, breakfast, clear up the
farm, pack at leisure as we fall in at 8.30. March to headquarters two miles away, where we strike a cobbled military road, and await the arrival of other Companies of our
battalion, and strangest of all, 35 London Gen. Omnibus
Co.'s buses. Along they came, and on and in we piled, and
off, a long string of laughing men and Cockney busdrivers,
through villages and a good-sized town, where everybody
turns out to see the procession. ' Les Canadiens pour les
tranchées '. Ten miles covered, and out we turn, raining
hard by now. Back go the buses for more, and we pile in a
large empty factory mixed up with the regulars and wait
four hours until the arrival of the balance of the Battalion.
Packs on, and off for a ten mile march, for we are going in
the trenches that night. We pass right through at a slow
march a town you have all read about, a town noted for its
splendid buildings, Cathedral and Cloth Hall. If everyone
in England could only see that town as we saw it Wednesday last, with its most valuable buildings so palpably

picked out for ruthless destruction . . . well even the head of a great school would stop preaching "Love your enemies." Walls tottering, roofs gone, and gone beyond repair.

Out up the long, narrow, cobbled street, and when a mile out of town a halt is called. We are waiting for darkness now, and we throw ourselves down, not so particular now as earlier in the day as to whether the ground is damp or not. On again, halt, and on again, through a straggling village with few houses left intact. . . . Soldiers begin to pass us coming from the trenches, for it is a . . . regiment that we are relieving. Another tiring hitch in front, and the column halts ; will one never get the pack off the back ? On again, we have now left the road, and word is passed down to watch out for the "Jack Johnson" holes with their two and three feet of stagnant water, past farmhouses, across streams and meadows, and we are there. . . .

Off go our packs, myself and four others have been lucky enough to get a sandbag shelter with a little straw on the ground. . . . Shells falling at intervals all the time and some uncomfortably close. A most anxious and trying day. . . .

A boom from the enemy cannon, a rushing shriek that you feel must be coming direct at you personally, a fountain of mud (and in some cases sandbags) rises high, and then listening intently one hears the long drawn out wail, almost like a human scream of terror, made by the screw-cap of the shell as it flies off and hurtles through the air. It has fallen in the trenches of our No. 2 Company on our left, and we wonder, has anyone been hurt ? The question is soon answered, for scarce has the dust cleared when word is passed down our line quickly from mouth to mouth "Stretcher bearers at the double." They give us several hours of this sort of thing every day, and we answer bomb for bomb. Mostly no harm is done at all, and one gets so used to it that no conversation is interrupted or pipe left unlit. It is on the daily menu, and must be accepted. Then again whilst you are still laughing over some yarn or lie that has been swopped, comes down the line " Stretcher bearers at the double." . . .

Friday passes in alternate sunning and snatching an hour's sleep, one cannot really rest by day. The shelling is not so bad to-day, and no casualties in the 3 Companies to report. . . . Saturday, sunshine and clothes being dried, and the evening brings its duties. I am detailed for " Listening Post." D, F, and myself are told off for first duty and three others relieve us every hour through the night, and vice versa. Listening Post means that you climb over the parapet after dark, make your way through the barbed wire along a shallow dug ditch for almost forty yards out and there lie prone and look and listen for the enemy's movements. If one wants to realise creepy sensations I commend this job. There is a great fascination about it, and I like it best of all—it's worth while. I don't think the man lives whose breath doesn't come a little short when on the warning word, whispered from sentry to sentry, " No. 10 listening post going out," you climb up and over and scramble down the other side, and disguising yourself as much like a rabbit as possible you make your way out leaving a long line of sentries behind you, watching but unseen. We put in four hours, an hour at a time, with an hour rest between. It is quite long enough, for it is a strain on eyes and mind, and the hour up, the three reliefs come quietly, bent low, and you move from your prone position, now stiff, and make your way back through the wire, up and over and drop down on your own side, glad to be able to stretch, blow a nose, cough at will.

We are at last doing our fourth turn, and the hour before the dawn is much colder. When will that darkness in the East give place to the rising sun ! A rocket goes up, turns, and breaks to a ball of light, which sways on its parachute. We flatten ourselves still more but look the harder ahead. The light gradually descends and goes out, and again to one's imagination the distant hedge assumes human form, such is the blackness around us. Quietly without noise a lark has risen from the very centre of this " Tom Tiddler's

Ground " and high up, he bursts into sound, the song distinct as he rises higher and higher. For the space of a second you forget that you are there lying prone with loaded rifle and fixed bayonet and that you are there to kill if necessary, listening to that song. But suddenly the blackness ahead is rent with an ugly red flash, a boom, a scream overhead, a bursting shell away behind and you are back to realism and its dangers. You are relieved by the outcoming three, and as you climb back over the parapet you catch the passing message " Stretcher bearers at the double." You drop to the ground and pass around the grave in our midst over which is inscribed, on a rough soldier-made cross, " *Ci git un soldat francais mort au Champ d'Honneur.*" The order for standing to is given shortly after, and the dawn is here with another day begun. . . .

FRANK

LIEUTENANT HENRY AUGUSTUS BUTTERS
R. F. A.

American citizen. Educated California and Beaumont College, Windsor. Landed proprietor in California. Joined British Army, 1915. Killed in action, France, 31 August, 1916, at the age of 24.

[TO HIS SISTER]   [France]
Dearest,   *22nd March, 1916*

We have come out of action and are back in the rest area for a little while. Been here 3 days with lots of lovely green grass and no noise. The battery is all spruced up and ready for any degree of General's inspection. Everybody is enjoying himself after his own particular fashion, and sports begin to-morrow.

Your letter, which arrived yesterday, finished up with a paragraph on Verdun, and your sorrow for the loss there, and not only by this, but by an occasional line in the same

53

vein that has been slipping into most of your letters lately, I read between the lines the dangerous fact that you are thinking a little too much about some of the disgusting details of Life at the Front. Now, then, Gookie, forget it ! I, who am over here for the good of my soul and the greater success of the Allied armies, have got to go through a number of extremely unpleasant experiences and become thoroughly familiar with all the sides that go to make up the " Romance of War " ; and for me these things are good and threaten no danger to the mind, because a very few seconds after you are scared out of a year's growth by a shell arriving in the next ravine, or turned sick by the sight of some uncleared remains of a late battle field, you have forgotten about it, and while the item undoubtedly has left a permanent subjective impression, its effect on the objective mind of you and on your good health and spirits is nil. You've got too many other things to think about, to worry about it for a minute after it is out of sight or sound. Out of sight, out of mind—is the rule of the soldier on active service, and the few who fail to follow it naturally go home with a weak heart or varicose veins.

But with you at home it is different. Once you begin to worry about the harrowing details, they are always with you, and as you don't really know a damned thing about the actual shape or circumstance of said details, your imagination is given full play to garnish them up with all the thunder and lightning and souls writhing in torment effect, and the longer you ponder on it the worse it gets, and pretty soon you're headed right straight for the Nut Factory. Wherefore, I repeat—forget it !

Take the war news casually, and remember that every battle brings us nearer to the end.

I notice Stewart Edward White tells you to read " *Between the Lines.*" I hope you will pay attention to me when I tell you *not* to read it. Nor any of the other war books that are just beginning to appear in such numbers. " *Sergeant Michael Cassidy, R.E.*" " *The First Hundred Thousand* " and a few more like that. *Quand la guerre finit*—these masterpieces will be all very well to read and ponder over as excellent descriptions of the times we have lived in—I must admit they are good because I read a couple of them myself and they gave me the jim-jams for a week ; but they are the wrong medicine right now for anybody with a personal interest in the War. If you have already bought " *Between the Lines*," you leave it for Gus and the Colonel to read, and you can bet it won't worry them !...

I cannot think of another damned thing to say, except the same old Devoted love,

HABS

LIEUTENANT HUGH MONTAGU BUTTERWORTH
The Rifle Brigade

Educated Marlborough and University College, Oxford. Racquets Blue, 1905 and 1906. Schoolmaster at Wanganui, New Zealand. Killed in action, Flanders, 25 September, 1915, at the age of 30.

[TO HIS COLLEAGUES AT WANGANUI,
NEW ZEALAND]
[Flanders, late July, 1915]
Wednesday, 1 p.m.

... We know our sector very well now. By jove, it makes a difference. The result is we can run it about ten times better than we could at first. I think if the Germans had rushed us when we first came in, they'd have eaten us. It was a wild place to send a new regiment to ; only all regiments are new now-a-days. Now the men have got down to the position, their sentry work is excellent and our sniping is quite fair, they work splendidly. We work them very hard, but no digging or wiring party ever goes without an officer, that is the way to get the men along. If one takes out a party of men somewhere they don't know—in the open probably—to dig, they'll go like lambs as long as

55

they've got an officer with them. The curious thing is that in civilian life they've probably cursed us as plutocrats, out here they fairly look to us. The other night some time ago, I had some men and had to get somewhere I'd never been to before in —— ; as a matter of fact it wasn't difficult and we had ample directions, so before we started I was told to send the men with a sergeant. Said the sergeant to me, ' I wish you were coming sir, I don't know the way.' I said, ' My dear man, nor do I.' To which he made this astounding reply, ' Very likely not, sir, but the men will think you do and they know I don't ! ' He got there all right. My own sergeant is different from most of ours. He's a tip top A1 regular, and we work in wondrous harmony. Whenever I forget things—as I often do, strangely enough—he always remembers and gets them done without rushing to me for orders. He has an uncanny knack of knowing all the stores, etc. one has in the trench. One has to keep a log and so on and you have to know to a round what ammunition you've got and every other dashed thing.

Probably at two I get a message to report at 1.30 (usually a message comes after the time at which you have to report) how much S.A.A. and so on I have. I dart up to Sergeant Dyer, who consults his note-book and gives me the thing cut and dried correct to the nearest round. We also are probably the two most successful thieves in the trenches. And he has taught me this splendid habit—if wild messages arrive inquiring whether this or that is done and why the deuce isn't it, we always report it is done and do it instanter. In fact we're a thoroughly immoral pair, but I believe we're knocking out a pretty useful platoon. . . .

————

[To the Same]   [Flanders,
                                          early August, 1915]

. . . *Wednesday*. We're out temporarily but shall probably be back to-morrow night. We had an awful time ! I haven't read through the previous pages of this letter so I don't know what I said ; anyway the whole show lasted about ninety-six hours and is probably by no means over yet. We may quite easily be shoved into the attack almost at once. When the show is over the whole division will undoubtedly go away somewhere to refit and recover.

Now we are out of trenches and can sort out impressions. I think that there is very little doubt that the liquid fire attack was also attempted on us, but the fire turned to smoke before it reached us. I was otherwise engaged when the blaze broke out, as I had to rush up my trench to persuade the men that that wasn't the exact moment to watch a fire on one's flank. So I've had a curious experience. Everyone in neighbouring trenches wants to know about the liquid fire in my trench and I can't say if I had it or not. Secondly I can't say for certain whether I was attacked by Bosche or not ! ! No one who hasn't been here could understand, but the noise, dust and general tumult is such that anything might be happening. I wish you could have seen my men during that three or five minutes (or hours, I don't know how long it was) when we were actually " repelling the attack " (if there was one). They all were right over the parapet firing like blazes, my sergeant bucking about persuading them to fire low, my humble self standing half on the parapet and half on the parados with a revolver in one hand and rifle near the other and a cigarette going well, using the most unquotable language. Do you know that really was a good moment. I can't pretend to like bombardments, nor war generally, but that really was a moment when one " touched top " (as opposed to " touching bottom ") but you'll feel that it was an interesting moment in one's life.

I felt absolutely as cool as ice during that part, one was so worked up that one felt that one could stick anything out. However when one has spent four sleepless days and nights with all sorts of alarms and bombardments and attacks and counter attacks going on—that was fair Hell. At the end of it, our relief went hopelessly wrong, and we walked out in broad daylight. When we got half way to Ypres, our big guns opened up bombarding. I was too tired to worry much, but I just mentally noted that the whole company must infallibly be wiped out. But our star was there again and we got out and went home in a Willesden bus.

This letter fails hopelessly. I can't express what we felt or give you a real idea what Hell looks like. We lost two hundred and fifty men. I left Aldershot fifth officer in the company. I am now second in command of it. I am I think fairly certain of my second star but we haven't time to think about promotion just now. . . .

Blessings and love to all.

LIEUTENANT ROBERT FURLEY CALLAWAY
Sherwood Foresters

Mission priest in Africa. Joined Army as Chaplain and later served as combatant officer. Killed in action, France, 13 September, 1916, at the age of 44.

[France]

[TO HIS WIFE]   2 /9 /16

. . . Before the route march yesterday the whole Brigade formed up in a cornfield to listen to a lecture by a Scotch Major. It was extraordinarily good, but to me the interest of the lecture lay not so much in the lecture itself as in what the lecture stood for—the entire conversion of our whole attitude of mind as a nation. For it was instruction as to how best to *kill* (with the bayonet), and every possible device that had been found by experience useful to enable a man to kill as many Germans as possible, was taught. As one writes it down it sounds the most hideous brutality, and yet yesterday I don't suppose there was an officer or man present who did not agree that if the war is to be won we must fight to kill. Personally I still shudder at the idea of sticking six inches of cold steel into another man's body or having his steel stuck into my body, but I shudder merely with the natural instinct of repulsion which is common to at least all educated people. I don't shudder because I think it any more wrong of me as a priest. I have never for a single moment regretted becoming a combatant. In one only way I can say with St. Paul, " I glory in the things which concern my own infirmities." I am proud of just those very things which other people think must be such a bore for me, e.g., coming down in rank, being under the orders of boys of eighteen, having to trudge along on foot, etc. And for that reason I rejoiced even when I gave up the Lewis Gun job, though everybody thought me a fool to do so.

Coming back from our march yesterday, we passed all the black fellows (Senegambians) at work. They look exactly like our Kaffirs, except that they are much blacker—most of them are quite young.

CAPTAIN IVAR CAMPBELL
Argyll and Sutherland Highlanders

Educated Eton and Christ Church, Oxford. Killed in action, Mesopotamia, 8 January, 1916, at the age of 25.

[France]

[*1915*]

. . . It is difficult to write things out here. Journalists do it, yet miss the note of naturalness which strikes me. For these things are natural. I suppose we have been fighting a thousand thousand years to a thousand years' peace ; they miss, too, the beauty of the scene and action as a whole— that beauty defined as something strange, rarefied ; our deep passions made lawful and evident ; our desires made acceptable ; our direction straight. Such will be the impressions to linger, to be handed on to future generations, as the Napoleonic wars are fine adventures to us. Here, present and glaring to our eyes in trenches and billets, etc., the more abiding and deeper meanings of the war are readable.

Here is the scene I shall remember always : A misty summer morning—I went along a sap-head running towards the German line at right-angles to our own. Looking out over the country, flat and uninteresting in peace, I beheld what at first would seem to be a land ploughed by the ploughs of giants. In England you read of concealed trenches—here we don't trouble about that. Trenches rise up, grey clay, three or four feet above the ground. Save for one or two men—snipers—at the sap-head, the country was deserted. No sign of humanity—a dead land. And yet thousands of men were there, like rabbits concealed. The artillery was quiet ; there was no sound but a cuckoo in a shell-torn poplar. Then, as a rabbit in the early morning comes out to crop grass, a German stepped over the enemy trench—the only living thing in sight. " I'll take him," says the man near me. And like a rabbit the German falls. And again complete silence and desolation. . . .

————

[France, *1915*]

The splutter of shrapnel, the red squeal of field guns, N.E. ; the growl of the heavies moving slowly through the air, the cr-r-r-r-ump of their explosion. But in a bombardment all tones mingle and their voice is like machinery running not smoothly but roughly, pantingly, angrily, wildly making shows of peace and wholeness.

You perceive, too, in imagination, men infinitely small, running, affrighted rabbits, from the upheaval of the shells, nerve-racked, deafened ; clinging to earth, hiding eyes, whispering " O God, O God ! " You perceive, too, other men, sweaty, brown, infinitely small also, moving guns, feeding the belching monster, grimly, quietly pleased.

But with eyes looking over this land of innumerable eruptions, you see no line. The land is inhuman.

But thousands of men are there ; men who are below ground, men who have little bodies but immense brains. And the men facing West are saying, "This is an attack, they will attack when this hell's over," and they go on saying this to themselves continually.

And the men facing East are saying, " We have got to get over the parapet. We have got to get over the parapet—when the guns lift."

And then the guns lift up their heads and so a long, higher song.

And then untenanted land is suddenly alive with little men, rushing, stumbling—rather foolishly leaping forward —laughing, shouting, crying in the charge. . . .

There is one thing cheering. The men of the battalion—through all and in spite of that noisy, untasty day ; through the wet cold night, hungry and tired, living now in mud and water, with every prospect of more rain to-morrow—are cheery. Sometimes, back in billets, I hate the men—their petty crimes, their continual bad language with no variety of expression, their stubborn moods. But in a difficult time they show up splendidly. Laughing in mud, joking in water—I'd " demonstrate " into Hell with some of them and not care.

Yet under heavy shell-fire it was curious to look into their eyes—some of them little fellows from shops, civilians before, now and after : you perceived the wide, rather frightened, piteous wonder in their eyes, the patient look turned towards you, not, " What the blankety, blankety hell *is* this ? " but " Is this quite fair ? We cannot move, we are all little animals. Is it quite necessary to make such infernally large explosive shells to kill such infernally small and feeble animals as ourselves ? "

I quite agreed with them, but had to put my eye-glass fairly in my eye and make jokes ; and, looking back, I blush to think of the damnably bad jokes I did make. . . .

LIEUTENANT CHRISTIAN
CRESWELL CARVER
R.F.A.

Educated Rugby. Joined Army from school. Died of wounds, Flanders,
23 July, 1917, at the age of 20.

Fromewhere in Sanders.

[To a Brother]   Sunday Morn.

Dear Maurice,   [*Late July, 1916*]

. . . Should this reach you, it will find you in camp, so
that you will not read it, military operations very rightly
coming first. . . . It is difficult to tell you about my personal
experiences, as they are so bound up with technicalities.
But one gets certain pictures absolutely engraved on one's
soul.

The first is during the preliminary bombardment.
Carroll and I stood on top of one of our gun pits one pitch-
dark night, watching the show. Everything from 18 pdrs. to
15″ appeared to be shooting. The familiar landscape showed
up in fragments now here, now there, lighted by the
blinding flash of the guns. A red glare and a shower of sparks
every $\frac{1}{2}$ minute or so represented hun shrapnel on the
Peronne road. Speech was of course impossible, and one
could only stand and *feel* the thousands of tons of metal
rushing away from one. Impressive enough, but what I shall
never forget was a substratum of noise, an unceasing
moaning roar, exactly like enormous waves on a beach.
The 75's firing over Maricourt Wood, a shell passing over
trees makes a noise exactly like a great wave. Or was it
indeed the breakers of the Sea of Death beating against the
harbour gates of the hun, beating until it swept them and
him away, washed them back and threw them up, only to
be washed further yet by the next tide. I think it was. The
second is from Montauban valley, at dawn on the 6th July.
Straight opposite was the as yet untaken Bazentin ridge,
beyond which we could just see the spires and roofs of the
2 Bazentins. On the skyline High Wood. To the left, rising

out of the smoke and mist, the dark mass of Mametz Wood, beyond it Contalmaison. To the right—dawn. I shall never forget that either. Silhouetted against Mithras' morning legions, all fiery red, and fierce gold, the dark sinister line of Longueval, houses, spires *now* all gone, showing among the trees of Delville Wood. And in an open space the incongruously complete buildings, and factory chimneys of Waterlot farm. Nearer the remains of Montaubon and Trones Wood.

The third is from the same place some hours later, when we looked down into hell on our left. A frontal attack on Contalmaison and Mametz Wood (quite different and separate from Mametz village) which we saw from our ridge to a flank. Every kind of shell bursting in the wood and village. Shrapnel, crump, incendiary, lachrymatory, and over the torn-up waste of what had once been trenches and over which our people had to advance, hun " Woolly bears " (5.9″ Shrapnel), crumps, and a steady barrage of field-gun shrapnel from Baz. Wood, fortunately bursting much too high. By way of a frame for this happy scene, one saw it through the hun flank barrage bursting on the brow of our hill about 200 yards in front of us. He put a barrage on us too, but as it was 25 yards behind us, and apparently meant to stop there, it soon ceased to worry us. Presently one saw great clouds of gas sweeping across, and I must say I felt we were looking into hell indeed. Then little black figures which formed into lines, which presently moved slowly forward. Gigantic shell seemed to pitch right into the line, but they still went on, now disappearing into a trench, but ever moving on forward when they reappeared, their work accomplished. And so one lost sight of them in the welter of smoke, and only saw occasional little single figures (messengers) running steadfastly back across the plain. Sometimes a shell burst and one saw them no more. Carroll arrived to relieve me and we wended our perilous way down to the battery and breakfast.

The last impression is the morning of the 17th. We went along the Briqueterie road and round into our valley of the shadow. The great valley was already nearly ploughed from end to end, and here and there whizz-bangs were bursting. We got to our position, in a sort of little hollow, and the ordered confusion of getting into action was at its height when with a shriek and a crash a shell burst some 20 yards behind us. Then a bang—and the yell of the shell case as it went through us. I remember looking down the battery. The driver standing beside me was lying killed. A Gunner who was behind me got the bullet I should otherwise have had, in the stomach. A little further on someone was bending over Wager, and I saw Bowman crawling into the trench with his leg broken.

Wounded men lying about, some dead horses. There is no hope of taking cover in a case like that, you just have to stand by your horses. Everybody behaved rippingly. I saw little Sparkie, my groom, unconcernedly holding my ponies. Well, old spot, be good if you can't be clever. Yrs.

C. C. CARVER

The Grease Spot,

[TO A BROTHER] [Flanders]

My dear Maurice, *21.8.16*

I gather from G.F.'s letter to you that last term was ticklish work ; hearty congrats. on piloting the house so successfully through it. I don't look upon it as possible or desirable that you should see any actual fighting in " this dreadful War " and I think that you must look upon it from this point of view, which I think you have heard me state before. You can either chuck up being head of the house, at a time when it would be nothing short of criminal, and leave it in an awful hole, for the sake of being able to say, when your grandchildren cluster round your gouty knee, piping in childish trebles, " What did *you* do in the great War, Grand-pa ? " " Children, I took unto myself a commission, I donned the khaki, I learned to form fours and drink cherry brandy at No. 9897 camp, Slinghampton." Rather a good sentence, it conducts you from 1, Hillmorton via your 2nd childhood to Slinghampton. Or else, you can continue at your job which is necessary, difficult, instructive and extremely thankless, in fact, *really* serve your country, while the credit for same goes to 2nd Lt. Faceache, who could no more do head of the house than milk a crocodile.

*Some*body has got to do it, and it is rather sickening for G.F., when after a lot of worry and stress he selects you as H.H., when moreover you have justified his choice in that you pull the house through a bad period, that you should then start getting discontented because you hanker after something totally different. I think you must guard against that. You don't mind all these home truths do you ? I know the real reason is that you want to be out here with me. My dear old bird, if only you could have a magic ring round you keeping you exempt from shells, bombs, bullets, bayonets, boches, etc., it would be the one thing I should pray for. But you can't, and when you add to that the fact that we could not be in the same Regiment, let alone battery, that even if you get out here, there would be less than 1 chance in a million of our ever meeting, can you wonder that I think that one is enough, and heartily hope that none of you will ever see the dirty end of this infernal show. I sometimes think that war is *all* criminal folly, and that the excuse that we were forced into it does not excuse us. That we ought to have foreseen and taken measures to prevent it. If you saw a peer of the realm fighting a hooligan, would you take it as an excuse that the hooligan started it ? No, you would say, " more fool him for not providing a policeman." Yes, I admit the force of your objection, but we are too ready to prove ourselves in the right ; any old specious excuse does. I don't know about your history books, but in all the ones I have read, it is put forward blandly, when we hung back here, and failed a friend there, that we were perfectly right because it was our duty to ourselves as a nation to refrain from any interference on the continent, and devote ourselves to bagging colonies, see " Our Colonial Expansion." What we really meant was that

EE 65

interference was " no bon " because we shouldn't get any land out of it, territory on the continent being for us untenable, oblivious of the fact that we might be fighting peoples or influences which, if not squashed, would rise and squash us. I loathe *all* Germans, but can't you believe that he found our attitude exasperating ? It is only when the people and influence *have* risen to try and squash us, that we start to chat about fighting for the sake of freedom etc. What do *you* think, you historical old bloke ? I have just got over a bad 4 days, resulting from a touch of " flu " and the reaction after the Somme. I felt mentally run down, and totally incapable of winding myself up again. The state of mind when you sit down and hate everything, shells, trenches and the hopeless unending vista of shells and trenches in the future. When you feel you would give absolutely *anything* to get away. It passes off, I am glad to say. Well, tweet-tweet, old bird, I'm getting peckish. Yrs.

CHICK

[TO A BROTHER]   [France]
My dear Maurice,   *16.11.16*

Thanks so much for your letter. So glad there is a chance of your doing something at Oxford. I am very much hoping you will be able to have a jolly good time there— so that I shall be able to have one by proxy. " My frater at Oxford you know " sort of idea. I had a very nice reply from G.F. the other day, in which he said you were a great standby to him, but " that like all the Carvers, he is too conscious of the mote in his own eye, to realize that most other people have a beam in theirs, or to be really happy, etc." He is a wonderfully perceptive old bird, for that just hits off you and I to a T. Whenever I came across difficulties in my work, or did a rotten bad prep. I used to be apprehensive and depressed, and I expect you are the same. In time I came to realize that I had a brain as good as the average, and that what was difficult for me was difficult for others, and real work generally brought one on top. In exams, for instance, when I was depressed at having done badly, it usually turned out that others had done worse ; one only did badly when one thought one had done well. In an exam, the only thing you have got to fear is nervousness, and that can be overcome by seeing things in their proper proportions. But above all, old bird, try and be happy, particularly while you have such excellent opportunities. The power of being cheerful is worth much fine gold, and it helps on others no end. Without it no man can attain to leadership, whether in thought or deed. And leadership, each in our own degree, is what we are put here for after all. I don't know what you feel about what is called—with a sort of semi-aversion—religion. I find, in this sort of job, that I have to pray, and pray good and hard, otherwise one could not keep going. One must look up, and the God one looks up to is a God of Hope, and the Kingdom, a Kingdom of Light and happiness. Consciously or unconsciously, one always pictures Heaven, and I always find myself apt to slip into an idea of a sanctified place, with harps and wings and things floating about, illuminated by a sort of incandescent white light. But when you are struggling along, through foot-deep sticky mud, and there are shells bursting on the path in front of you, and corpses lying about, then when you pray, you think of all the happiness and beauty you have ever known, and get a closer conception. Wherefore, oh, my brother, be happy for it is your job. . . . I am delighted to hear about Symmond's sermon, I wish I knew him for I am sure we should have a very similar outlook. How people do hate home truths, especially the type of Rugby parent. Yours,

C. C. CARVER

67

My dear Maurice   *27.2.17*

Many thanks for your letter. I like " small beer chron-
icles," however trivial. You will be glad to hear that the
grand obstacle Hun Hunt is now open. There is no charge
for entry ! At present we are sitting looking dubiously at the
first fence. It's a devilish stiff one, old lad, devilish stiff. And
lots more like it to follow. However it's all in a lifetime—
and if one does take a nasty toss, there is always the satisfaction of knowing that one couldn't do it in a better cause.
And if a man gives his life for a definite object, it is not
natural to suppose that that object will cease to interest him,
he must " carry on " in some form or other. Otherwise
death, the most natural thing in life, would be unnatural.
We pass into life from the unknown, we pass out of life to the
unknown, but the " wheel swerves not a hair," there can
surely be no stopping. I am reading *Europe Unbound* by
L. March-Phillips. He is very insistent that we are fighting
for Liberty, though it is so natural, so fundamental in us
that we cannot always realize it. And it is so, I suppose. I
always feel that I am fighting for England, English fields,
lanes, trees, English atmospheres, and good days in England—and all that is synonymous for Liberty. One of our
battery commanders was very badly wounded to-day,
reconnoitring the place we are moving into, hence these
thoughts. A rotten job, for he leaves (and I fear he must) a
wife and 2 kiddies. . . .

CHRISTIAN

————

[To a Brother]   [France]
My dear old .Hump   *14.3.17*

How slips it this life with you ? WE are pushing ahead
almost *too* fast, but thank God we are in sight of getting out
of this hideous bit of country over which the worst fighting
has passed. Perhaps you imagine it as a place of broken trees
and ruined houses—as a fact there is nothing—NOthing.

We live in that desolate belt, extending from the Ancre to the Somme, some 5 miles in depth, where no trees remain to make a show of green in the coming Spring, and the chateaux and churches are pounded to mounds of red and white dust. We have just passed through a stage in which our habits have been largely nocturnal, owing to the bad taste of the hun in holding the high ground. Imagine us setting out as dusk is falling with some 60 braves, each leading 2 stalwart horses, on an enterprise connected with ammunition. We reach the appointed place in the pitchiest of darkness, and labour long in mud, and among pertinaciously surviving barbed wire, till by 2 a.m. or so the good work is done. A sickly yellow moon is showing now, looking almost as jaded as we. Wearily I clamber upon a steed, once white, and with some half dozen of the rear guard, set out for home. We proceed hastily through this first village (there are quite a few walls and things left, the advance has washed over it so quickly), for it has an evil reputation for travellers—no one has yet been found with sufficient hardihood to *live* there ! A certain corner rounded, we breathe more freely. Along the cliff road till we are brought to halt by a " block " in the road ahead. On our left a steep and shell-pocked bank, over which the moon is peeping. To our right and below us is the river stretching across a vista of broken stumps, running water and shell pools, to the skeleton gleaming white of another village on the far bank. If only an artist could paint the grim scene now while the hand of war and death is still hovering over it. In our steel helmets and chain visors we somehow recall *Pilgrim's Progress*, armoured figures passing through the valley of the shadow. On—for Apollyon's talons are over near. Steadily along the road, round curves and through a hollow, till we reach a point where some dead horses lie across the road. They were not there when we came up, and some ammunition wagons, standing horseless, and sprinkled with earth from 5.9″ crumps, tell their own story. Clatter and splash and clatter, on and on from desolation to desolation, till we reach the wagon line as dawn is breaking. And next night it is all to do again. By way of relieving the monotony we have just chivied a wild boar. God knows where he came from or why. Perhaps to visit the home of his childhood—in which case he will be disappointed. A heron also lives hereabouts. It is the last place *I* should choose. Yours, CHRISTIAN.

———

LANCE CORPORAL HAROLD CHAPIN
R.A.M.C.

American citizen. Educated University College School, London. Actor, producer and dramatist. Killed in action, France, 26 September, 1915, at the age of 29.

[TO HIS WIFE]

[France]
May [4th], 1915

... This a week of sensations but I really think last night will be unbeaten at the end of the war. It was by moonlight—almost full—that adds something, don't you think? I had taken three men in answer to a message incoherently delivered by a man on horseback, accompanied by two cyclists. ...

" Man gone mad down at —— they have got 'im in a little room—by the railway station."

We found him not raving but apparently asleep, wrapped in blankets, quiet as death. A stretcher was brought out of the motor and about a dozen spare stretcher slings I had thought to bring—fortunately—and we debated a moment in the moonlight. What a curious group we must have been on the deserted station platform, standing round him ! Then one of his chums touched him. You must imagine more than I can describe in this chatter. He raved and bit and beat out with fists and feet snarling like a dog—*really* like a dog—we got him on to a stretcher, and I lashed him on as gently as I could but very firmly. Once bending

70

across him I touched his face with my sleeve, he had it in his teeth in a minute—and in the midst of it men passed going up to the trenches singing. They passed along the road not 50 yards away while a dozen of us held him down by arms and legs and hair, and muffled him in blankets and packed him off with two of our men and two of his chums to our snug little brand new hospital at ——. Ashcroft and I then set out to walk back, to our station.

It was this walk in the moonlight with the star shells on the horizon and the rattling line towards which we were walking—(the station lies away from the firing line from here) that provided *the* sensation. I was naturally impressed. Ashcroft is a good obvious fellow. He prattled wonderingly of " Wot would make a chap go off like that." He supposed he had been " too daring like " and it had " *told* on him." " These engineers go mad very easy——" etc. Can't you hear him—an old liner steward—a bit of a gardener—a silk hat maker last job—age about forty ? The sort of man you meet fifty of in an hour.

We had to pass the wooded garden of the Chateau de ——. In the wood are about two score graves, half of our men and half of Indians—Khdir's and Ali's—beautifully tended graves shining in bead wreaths and pine crosses. Over them in the moonlight a nightingale was singing loud and sweet. Its first notes were so close and so low I was startled.

Eh bien, I can't express it. I feel as if for a week past a great super-human artist had been painting over me, in all the colours and sounds and feelings and scents of creation, a picture of himself. He is Reality one moment, Mystery the next.

Have I mentioned the spy we saw in uniform, being marched away under armed guard—swaggering but unable to swagger in a straight line. I should not be surprised to hear he was no spy and got off—but he swaggered and he was frightened. . . .

I went up to the —th H.Q., this afternoon to see two men buried. Their chums were so particular to dig them a *level*

grave and a *rectangular* grave and *parallel* graves, and to
note who was in this grave, who in that, that my mind,
jumping to questions as always, was aching with why's
which I would not have asked for the world—almost as if
the answer—you take me—would disgrace me for not
knowing already—brand me as lacking some decency the
grave diggers had.

Oh Lord, the mystery of men's feelings.

————

[France]

[To His Wife]   ·May [*29th*], *1915*

We are rather crushed to day, Darling. Casualties—our
first. Two killed, one injured (slightly), one suffering from
shock. All C. Section men, but not great friends of mine—
though I liked them. M—who knew the two dead very intimately—is fearfully down : seems to think he should have
been with them. Curious how people feel, isn't it ? I feel
most for their mothers. C—the younger of the two—was
only nineteen and such a child ; though very tall. They
were all smashed by a shell. I wish to God England would
come into this war and get it over ! I told you I thought
November. It won't be November twelve month unless
England drops attacking Kitchener, attacking the *Daily
Mail*, attacking defenceless Germans in London, striking
and all the rest of it, and devotes all its attention to attacking the German Army out here. If you at home could only
see and hear the enormous concentration of force necessary
.to take a mile of German trench ; the terrific resistance we
have to put up to hold it ; the price we have to pay over
every little failure—a price paid with no purchase to show
for it—if you could only see and realise these things there'd
be some hope of you all bucking in and supplying the little
extra force—the little added support in resistance—that we
need to end this murderous, back and forth business. Every
man not engaged in supplying food and warmth and order

—bare necessities—to those at home should be directly engaged in supplying strength toward the ending of the war. If he isn't doing so he is contributing by neglect to that killing and maiming of our men out here *which he might be preventing*. I am not exaggerating an iota. This is mere truth which cannot be gainsaid. There can only be one reason for not serving : selfishness. And selfishness at this time is not the commonsense quality it is in ordinary times, since no man is now looking after himself or could look after himself entirely. He is part of the crowd which those of its complement who are serving are looking after, and he could no more look after himself than anyone of the men out here can look after himself, but each can help to look after the crowd and be looked after in return. The Devil of it is that so many have slipped into the crowd and are being looked after in return for nothing. That is the weakness. . . .

———————

[France]

[To His Mother]   *1st June, 1915*

. . . I can stick anything but depressed fracture of the skull. A man died in one of the wards here of that, Galton watching him. He had a ward to himself (they make such a noise) and a mouse came out and ran back and forth under the stretcher he was tied to. Galton called me to watch ; he was quite fascinated. These things almost *please* one by their perfection of eeriness and horror. Do you understand ? They are like some gigantic supernatural artist in the grotesque and horrible. I shall never fear the picturesque in stage grouping again. Never have I seen such perfect grouping as when, after a shell had fallen round the corner from here a fortnight ago, three of us ran round and the light of an electric torch lit up a little interior ten ft. square, with one man sitting against the far wall, another lying across his feet and a dog prone in the foreground, all dead and covered thinly with the dust of powdered plaster and masonry brought down by the explosion ! They might have been grouped so for forty years—not a particle of dust hung in the air, the white light showed them, pale whitey-brown, like a terra-cotta group. That they were dead seemed right and proper—but that they had ever been alive—beyond all credence. The fact that I had seen them " mount guard " was in another department of experience altogether and never occurred to me till some days later.

Of all the curious things of war the most curious is the way my old problems of perception, experience, and appre-hension—their relation to reality—the way those problems are being *lit up*. We have some really brilliant men among our officers. One in particular who—not deeming himself a surgeon (pure swank, he was going to perform a trephining without turning a hair—but such swank is most *sympathique*, isn't it ?) generally acts as anaesthetist, is often most illum-inating with a word here or there just when one is wonder-ing—as one can in the middle of holding down a half-anaesthetized and very energetic Scot or Guardsman—just what feeling is and what consciousness ; how can there be degrees down from our normal to zero and if there can be degrees up as well—you follow ?—to some zenith of appre-hensiveness to existence. Of course the normal capacity for perception fluctuates a little. Has it any limits up as it obviously has down ?—at *un*consciousness ? The devil of it is that an imaginative projection can be so easily mistaken for a conception the result of higher sensitiveness—percep-tiveness. So many of the mystics seem to me to have been merely people gifted with imaginations. The Brontë sister perhaps—what was her name ?—and Wordsworth, and A.E. and Evelyn Underhill genuine exceptions, the rest—most of them—imaginative. " Thyrsus-bearers " casting their imaginings in the form of active experience. . . .

Dearest,   *July 22nd, 1915*

   ... I am quite incapable of doing justice to this morning's
entertainment. " They " have been shelling the most
thickly—and poorly—populated part of this little mining
town. Some of us went up into it getting the wounded out.
Horses, men, women, and children blown to pieces by huge
high explosives—and more shells coming over every few
minutes, all within a couple of yards of the hospital. I want
to tell you all I see—all that happens to me out here, but
almost fail to convey it—and I don't want you *quite* to
share my feelings. Amusing, ironic contrasts abounded :
within five minutes of each other came in a self-possessed
young woman of about ten to have the remains of her arm
cut off—perfectly calm—walked in, never cried or showed
the least excitement, *and* a man of fifty on a stretcher with
a mangled leg, who roared out in an enormous mad voice
for his " *Maman* " over and over again till he was
anaesthetized. Could any creation of the imagination equal
this ? Or this scene in a squalid kitchen :—a huge woman
dead on her face across the threshold, a little child also dead
at her feet, the legs of her men folk (husband and son ?)
straggling across the foot way outside (I am keeping back
the hundreds of horrible details, hard though it may be to
believe it) and her remaining daughter, a child of about
twelve, leaping back and forth over the bodies struggling
to get a chain from the neck of the body. " *Souvenir !* " I
tried to get her away—she was half mad—but was assailed
fiercely by neighbours on her behalf, who seemed to regard
her desire for a memento of her mother under the circumstances, most natural and commendable. While I was being
suppressed another shell came over and we went to earth
in a heap, the hundred yards away crash bringing down
plaster and crockery on to our heads and the flying pieces
of " case " buzzing past the windows like enormous bees
or small aeroplanes. When they had settled the child returned to the chain—armed now with a carving knife—and
I left her to it. ...

CAPTAIN CHARLES MURRAY CHILDE

Gloucestershire Regiment

Educated Clifton and Pembroke College, Cambridge. Medical student.
Died of wounds, France, 21 March, 1916, at the age of 21.

[France]
21 /9 /15

I am sending a five-leaved clover which I found the other day on the way to my billet, and which I hope will bring luck. There's not much to write about. Life in billets is very peaceful. I have found my horse very useful and I generally go for a ride in the evening and have tea in the town quite near here and get the English papers. There has been a heavy artillery duel between the French and the Germans, and we can hear, and have heard for some days, a fairly heavy booming going on down south. I have been reading 1st Army Intelligence to-night and it is highly enjoyable. The Huns have been heard " yelling "—I quote the very word—in the trenches opposite a bit north, and men here say that they have heard yelling in the trenches opposite us. If I could talk to you about it all, you would go off and have a real good dinner on the strength of it. Another thing we have heard from the Staff is that the Germans have lost a fearful lot of men against the Russians and that now, as you can read in the papers, the Japs and Yankees have succeeded in getting their ammunition along to them. I have been a confirmed pessimist so far, but, taking it all round, and reading the Dardanelles news, I believe the rotten breed of Germans is in for far, far more than it ever bargained for. But it all must take time.

Here's a pleasant tit-bit, which ought to be framed in gold ! The French Staff report that at Souchez last week they captured 2000 of the breed, pumped them dry of information, disarmed them and then packed them off down a communication trench. A Zouave or two were waiting

round a traverse and as each Deutsche filed past he was
gracefully and neatly despatched ; cf. Agag of old. The
French don't want prisoners—all they want is scalps, and
you would feel the same after a long week-end in the Glory
Hole Orchard.

THE REV. OSWIN CREIGHTON
C.F.

Educated Marlborough and Keble College, Oxford. Served as Army
Chaplain in Gallipoli and France. Killed by aeroplane bomb, France,
15 April, 1918, at the age of 35.

[From a diary letter describing the Battle of Arras]

[France,

early 1917.]

. . . On Tuesday (27th) I was up at the batteries for a
burial. The trench mortar working party was out and a
shell fell among them, killing two men and wounding six.
. . . The whole battery turned out, and we escorted the
bodies to the grave. I talked a little about the meaning of
death. But I never quite know if it helps people to realise
the meaning of life and its persistence. There are few people
who definitely wish to deny it. But men generally take up
such an extreme agnostic position with regard to it, largely
as an escape from the sloppy sentimentalism of hymns and
Christmas cards, that they stand by the grave of their friends
and merely shrug their shoulders. I think it is rather a
splendid attitude. As Gibbon, I believe, said, the Turks
fought with the fanaticism born of an overwhelming conviction of the joys of Paradise, and the Christians fought
equally courageously though they had no such certainty.
I suppose the finest character springs from those who see
nothing beyond the present. And yet the future seems so
increasingly clear and certain to me. Death is absolutely

nothing to me now, except rather a violent shock, which one's peaceful and timid nature shrinks from. The gloomy articles in *The Nation*, for instance, which see nothing but the horror of Europe soaked in blood, and all the flower of youth being cut off, say very little to me. The horror of war is the light it throws on all the evil, ignorance, materialism, bigotry, and sectional interests in human nature. Surely death is not the horror of war, but the causes which contribute to war. The Cross is beautiful—the forces which lead up to it are damnable. It really does not in the least matter how many people are killed, who wins, whether we starve or anything else of a transitory nature, provided that in the process human nature is transformed in some way or another. I am not nearly so much depressed by death, or even by the thought of the success of the U-boat campaign or a revolution in Ireland, as by the absolute stone walls of ignorance, prejudice and apathy one finds oneself face to face with everywhere. . . .

Curiously enough, another incident happened immediately after the funeral. I was in the mess, taking down particulars, when we heard the sound of machine-gun fire. We rushed out and found an aeroplane battle on. Some Boche planes had come right over the town and were swooping down on our observer. No anti-aircraft guns were firing at them. The Hun planes are tremendously fast. A plane just above us caught fire and dropped a flaming mass to the ground just behind the convent. Instinctively we all rushed round. I thought possibly one might be able to do something. There lay a smouldering mass of wreckage. They dragged it away, and there lay two charred, black, smouldering lumps, which a few minutes before had been active, fearless men. It was not a pleasant sight to one's refined and delicate feelings. I felt rather staggered, and it loomed before me all day and night. But after all what did it signify?—the utter futility of violence and force. Ignorance again.

The Colonel wanted a canteen started, and that same day I found a place for one behind the guns. It was the house belonging to a doctor, an eye specialist, sumptuously built, heated with hot water, with a nice garden at the back. We soon got the canteen going there. The men patronise it all the time. It is really extraordinary the part played by the stomach in life. It simply rules the world, and affects all our outlook on life. We are paralysed, absorbed, hypnotised by it. The chief topic of conversation is rations with the men, and food and wine with the officers. Men pour into my canteens and buy everything up. For four Sundays I have been up to Arras to hold evening service. Twice I arranged it at the canteen. The men filed out when it began, and were back again for cocoa when it was over. (I have just stopped writing this to eat a piece of cake.) I felt rather furious last time. What is the use of feeding men if they deliberately set themselves against any attempt to teach or help them see the truth ? I preached at all services one Sunday on " Man shall not live by bread alone," and said that while that was the first truth laid down by Christ, it was the last that man could understand. We have no need to worry about the U-boat campaign, but we must worry over the absolute famine of words proceeding from the mouth of God. What is Government doing now, but hurling invective and living in suppressed strife ? How can there be a united nation without the passion for truth above all else ? We are hypnotised by an unscrupulous press. We are always being taught to hate the Germans, and to refuse to think or speak of peace. We are told about our glorious cause till it simply stinks in the nostrils of the average man. We all know we have got to fight as long as we wear the uniform, and have thereby committed ourselves to slaughter as many Germans as possible. But I, for one, and I tell the men exactly the same, utterly refuse to hate the Kaiser or any of them or to believe that I am fighting for a glorious cause, or anything that the papers tell me. But if man learns to live a little more on the words coming out of God's, and not Northcliffe's, ecclesiastics', politicians', or any one else's mouths—the war does not really matter. . . . Meanwhile I seem to be reversing the process with the canteens. Men do not want to think or learn. They are weary, sodden, patient, hungry, cheerful, good-natured animals. . . .

––––––––

CAPTAIN JOHN EUGENE CROMBIE
Gordon Highlanders

Educated Winchester. Joined Army from school. Died of wounds, France, 23 April, 1917, at the age of 20.

[To His Mother]

[France]
March 2nd, 1917

It has turned dreadfully cold here again, and of course we can't get fires in the tents. It will be much more comfortable in the line, and I am quite looking forward to going there. It is beautifully sunny to-day, so Sinclair and I are going to Arras to have a look at it. From a distance there seems quite a lot of it left, and I believe there is a square of cloisters built by the Moors, which is almost untouched and very pretty. I will leave this open till I come back. The Union of Democratic Control was the only sensible Socialist organisation before the war, and a very good one. I don't know what its Peace ideas are, but as a matter of fact I am quite in agreement with Snowden and that lot. Their trouble to my mind is, that they have such an irritating way of putting their opinions, not that the opinions are wrong in themselves. Anyhow when you think of it, the moral situation is damnable—we can only beat Germany by assuming her mentality, by recognising the State as the Supreme God whose behests as to military efficiency must be obeyed, whether or no they run counter to Christianity and morality. We call their use of gas inhuman, but we have to adopt it ourselves ; we think their policy of organising the individual life contrary to the precepts of freedom, but we have to adopt it ourselves ; we profess to shudder at the Zabern incidents, but what of our treatment of conscientious objectors ? Oh ! There are stacks of incidents, and the only hope is that we can drop it after the war. I agree I can't suggest an alternative, but I also agree with Ramsay Macdonald, that it shows that the way to defeat German militarism was not by fighting it—not the best way at least. And I don't believe we shall stamp out German Militarism at the end of it ; you can't change a nation's morality by military conquest, I am sure. But of course one must admit that if we had not fought them, what else were we to do ? I suppose at this stage of the world's history one could not expect anything else. It is an interesting question. . . .

I have just returned from Arras. Oh, Lord ! what a spot ! For sheer desolation I have not seen anything to equal it, and I can't describe the feeling it gives to go into it. " B.V." ought to have lived to see it before he wrote " the City of Dreadful Night," but as he didn't I expect I shall have to do it for him, when next I am inspired. It's far the biggest town I have seen, in fact I suppose it is the biggest on our front, and it is just in the state that makes the horror of it most impressive, like seeing a strong healthy man dying of some disgusting wasting disease, and his limbs dropping off with scurvy. We went through a sort of *Arc de Triomphe* straight into one of the main streets. The street was narrow, and all the houses on either side very tall. There are no inhabitants except for men living in the cellars, and every house shows hopeless dilapidation, but almost the worst part is that the outer walls are for the most part still standing, and through the unglazed windows and the holes from the shells, you saw the broken rafters, torn bits of wall paper, and debris of bricks and furniture at the bottom. And there was the long narrow ribbon of street utterly silent, and the walls, with nothing but ruin behind them, aslant and tottering, till it seemed a push with your hand would overset them : and indeed they do collapse frequently, for we saw many heaps of bricks, and there are large notices everywhere warning you to walk close into the walls and not in the middle of the streets. You can't conceive the effect of a really big town in that state, however you try ; it is far worse than seeing the place totally ruined, and in heaps of bricks and nothing more. It is those ghastly, sightless, purposeless walls that catch you, and the silence. For the life of me I could not have talked loud ; I think the echo would have sent me mad. We went down to the Cathedral, an enormous high building, and once I suppose rather fine, in the usual Romanesque style. Its outer walls are standing too, but it has no roof, and it's no place to stay in and admire, for chunks of masonry were falling down at the rate of about one a minute. That sort of ruin I have seen before—but those streets !—Who was the chap in Greek mythology, who, as a punishment in Hades, was put under a cliff, which was always tottering and about to fall and crush him, and never did ? It must have been worse torture than most. . . .

———

[France]
[TO A FRIEND]   *March 3, 1917*

As for the morals of the war, they are horrible. Perhaps they are a little worse than we are, but the point is that by fighting we have hopelessly degenerated our own morals. For instance, listen to this. Without going into details, for " mopping up " a captured trench i.e. bombing out the remaining inhabitants, you have parties of nine men specially equipped. When you come to a dug-out, you throw some smoke bombs down, and then smoke the rest out with a smoke bomb, so that they must either choke or come out. Now when they come out they are half blinded and choked with poisonous smoke, and you station a man at the entrance to receive them, but as you have only got a party of nine, it would be difficult to spare men if you took them prisoners, so the instructions are that these poor half-blinded devils should be bayoneted as they come up. It may be expedient from a military point of view, but if it had been suggested before the war, who would not have held up their hands in horror? The fact is, that if we decide to beat the German at his own game, we can only do it by being more Prussian than the Prussian; if we hate all that is Prussian, we shall become all that we hate. If we do win, it is only an argument for the Prussian, that if he had been a little more Prussian he would have won, and he will probably strive to be more so the next time, which is the very thing we wanted to avoid, and it can only be prevented by our keeping our top-dog attitude to him. It's absolutely Gilbertian, but I don't think we will make the German a pacifist except by example, and we have given him back his own example, only rather more efficiently. But, the question is, what else could we do? If we did not fight, we admitted the superiority of his example, as it showed us that he could conquer us, and that by conquest he could force on us his principles. It is an extraordinary tangle when you think of it. And I am sorry to be pessimistic, but I doubt if it will have helped us to find God. Among the millions actually fighting it seems only to have increased the drunkenness and vice—perhaps some among those at home, anxious for dear ones fighting, may have learnt to rely on Him. It is wonderful to think of Peace, and all this ghastliness ended.

LIEUTENANT ARCHIBALD WILLIAM ROBERTSON DON
The Black Watch

Educated Winchester and Trinity College, Cambridge. Medical student. Died on active service, Macedonia, 11 September, 1916, at the age of 26.

[Macedonia]

[TO MISS HELEN HILL]   *27th May, 1916*

I am bound to try and explain and justify my hanging on to the U.D.C. King's Regulations and Army Acts forbid me to go to a U.D.C. meeting in uniform : personally, I don't think I should go at all. K.R. and A.A. forbid me to organise a U.D.C. meeting ' near a camp or barracks.' I should never dream of doing so. But the A.A. and K.R.'s do not forbid me to support a College mission, or to write an article on brotherly love in the *Church Family Newspaper*, or to belong to the Cavendish Club or the U.D.C. If, of course, the U.D.C. were a treasonable or anti-national organisation the situation would be changed. I honestly and deeply feel convinced that there is no sort or kind of duplicity in serving King, Country, and the cause behind the U.D.C. simultaneously. In fact, almost it is because I believe in the U.D.C. that I also wish to fight for King and Country. It is just because the beating of the Germans is essential to the cause of humanity that the war is bearable and quite worth doing. Personally, I don't feel I am fighting to preserve more than the soil of England of the past, and its associations and some of its traditions : that is a lot to fight for : but far more I want to fight that England may go ahead towards a future in which she may be the leader and forerunner. It is to preserve the future, not the past so much, that most of those I know are fighting and have fought.

The U.D.C. is full of the faults of a young thing, struggling under excessive, almost destroying circumstances. It is sometimes over-eager to be fair to the enemy ; sometimes over-critical (out of a deep-down love of her) of England ; it is indiscreet at times. But it is something to cling to, and merge with, and help on. A consolation for partially lost freedom of thought and action. I regret that the U.D.C. members of Parliament give the impression of being over-critical of England sometimes.

You are doubtful about this U.D.C. Papers again and again have accused it of pro-German sympathies, or undermining our will to fight. Of course in a sense it is pro-German : so am I : so in that sense I imagine are you : but it does not mean pro-German in the sense that we wish Germany to win. It is not out to stop the war in the peace-at-any-price manner. I have not the slightest intention of being very silly till after the war.[1]

LIEUTENANT RICHARD DONALDSON, M.C.
R.N.V.R.

Educated Glasgow University. Joined R.N.V.R. while a student. Killed in action, France, 5 September, 1918, at the age of 22.

[TO HIS MOTHER] On Active Service [Flanders]
My Dear Mother,   *14.11.17*

When I come home on leave you must not marvel if I am restless. This is a restless life of ours out here, and the wonder should be that I am able to sit down even for five consecutive minutes. Yesterday we moved ; and on the day before, we moved ; and on Saturday (two days previous) we moved. But be content. At each step we have moved back, away from the line, by easy stages, and last night I slept out of earshot of the guns in the most clean and picturesque village I have ever seen in this benighted country.

Up to the present I have seen only one aspect of this part of France—mud ! Of course even the mud can startle by its beauty on occasions, as when I looked from my hut through what might have been a porthole of a ship and saw a stretch of grey water, as sombre and still a sea as any sailor gazed on. And last Wednesday morning, just a week ago as I write, I stood by an old German trench and watched the blessed sun dawning on still another sea of mud. And that too was beautiful ! Sunrise, gold and orange and purple fading into an ultra violet that the eye could not discern, and under it mud and swamp and brimming shell-holes, all reflecting the gaudy colours of the sky. Only there was no life about it, no men, no birds, no creeping things ; and the stillness was painful because the guns were suddenly silent.

[1] He resigned his membership of the U.D.C. about two weeks later.

But now I have seen another aspect of the country and a more familiar beauty.

This village is reminiscent of Rosebank at its prettiest, only it seems scarcely so fragile and considerably bigger. The villagers are kind, there are green fields and trees and cattle and the Battery is settling down for a real rest. . . .

With love to all,

Believe me

Your very affectionate son

RICHARD

[TO HIS SISTER]   [France]

My Dear ——   *9.5.18*

I am writing this in my orchard. The sun is again very warm to-day and I have been having my meals out of doors. Beside me stands a little folding-table just like a card-table, and as a centre-piece it has a glass vase holding a bouquet of wild hyacinth. Lunch is just over, and before I set to work on my official correspondence I am going to write you this other note home. You would love to see my present abode, and I can assure you it is very pretty indeed. I do not mean that the abode itself is very pretty, for after all it is only a dug-out in a hedge—but the entourage is really exquisite. Except for some coils of barbed wire dumped in a corner of my vineyard and for the intermittent thunder of the guns, there is nothing at hand that savours of the war. A little green enclosure of some forty yards square, hedged in by trees and with parallel lines of trees running across it—such is my home for the nonce. The trees are blossoming now and the green in the branches is mingled with delicate pink and white. On the ground beneath there is another shade of green tinged with the brilliant gold of the dandelion and buttercup. It is the same wherever one goes in this area.

This morning I had a very pleasant stroll with Petty Officer Houston over a country that was well known to both of us and where we battled long ago. It was a little pathetic to look again on the old familiar scenes, but never before did we see them under such wonderfully picturesque conditions. Whole fields seemed like lakes of gold, and the sun shone down on them as we never believed it could in this country. And then Houston said " What about to-day in the Kyles, sir ? " And I *nearly* became sad again for I had just read in Tuesday's " *Herald* " that the " *Lord of the Isles* " would commence its sailings in a few days' time and I had been dreaming of that first whiff of the salt sea just below Bowling, and the smell of the seaweed at Gourock Pier, and the wee room at Elm Cottage where one could stand on a bed with one's head through the sky-light and see the Cumbrae light go out and out and—miss one ! Still, after all, it's good to think about 'em, even if we can't see 'em now—and here's hoping ! Your RICHARD.

————

PRIVATE THOMAS DRY

23rd Battalion, Australian Imperial Force

Watchmaker. Enlisted in Australia March, 1915. Killed in action, France, 4 August, 1916, at the age of 28.

[TO HIS FAMILY]   Egypt.
Dear Mother, Dad and Family.   *January 15th, 1916*

Being fortunate enough to have a friend of mine returning to Australia, he informed me he would deliver this letter to you personally, so that I am at liberty to write what is the truth, otherwise I could write but little, as the censor delights in running his great pencil through. My friend, M— L— by name, who was with me at Broadmeadows, is one of my best friends. Ask him to relate our experience in Egypt, especially the time when we went to help one of our boys and chased the natives with bayonets. He is being sent back with heart disease, so give him a good time.

We landed at Gallipoli on the notorious soil on which our boys first put foot, namely " Anzac," on the 4th September 1915. We came over from Egypt to Lemnos on the " *Haversford* " and stopped a day and half. Then we transferred from

the " *Haversford* " to a low flat boat named the " *Partritch*."
. . . We had to continue our journey in flat barges to the
shore and so we landed. A few spent bullets pinged in the
water close by, but no one was hit. It was dark when we
landed, the time somewhere about 10 p.m. Looming up in
the darkness against the skyline could be seen the cliff over
which our gallant lads charged on the never to be forgotten
25th April, 1915. That was the first sight that met our eyes,
and I tell you we were amazed to think that soldiers could
charge over such ground, especially when we saw it later
on in the daylight. The Cliff rose perpendicular and what
with scrub and other obstacles, it is no wonder that Australia has earned such a name.

Of this you must ere now know as much as I can tell you,
seeing that pictures have appeared in some of the papers,
but starting at the beginning, I must describe things as they
happened to me.

The cracking of rifles, which resembles somewhat the
croaking of millions of frogs, and the occasional boom of a
big gun could now be heard, and we were all curiosity.
Marching along the beach, we saw the flat bottomed boats
in which the *first lot of soldiers* landed lying bottom upwards,
some partly broken, but all pierced with bullet holes told
us what that landing must have cost. Continuing our
march, we were halted in " Rest Gully," where we bivou-
acked for the night. . . .

After resting for a day and a half we were sent to relieve
the lads who had landed. Our baptism, and a severe one it
seemed to me at the time, but was only a fleabite to later on.
We were all posted thus. The trenches are very high, and to
get on your post you have to step up. Then standing
straight up, an average man's head would be level with the
top. For protection sand-bags are stacked two deep with a
loop hole. The loop hole is about 2 or 3 feet long by 2 feet
of sheet steel, and a hole large enough to put the rifle
through with a door which you close when not in use. The
steel is about an inch thick. Two men mount a post, two
hours on, two hours sitting on the step, ready with a blanket

or overcoat to throw over bombs should they come over, and two hours sleep. For six days and nights we did this without a spell, and then when we had what they call a spell, we had to go and deepen a trench with pick and shovel—48 hours in the trenches and 48 hours out. So we worked after, but it was just as bad out as in, and as dangerous. At first we used to sleep at the bottom of the trench, and being only a little over 2 feet wide, and N.C.O.'s walking about all night, we were walked all over ; but nature must have its way, and we slept.

You would see bloodstains all over your post where perhaps the soldier on before you was hit, and pieces of a rifle smashed to atoms. Things were fairly quiet for awhile, and then they gave us a demonstration. The never ceasing crack of the thousands of rifles, and the boom boom of the bigger guns. The bursting of the shells,—a moan telling that some poor unfortunate soldier was hit, made up for the quietness. The hand bombs were worse than anything excepting shells. We were in places only a few yards from the Turks and hand bombs did the most damage. The night is the worst and busiest part of the twenty-four hours. Each side is looking and waiting for an attack. Every man in the trenches has to " stand to " with bayonets fixed in case the Turks attack, from an hour before dawn till daylight. Firing over 100 shots in a night I think caused me to go a bit deaf, or else the explosion of a bomb. Be that as it may, the fact remains I went deaf, and was put on assisting the engineers. You said in one of your letters that the rest behind the firing line would do me good. At Gallipoli, Mum, there is no such thing as behind the firing line. Down the beach—in your dugout, it is all the same, and the man that has set foot on Gallipoli, in my opinion, has done his bit. The Engineers work right in the firing [line], and I would just as soon be at my post. The Engineers sap towards the Turks' trenches, and the Turks sap towards us. Should we hear the Turks picking we locate whereabouts they are, and try to get underneath them and blow them up, and they do the same. It is just like a race. To give you an idea what a sap is, try and imagine a tunnel going in about 10 to 15 ft., then down 20 feet, another drive about 12 feet and then another shaft sunk another 10 ft.

I was in one when it was blown up, and will never forget the experience. I was only just in the mouth at the time, but the force of the charge caused me to stagger against the opposite side of the trench, and I had to feel if my nose was on and my eyes correct. They were alright. I might here say that when a sap is blown up the charge is so strong that it shakes the earth, and the feeling is just as if a huge giant tilted the earth from underneath. What I did not like about sapping was that should the Turks charge or anything else happen you were caught in a trap, being as it were, in the bowels of the earth. Just before I left it snowed and became bitterly cold, and was the cause of a lot of us being sent away sick. Men were getting frost bitten feet, and when they removed their boots, they could not put them on again, on account of the swelling. Men were wearing socks as gloves, and here it was where Grandma's gloves came handy. On top of this snow, bitterly cold, as it was, the Turks opened up a heavy bombardment. The heaviest bombardment the Peninsula has known, so some who were at the landing tell us. They kept their fire on Lonesome Pine only, and the 23rd and 24th were holding Lonesome Pine and bore the brunt of it all. Shells of all descriptions were poured into us. You would feel the earth quake as a shell would bore its way into the earth. Men were ordered to take cover in the tunnels, but of what avail ? A shell would come crashing through the tunnel and bury unknown numbers alive. Stretcher bearers running past with their dead or wounded, Officers giving orders, and Hell was let loose. How I escaped I know not—shrapnel was falling by me, shells passing overhead on their deadly mission, and there I lay with never a scratch. The worst of all this was the fact that the warships, artillery and big guns answered never a shot. Here were we getting bowled over like nine-pins, and us taking it like so many sheep. Every man there waited for the order to charge, and have some of their own back. As far as is known, between the 23rd and 24th over 200 men were lost in that bombardment without as much as one shot in self defence. Then came the calm. Our trenches were all knocked about. Dirt piled up like the pyramids. We had to go and dig out who we could, and a gruesome game it was. Pieces of flesh, scalp, legs, tunics tattered and parts of soldiers carried away in blankets. By God, to stand by and see your own boys dug out in pieces and do nothing is almost unbearable.

Such is war, and the curse to the ones who are the cause of it. Many a brave man had tears in his eyes, as, gazing on some friend in almost unrecognizable masses, he had but a minute before his death been joking with him. Imagine you are all sitting down to a meal with friends around you, when all of a sudden by some unseen hand the person to whom you are speaking drops dead by your side. Before you have recovered a head flies off another of your friends, and you then look around, and seeing nothing, you gaze on what is before you. Then the feeling would come over you that you would like to avenge their death. We do not blame the Turks as, unseen by us, they no doubt have suffered more than we have, and all is fair in war. The Turks from what I have seen of them are fair fighters, and from the appearance of the prisoners we captured are glad to be out of the fight. They wear all sorts of clothing, and seem fond of gay colours. Some were coming in to us to surrender, but as soon as our fellows saw them they shot them dead. This is due to their treachery early in the war. They are big men, and one we pulled over the parapet had a chest on him like an ox. At night they sometimes would creep up to our trenches and throw bombs into us, or wait until you opened the loop-hole and then shoot at you. I never struck any on my post, but others told me that is what they used to do.

The miseries of Gallipoli.

Now we come to the hardships of Gallipoli. It is reckoned that Gallipoli is one of the hardest fronts to fight on. Unlike France, there are no friendly villages to get a little comfort or food, neither is there any flat country with farms. Nothing but mountains, and barren at that, save for a little scrub here and there, to say nothing of the flies with which we had to contend. These pests would be on your face, hands, down your throat, and if you were eating biscuits with jam on, it was more like biscuits and flies. We slept in dugouts, which is a place dug out of the side of a trench, with sufficient width and length to lie in with ease. The lower they were the better protection for the occupier. Here was another misery. You would turn in your sleep and knock your head or arm against the top, and the soil, being of a sandy nature, would fall down on your face, and if you happened to have your mouth open you would get it full, but we soon got used to that, and after awhile got very comfortable. These are as nothing compared to the lice. For a week I did not feel them, but after that I suffered the tortures of hell, and to use the only expression, became " lousey." Each day I would kill about 50, and woe to him who neglected going through himself each day. He would not sleep that night.

There was no getting rid of them. They would breed on you, and no matter how often you changed yourself, you would be just as bad next day. We could not wash our-selves, as there was a scarcity of water. The only chance to wash yourself was to go down to the beach, but so dangerous did this become, owing to the havoc caused by the gun known as " Beachy Bill," that it was not worth the risk. In fact, they had police there to prevent anyone so doing. This may seem to you overdrawn, but it is the truth. My skin was red raw through scratching myself. All were the same. One fellow said he had none on him. We took his shirt off, and it was swarming with them. When we showed him he said he did not know what they were before, but thought it was fleas that bit him at night. To read this you would think it im-possible that we slept at night, but so hardened had we become that after we had a scratch or two we would fall asleep, and they would then do their worst. The fleas were not nearly so numerous.

Food

You ask me in one of your letters how we get on for food. I dared not mention the truth, for you would never have received the letter. You may think some of my letters funny from the front not giving much news, but the fact was, we were not allowed to tell much. For instance I wrote simply saying the sights here are ghastly and I was told the censor had done his work with his masterful stroke. For breakfast we got a slice of bacon with either biscuits or bread and plenty of tea. Dinner either rice, which was good, or stew. The stew at first was made of bully beef and dessicated vegetables. For tea, sometimes rice or stew with tea. At this time we got a fair amount of bread, but not sufficient to last a day. Jam was issued every day. A pound tin between three, and plenty of water. Later on we got fresh meat stew and steak in the morning. This was good while it lasted. Then came the change. In the first place a shell knocked some of our dixies over and made us short, and we had to suffer. Instead of getting rice and stew each day, we got for breakfast sometimes bacon. For dinner tea only, and for tea rice or stew. We were issued with a 2 lb loaf between 3 men, but could not get a biscuit on the peninsula. This bread was only sufficient for one meal, but had to last you for a day. Then we got biscuits, but could not get bread and our meals consisted of the following : 6 biscuits per man, which were as hard as iron. They taste something like cabin biscuits. A piece of bacon, which you could eat in one mouthful, and a quarter ration of tea. Water was getting scarce. For dinner just a cupful of tea and bully and biscuits if you liked to eat it. For tea a little stew. Then came the starvation rations. Three biscuits a day. No bacon or sometimes a little and a very little stew. For dinner we got a little cheese but only a bite. To top the lot, we could not get water or tea to drink for nearly a fortnight. So bad did our thirst become that we had to go down to the cooks and get a drop in the middle of the night at the risk of getting into serious trouble, as they had sentries stationed all round. Then the snow came and we ate it, but it takes a lot to quench your thirst. Some, who were fortunate enough to find wood, melted a lot of snow and got water that way. So bad were things that I saw a fellow near me go round picking old pieces of bacon off the parapet and eating them, and to quench his thirst drink out of a dirty well where perhaps dead bodies had been. This is the gospel truth, as M— L— will tell you. You may not believe it, but things were that bad over there, that if fellows were carried out on a stretcher wounded some would say " Lucky devil, I would give a limb to be there." I would not go that far, but I often wished for a nice little wound to give me a spell. You will hear soldiers who are wounded now that they are home again exaggerate to some extent such as " dying to get back again." I have been through the mill, and know that all or most who were on the peninsula would not like it again. It was a great joke to us to read some of the letters by the soldiers, and many a laugh we had over them. It seems that I am appearing as a coward, but were we ordered back to Gallipoli to-morrow, I would go willingly, but not with the same enthusiasm, knowing that we cannot get the proper treatment as at other fronts. No matter where we go now it will never be as bad as Gallipoli. . . .

Our Company are in camp at Tel-El-Kaber, and as far as I know we are to guard Egypt. Be that as it may, I have been through Gallipoli and I care not where we go. Although this letter looks very black, do not think for one moment that I am trying to get away from it. I have written the truth as it happened to me and others, and if any soldier or officer reads this letter through and speaks the truth [they] will agree with me—that is providing that they have been to Gallipoli. We had our pleasure there as well, and were it not for the bad food it would not have been so bad. Now that I am away from it all, and have done my bit, so to speak, I think of my home, and would dearly like to see you all, and that is the feeling of the rest. I said to you before I left that I would come back and march through Collins Street, and I still think I will do it no matter how long the war lasts. I am not only alive, but fatter, stronger and harder, and the bullet has yet to find me.

You know that I am a believer in fate, so I will give you a few instances which have strengthened my belief. Standing on a rise gazing out to sea, an explosion caused me to suddenly turn, and with lightning speed pieces of shrapnel passed me within an inch front and back overhead. In short I was in a shower of shrapnel. One soldier was killed and another wounded while I, who stood in the middle of it all, never got a scratch. Another time I shifted from my dugout into another. Hardly had I left my old dugout than it was blown in. Had I been in it at the time, my career would have been ended. I could mention dozens of cases where fellows have been saved by being away from places where they should have been. A step forward is enough sometimes to save you, or, on the other hand it may be fatal. It was no use. You just had to take your chance, whether walking, standing, or sleeping. I was sitting down when a soldier came up and started to talk to me. He sat down on my right, and the next minute got shot through the thigh. Here is where fate comes in. On my right there was barely enough room for him to sit, while on the left there was tons of room. Had he sat on my left that bullet would have been mine. Some call it luck, but I would like to know what prompted him to sit on my right. . . .

Your loving Son
TOM.

————

SERGEANT JAMES DUNCAN, M.M.
R.G.A.

Educated Public Schools, Islay, Argyll. Coal merchant. Killed in
action, France, 23 September, 1918, at the age of 38.

[To the Rev. Duncan MacArthur.
Believed to be his last letter]

France.

Dear Duncan   *5.9.18*

. . . I suppose you will want to know something about
the war. As you will see by the papers we are living in
stirring and moving times.

In the Spring the Hun sowed the wind and lo, in the
Autumn he reapeth the whirlwind. The seed was sown by
the sweat of tears, the harvest is gathered by the sweat of
blood.

I have followed in the wake of the grim reaper, and have
helped to sharpen his sickle as he cut mighty swathes from
the Vosges to the sea. When you look back and find that
this same harvest has been nurtured by the sons of Christianity and evolution, you will no doubt like myself pause
and consider.

A few days ago, in our advance we stopped beside an
advanced dressing station. There was a slightly wounded
German officer there who could speak English and I got
into touch with him. I pointed to the row of stretchers,
each with its burden of battered humanity (German and
British) and asked him " Well Fritz, do you think it's worth
it all ? " He shrugged his shoulders and said " This is war,
nothing but war." I asked him what victory he thought
would be commensurate with the sacrifices made both by
him and us. He answered, " The victory of a lasting peace
made by a people strong enough to discipline humanity
and lead them along the paths of a higher culture." A
typical answer by a typical, well-educated German. I told
him that I thought the shapening of the destinies of the
future generations would be in the hands of a different

people to what he had in his mind. He shrugged his shoulders and gave a weary smile. This same smile is symptomatic of the German frame of mind at present.

I have seen prisoners coming in from the battles of the Somme, the battles of Mons, Messines and down the Menin Road. They had a dour defiant look in their faces that said, " You've got me but there's plenty left to carry on and we will smash you yet." Now you will find them an abject lot. The weariness of the mind along with the weariness of the body stamps them with the hall-mark of a beaten enemy.

I remember on the 23rd of March, on our retreat, coming across a batch of prisoners. They looked at us with a half-jeering smile. That smile went to the marrow of my soul. That was the last drop that overflowed my cup that day. I can't but half sympathise with them now, knowing how they feel, because I felt it myself and it was the bitterest experience of my whole life. I can refer to it now seeing that we have wiped out that old score. Do you know what bothered us most of all was the thought of going back to " Blighty " and facing our old pals and our women folk at home. If you realize what we felt then, you will realize what [is] the spirit in which we enter into this war of movement—when the movement leads us to the Rhine. . . .

My own gun, 30 yards away, is firing a round every two minutes (weighing 300lbs) into the Hindenburg line. All along the valley and over [the crest] are guns and still more guns.

The bark of the eighteen pounders and the creak of the six-inch and 60 pounders, the boom and crash of the heavy artillery, makes one continuous roar that baffles description. To us who are used to it, the only discordant note is the whine or screech of Fritz's returning shell, which by some intuition we can pick out amongst the prevailing thunder. We are, as it were, blazing a trail for the legions in the trenches. Well might it be said in Bismarck's own words, these paths are made in " blood and iron."

Down the broad track in the valley, a Division comes

unshaven, unshorn, their clothes torn and covered with mud. You don't need to be an expert to know where they have come from. A triumphant smile on their haggard faces tells of a duty well and truly done. They have cut their notch still a little bit higher, and have earned their rest, as well as their place on the scroll of fame.

A fresh Division passes them, going in. In their ranks there are no gaps. They are spick and span even to the last button, rifles and accoutrements polished till the sun glints on them. Field-kitchens . . . with the hot food they will get when they reach their destination.

They bandy words with the warriors coming out. They are told that there are still some Jerries left to be killed, but that they have very little guts left in them.

On the road to our left is an endless procession of motor lorries, horse transport, field guns, ambulances etc. etc. The rule of the road is watch yourself because no other one will bother about you. Keep to the right. Ambulances with wounded and guns going into action take precedence of all other traffic. A Bosche shell gets an O.K. on the road. You dodge the splinters of flying wheels and axles. There is a short pause as dead horses and battered limbers are cleared off the track. There is no place or no time to dodge the next shell. If your name is on it, well then, your luck's out. Wounded men are roughly bandaged and put into passing motor lorries going down the line. The dead are left by the side of the road covered by their blankets. A few days later a burial party will come along and put them under the troubled soil. The gap closes up, the stream flows on. It is now getting late. The sun is sinking over the ridge to the right of Cambrai. Its setting glory is hidden from me by the murky pall of smoke, or the fog of war that stretches across our horizon beyond Douai and Lens. The coming of the night does not bring to us rest and peace. We go on in an endless cycle, whirling in the ether of " man's Inhumanity to man."

And to think that this same sun sets over the peaceful heather hills of Melford. I picture you with a heavy basket, winding up your rod and reel by the side of some quiet, moorland loch, listening to the plop of some wily trout that has evaded your most cunning lure.

I will also wind up my reel, and hope that the strap of your basket makes your shoulder ache as you come down the hill. . . .

Yours as of old
James Duncan

P.S. If you come across a pessimist anywhere, be he friend or foe, shoot him at sight. . . .

SECOND LIEUTENANT WILLIAM HUBERT DYSON
16th London Regiment

Educated The Leys and King's College, Cambridge. Candidate for Wesleyan Ministry. Died of wounds as Prisoner of War, France, 14 July, 1916, at the age of 24.

[To His Sister]   [France]
Dear W——,   *Sunday, May 21st, 1916*

Generally speaking I cannot conceive why the Government pays us such a lot of money but there are days when I really believe we almost earn our seven and sixpence. Yesterday was one of them. . . . We marched some $2\frac{3}{4}$ miles and halted for five minutes under a magnificent clump of tall " scraggly " trees exactly like the ones in my old bedroom frieze. Then on again down a steep winding hill which we appreciated more coming back ! and along a broad road winding along the valley and full of motor lorries already disgorging the next day's rations at the various Brigade ' dumps '—on through a long straggly village till we came to the church where we were ordered to sit tight and await the C.E. We were somewhat in doubt as to who or what

99

the C.E. might be. Someone suggested Church of England. When he *did* arrive we found he was the Chief Engineer. The original party was split up into 3 and our 80 men went off up a ' struggle ' of a hill into some thick woods on the top. You remember the man called M—— who was given 3 days fatigue. Well we got the same thing though our names were not M—— at all. The orders were to cut down trees —the h'ash, the h'almond, the beech, the " teasletree," anything but the h'oak, so away we started and the woods rang with " music of the axe " (?) Some chose nice " cushy " little trees and had them down in about twenty minutes amidst great mutual applause. Others chose stout old fellows who defied the laws of gravity till nearly lunch time. Thinking it would be better if the trees didn't fall about any old how I ordered them all to chip on the side facing the sun imagining this to be a great wheeze. After a while one or two of the trees began to fall on the necks of other trees, it was clear they were going to stand or fall together. We therefore had to start on the ' other ' trees which were invariably 3 times as large as the original ones. After that we felled the trees any old way. They could fall anywhere they liked as long as they fell somewhere. Anyhow they did fall about quite a lot and we had about three dozen down before we left, cut up into 12 ft. lengths and carried to the road side for transport. The men worked really hard all day. I ran about with a note book as who should say " I'm really very busy though I don't look it " chopping at the more obstinate trees for ten minutes now and again. One of the parties which had been chopping at a particularly " durable " tree for most of the morning without success was rather taunted by the rejoicings of a " cushy " tree party over its third trunk and replied rather 'aughtily " Well *we*'ve come out to cut trees down, *we*'re not picking daffodils." As far as I can see the old sinners have a good long time to repent when the axe is laid to the root of the trees if the axe is drawn from an R.E. dump. I asked Sergeant Tucker if he wanted to be canonized at lunch time. He said " all right." So I promised to see it through if he'd give me a drink, unfortunately having omitted to bring a water bottle of course. We were on the verge of sleep after lunch when a Major General entered from the wings and asked us what we were doing. One would have thought it was sufficiently obvious but we told him and he paddled about examining the axes and pronouncing them useless one by one. He said he thought he could guarantee to bring down any ordinary tree by himself in 20 minutes, adding rather cautiously that he wasn't going to try. He seemed to think we were really rather good for " amateurs." " Of course I know you're all experts at something. This isn't your particular job. Now Corporal," he said, addressing our most timid and delightful N.C.O. in a splendidly " my man "-ish fashion, " What are you an expert at in civil life ? " The Corporal muttered something about being in an Assurance Office. " Quite so, an expert at figures " added the General beaming beneficently. With a few more touches of *camaraderie* he went on his way.

Later on in the afternoon the " Church of England " came round and strafed about because the stumps were in some places 18 inches high ! " I suppose you've only been cutting the marked trees " he said rather shortly. We told him we knew nothing of marked trees, our orders being to cut down any old trees that weren't oaks—whereat he mouthed bellicosely not a little and we marvelled yet again at the extraordinary capacity of the British Army for " muddling through." We started back about quarter to five and got in under two hours and a still blazing sun. I procured a large tin mug, filled it full of tea 2 or 3 times (and emptied it) found an old tub and proceeded to evolute in it on the stable floor, Carramel being out to grass. Changed into slacks and felt very splendid. All other officers being out I was called on to mount the guard. Whether it is legally possible to mount a guard in trousers, whether it is validly mounted, whether it is really a guard still, I know not, may it never be known. . . .

———

Dear Boy,   *July 5th, 1916*

Now that the smoke has rolled away I feel I would like to try and tell you something about the happenings of the past week. It really needs a Tolstoi or a Victor Hugo to speak of such things with any adequacy. Walt Whitman would have had a perfect orgy. . . .

First of the eve of battle. It was the last day of June. The weather had been peculiarly piggish for more than a week —intensely hot and stuffy with no sun and frequent storms attracted maybe by the pseudo-thunder we had been having for so many days before. But on the morrow all would be different. Summer would begin properly. It must be Summer in July. We would say " rabbits " in the morning—if we remembered, and all would be well. We were inclined to hurry over dinner that night. The savoury which Miles had constructed as a Parthian shot was left almost untouched. Everybody was too occupied to bother about savoury even à la Miles. It is the eve of " the great offensive." The warriors start putting on that curious medley of articles which compose " battle order." The battalion is paraded in the streets of the little crowded village—seven hundred men who had been singing all afternoon eager to taste a new experience. Platoon by platoon it marches off. Those of us ordered to stand by in reserve have an appalling feeling of aloofness. Everyone but us seems to be moving into this strange new thing. For a moment the endless routine of trench warfare is broken. Now for the first time there is an " eve of battle " feeling in the air. One began to wonder what Great Uncle Joseph felt before the Battle of Waterloo. The church clock strikes eight and still the traffic surges along in an endless stream. There is hardly 20 yards of road vacant for miles. Men, men and still more men, limbers without numbers, ammunition columns, G.S. waggons, horses and chariots ' a thousand three score and ten.' The reserve officers were to spend the night in huts, but huts in French villages are like ' Jones ' in Welsh. In the course of our search we passed a large white mansion with coloured lights outside. It is Divisional Headquarters and there in the gateway stands the General himself watching the troops go by. He has the typical army face and reminds one of " Fine old General at bay." There's deal of singing, a band plays in the distance and all seems fit and " brave." At last after hours of fruitless search we find the huts (we found out afterwards they weren't the right ones but no matter). It's now nearly midnight, still the limbers rumble by, and we find ourselves intensely thirsty. There being no means of finding drinking water in the dark we trundle down the village in search of an " Estaminet." Find one, shut up of course, and seeing a light in the window tap upon the door, no result. Tap on the window, small girl taking pity on us runs to open the door and is severely reprimanded by Madame for doing so. We are to have our drink ' par la fénêtre.' " Beeang " says we. We solemnly drank two glasses of milk and a glass of water, paid a franc for it and came away gurgling with mirth. The thought of strolling through a village and being given surreptitious drinks of milk through the window struck me as not a little comic.—" And so to bed " as Pepys would have said. Early in the morning tremendous guns began to speak. As the hours wore on a glorious day developed and the guns spoke louder and louder. Towards half past six more and more joined in until the conversation became a continuous roar. The more energetic and restless arose and strolled aimlessly about, agitated for breakfast and played gramophones. Personally I lay in my valise and wondered at the strange incongruity of it all, sleeping at intervals. After a time I arose and shaved under difficulties—the big guns seemed to blow one's beard about or something. After a still longer time breakfast arrived. We made it last as long as we could.—Army biscuits being the only substitute for bread we did this fairly successfully —eggs also being plentiful. After breakfast rest awhile, walk about the orchards listening to the guns and the birds. Soon a stream of traffic begins to rumble down the road— ambulances. Rumours begin to fly about. We select the worst and believe them after the pig-headed manner of men.

We are then told we have been occupying the wrong huts and trundle along to some others 500 yards down the road. Opposite there is an iron crucifix and a little chapel which is temporarily converted into a signal station. From time to time an aeroplane buzzes over flying very low, wheels round, flies over again and drops a little coloured streamer into the blue. All eyes follow it to the ground. The signal orderlies run to fetch it and bring in the message. All through the morning—all the afternoon we watched anxiously for the messages to drop—odd disconnected messages they seemed, though on thinking the thing over afterwards one is rather struck with the amount of information we did get from the R.F.C. All the while ambulances streamed down the road and here and there we saw a face we knew. Some smoked their cigarettes cheerily enough, pleased at the thought of " Blighty " before many hours were passed, —others were too low to think of anything but their wounds. Now and again long trains of ammunition limbers rumbled past towards the battle, and mule ambulances galloping back for another load. The news such as it was became more and more incomprehensible till shortly after tea-time when the order came down for all reserve officers to stand by ready to proceed to the line. Straightway we selected the more necessary parts of our " Christmas trees," snatched a bit more " bully and biscuits " and set off by road. It's one thing to lead fresh troops into battle in the beginning of the day. It's another thing to go up at nightfall with the vague consciousness that the game is up. The aftermath of any battle is fairly tragic. The aftermath of an apparent failure is more so than usual. The main object of the fighting was achieved but that was unknown to us at the time. Only later came the special message of congratulation from the Commander-in-Chief complimenting the Division on the magnificent work it had unwittingly done. It was with strange feelings that the little party of N.C.O.'s and men marched up to the firing line that night. Attempts at facetiousness fell flat. The continuous roar of guns and bursting of black and woolly shrapnel over the villages kept bringing us back to the situation before us. The last village we passed through was dimly illuminated by the lurid glare of burning houses in the main street. We reported to Brigade Headquarters and were straightway despatched to our own. An officer who had returned after fourteen hours in a shell hole asked if I would get 2 men and a stretcher and follow him into " No man's land." One jumped at something to do and followed on through the old communication trenches we had learned to know so well. Then out over the parapet, over the endless maze of trenches straggling to and from the front line, stumbling about amongst the shell holes and barbed wire illuminated from time to time by the more brilliant of the German flares. At last we reached the front line, straggled over it with the stretcher and trundled on into " No man's land." I was warned to have a revolver handy. Quite why one didn't know, for the rifles of both sides were at rest. Only the artillery men had the energy to carry on the noisy game, and the Germans fearing another attack kept putting up continuous flares. I shall never forget that night. It was Sunday morning really—the strangest I have ever spent. We had only two stretchers with us and were trying to find two men we knew to be particularly bad. It was impossible to find them in the dark and we just took the men who seemed to need us most and returned. It's no light task carrying a man over ground like that. We all took turns but it seemed appallingly slow. We had just reached the most difficult point in the journey where our wire had been most blown about by the bombardment when the bosche artillery decided to put what is known as a minor " barrage " on that part of the line. Three times I tried to find a way through the wire and left bits of my breeches on it without success. The only thing to do was to try and get him down into the trench which was already full of wounded going down. After an unconscionable time we managed to get him down to the aid post. The men were absolutely done so we handed over the stretcher to proper stretcher bearers and returned to the Company. It seemed almost hopeless. All the stretchers were already in use. The men were too done to do any carrying. The day was fast approaching when no man can work and still crowds of men were out in front,—had lain there all day and would have to lie there another 24 hours unless we could get them in before daybreak. Two sergeants and an officer volunteered and the four of us set out to see what could be done. We managed to get about half a dozen in some old how and then the daylight came in with a rush. The order was given to stand to and we had to come in. The doctor tells me everyone this side the German wire was got in before the second night was up. . . .

All this is simply between you and me of course. It gives the darker side of the " great push " which happens to have been my personal experience. I believe quite good things are happening further South. . . .

Yours ever
KID

———

SECOND LIEUTENANT JOHN SHERWIN ENGALL

16th London Regiment

Educated St. Paul's. Student. Killed in action, France, 1 July, 1916, at the age of 20.

[TO HIS PARENTS. *He was killed within the next three days*]

[France]
Friday, 28th (30th?) June, 1916

My dearest Mother and Dad,

I'm writing this letter the day before the most important moment in my life—a moment which I must admit I have never prayed for, like thousands of others have, but nevertheless a moment which, now it has come, I would not back out of for all the money in the world. The day has almost dawned when I shall really do my little bit in the cause of civilization. To-morrow morning I shall take my men—men whom I have got to love, and who, I think, have got to love me—over the top to do our bit in the first attack in which the London Territorials have taken part as a whole unit. I'm sure you will be very pleased to hear that I'm going over with the Westminsters. The old regiment has been given the most ticklish task in the whole of the Division ; and I'm very proud of my section, because it is the only section in the whole of the Machine Gun Company that is going over the top ; and my two particular guns have been given the two most advanced, and therefore most important, positions of all—an honour that is coveted by many. So you can see that I have cause to be proud, inasmuch as at the moment that counts I am the officer who is entrusted with the most difficult task.

I took my Communion yesterday with dozens of others who are going over to-morrow ; and never have I attended a more impressive service. I placed my soul and body in God's keeping, and I am going into battle with His name on my lips, full of confidence and trusting implicitly in Him. I have a strong feeling that I shall come through safely ; but nevertheless, should it be God's holy will to call me away, I am quite prepared to go ; and, like dear Mr. Le Patourel, I could not wish for a finer death ; and you, dear Mother and Dad, will know that I died doing my duty to my God, my Country, and my King, I ask that you should look upon it as an honour that you have given a son for the sake of King and Country. . . .

I wish I had time to write more, but time presses. . . .

I fear I must close now. Au revoir, dearest Mother and Dad. Fondest love to all those I love so dearly, especially yourselves.

Your devoted and happy son,
JACK

CAPTAIN ROBERT ERNEST EVERSDEN

R.A.F.

Educated Licensed Victuallers' School. Clerk in shipping firm. Served in Gallipoli, East Africa, Egypt, Palestine, and South Russia. Accidentally killed, Russia, 15 August, 1919, at the age of 24.

[To His Mother] [Palestine]
My dear, *17/8/18*

. . . It's topping to see the war again. The star-shells are faintly visible at night and the guns are distinct. I have trodden the road over which Mary and Joseph fled into Egypt, and saw Jaffa from the train 3 days ago. From my tent, and as I write, I see the low clouds hanging over the blue mountains which surround the Holy City, and from a height of 6000 feet this morning saw the Dead Sea, and all the land of Palestine. A mile or so from the camp an ancient tower stretches leanly up from its surrounding bed of olive trees. It is a relic of the brave Crusader and bears upon its breast the effigy of St. George. How amazed the armoured saint must be to see, after all these centuries, British soldiers sweating past, marching on towards his Master's Tomb. And across the fields there is an old Bedouin and his family, and on his land our fast scouts lie waiting for the call ! He, with his dark skin, his hooked nose, his Koran and his knowledge of the Turkish Regime, sees the ' infidels ' making tennis-courts and playing football between their bloody combats !

Heavens this is a fair country ! Mother, after the sand and the flies, to see mountains, and fields, ploughs and corn, olive and orange groves, and to get your legs stung by thistles and nettles. Clouds and in the distance the blue sea. . . .

Now, isn't all this ridiculous ! I'm relapsing into my old sentimentality. Me ! The cold-blooded me who races up after the poor unfortunate Hun ! He (the Hun) is getting such a thick time here, dear. We shot one down yesterday.

Shot his observer in cold blood and then shot off one of his planes, and then his fuselage—like a boy picking off flies' legs one by one ! ! All my love, dear.

Your affectionate son

BOB

———

LIEUTENANT HORACE WILLIAM FLETCHER

Royal Welch Fusiliers

Educated Eton and Merton College, Oxford. Candidate for Holy Orders. Killed in action, Palestine, 26 March, 1917, at the age of 28.

[To His Mother]

[Egypt,
early 1916]

. . . I wonder how the thoughts of people are tending in England now. Not so much about the course of the present War as about the world's future afterwards. Do you think that the experience of this War has made the general public realize that there must be other ways of settling points of dispute which are as satisfactory as the way of bloodshed ? Ought we not to be praying that the mind of the Church —that great intangible authority—may be led by the Holy Spirit and guided by His power, to stop war henceforward ? We know God can do it, that He waits for our co-operation.

If man were to make a venture of faith, and believe that there *is* a way (if demanding more patience), such a way would be found. We must believe that our Lord's kingdom on earth is a kingdom of *love*, and also that it is *here*, waiting to be established if mankind will reach up for it. And in this kingdom of love, war and hatred of nation for nation, and man for man, can have *no place whatsoever*. Don't you feel how far this shows us to be from the coming of the kingdom ? . . .

———

LIEUTENANT KENNETH GORDON GARNETT, M.C.
R.F.A.

Educated St. Paul's and Trinity College, Cambridge. Rowing Blue, 1914. Died of wounds received in action, France, 22 August, 1917, at the age of 24.

[France]

[To His Mother]   *1 November* [*1915*]

... This is all a great game—so very childish—but I am such a child as to love it. And you poor people at home pay for us to play " bears " as we used to do when I was four—only now the game is very greatly glorified. Do you remember the Fort at Sea View, near the Point that the Curwens and I once built ? This game is just like that, only more people are playing it, and we don't get into a row for getting our clothes messy. We have our peep-holes just the same, and fire at anything we like—only this as I said is much more fun—but it is the same game ! And I am enjoying it immensely ... my riding apron is awfully useful. I wear it in the trenches and it saves my bags a lot. You can imagine the German Intelligence Corps reporting— Some Highlanders were seen in the enemy trenches at . . . the Brigade there must have been changed. . . . They'd very likely name the particular Regiment and battalion of Highlanders to which I belong. . . .

SECOND LIEUTENANT ALEXANDER DOUGLAS GILLESPIE
Argyll and Sutherland Highlanders

Educated Winchester and New College, Oxford (scholar). Ireland scholar. Bar student. Killed in action, France, 25 September, 1915.

Billets [France]

May 5, 1915

This day began for me about midnight, as I lay in my dug-out in the breastwork watching the Plough swing slowly round. I shall remember that night; there was a heavy thunder-shower in the evening, but when we marched down it cleared away for a warm still summer night; still, that is, except for the snipers' rifles, and the rattle of the machine-guns, and sometimes the boom of a big gun far away, coming so long after the flash that you had almost forgotten to expect it. The breastwork which we held ran through an orchard and along some hedgerows. There was a sweet smell of wet earth and wet grass after the rain, and since I could not sleep, I wandered about among the ghostly cherry trees all in white, and watched the star-shells rising and falling to north and south. Presently a misty moon came up, and a nightingale began to sing. I have only heard him once before, in the day-time, near Farley Mount, at Winchester; but, of course, I knew him at once, and it was strange to stand there and listen, for the song seemed to come all the more sweetly and clearly in the quiet intervals between the bursts of firing. There was something infinitely sweet and sad about it, as if the countryside were singing gently to itself, in the midst of all our noise and confusion and muddy work; so that you felt the nightingale's song was the only real thing which would remain when all the rest was long past and forgotten. It is such an old song too, handed on from nightingale to nightingale through the summer nights of so many innumerable years. . . . So I stood there, and thought of all the men and women who had listened to that song, just as for the first few weeks after Tom was killed I found myself thinking perpetually of all the men who had been killed in battle—Hector and Achilles and all the heroes of long ago, who were once so strong and active, and now are so quiet. Gradually the night wore on, until day began to break, and I could see clearly the daisies and buttercups in the long grass about my feet. Then I gathered my platoon together, and marched back past the silent farms to our billets. . . . The afternoon I spent in getting plants from a ruined village for our trench gardens— wallflowers, peonies, pansies, and many others; rather cruel to transplant them perhaps, but there are plenty left.

The village is a terrible sight, for what the shells have left standing has been wrecked in the search for wood, for burning and making dug-outs in the cold wet weather last winter, and you notice the contrast more now that the fruit trees are all in blossom, and the garden beds have all their spring flowers. There were many books lying about in the wreckage on the floors, mostly Catholic Lives of the Saints and other books of devotion, but I saw one Greek grammar. There was a school too, with its windows all broken, and great jagged gaps in the walls where the shells had come bursting through ; so that there was a touch of grim irony in the inscription on the walls—

> *Le Don de nos Benefacteurs,*
> *Enfants, prions pour eux.*

There are graves too, everywhere in the little gardens behind the houses, and except for the birds and an occasional soldier passing, the place is very quiet. One old couple still live in their house, I believe, because they have nowhere else to go. . . .

——————

LIEUTENANT WILLIAM GLYNNE CHARLES GLADSTONE
Royal Welch Fusiliers

Educated Eton and New College, Oxford. Squire of Hawarden and M.P. for Kilmarnock. Killed in action, France, 13 April, 1915, at the age of 29.

[France]
[TO HIS MOTHER]   *March 23, 1915*

This morning, as soon as we had awoken, the German guns began to shell us. Our billets are well within their range. Personally, I am at one end of the townlet and they were shelling the middle and demolished a church. The noise is just like the tearing of calico, growing louder and louder until the explosion ends the rending sound. We were so distinctly not the object of their attention that one was not in the least excited. . . .

I hope you have settled down now and got resigned to my departure, but really you will be wrong if you regret my going, for I am very glad and proud to have got to the Front.

It is not the length of existence that counts, but what is achieved during that existence, however short.

LIEUTENANT HEDLEY JOHN GOODYEAR

102nd Battalion, Canadian Expeditionary Force

Schoolmaster. Killed in action, France, 22 August, 1918, at the age of 32.

[To His Mother. *He was killed the next day.*]

Dearest Mother,   France, *Aug. 7, 1918*

This is the evening before the attack and my thoughts are with you all at home. But my backward glance is wistful only because of memories and because of the sorrow which would further darken your lives to-morrow.

With hope for mankind and with visions of a new world a blow will be struck tomorrow which will definitely mark the turn of the tide. It will be one of a grand series of victories which will humble the selfish and barbarous foeman and will exalt the hearts that are suffering for freedom.

I have no misgivings for myself in tomorrow's encounter. It does not matter whether I survive or fall. A great triumph is certain and I shall take part in it. I shall strike a blow for freedom along with thousands of others who count personal safety as nothing when freedom is at stake. In a few moments I shall make the final address to my men and shall strengthen their hearts, if they need strengthening, with the language of men of war ! We shall strive only to achieve victory. We shall not hold our own lives dear.

The hour is all more dramatic for me because for the first time since I came to France I am close to the spot consecrated by the blood of our gallant dead. It was here that noble Raymond fell and Joe and Kenneth shed their blood in freedom's cause. I trust to be as faithful as they. I do not think for a moment that I shall not return from the field of honour but in case I should not, give my last blessing to Father and my greatest thanks for all he did for me. Give my blessing to Roland and his family and to the others that survive me. I have no regrets and no fear of tomorrow. I should not choose change places with anyone in the world just now except General Foch. I shall be my father's and mother's son tomorrow again. God bless you all.

HEDLEY

LIEUTENANT THE HON. GERALD WILLIAM GRENFELL
The Rifle Brigade

Educated Eton and Balliol College, Oxford. Lawn Tennis Blue, 1910. Killed in action, Flanders, 30 July, 1915, at the age of 25.

[France]

[TO HIS MOTHER]   *Tuesday, May 25th, 1915*

Darling,—Just one word of blessing and good hope. I know how strong you have been and will be. How can we feel anything but serenity about our darling Julian, whether the trumpets sound for him on this side or the other.

Your
B.

[TO HIS MOTHER]   *June 1st, 1915*

Darling,—The more I think of darling Julian, the more I
seem to realise the nothingness of death. He has just passed
on, outsoared the shadow of our night, ' here where men
sit and hear each other groan,' and how could one pass on
better than in the full tide of strength and glory and fear-
lessness. So that there is no interruption even in the work
which God has for him. Our grief for him can only be grief
for ourselves.

How beautiful his poem is. It perfectly expresses the unity
and continuity of all created things in their Maker. I pray
that one tenth of his gay spirit may descend on me. . . .

Very very best love, from

BILLY

———

[Flanders]

[TO HIS PARENTS]   *July 11th, 1915*

. . . We came out at 1 a.m. on Friday, and marched 14
miles here through Poperinghe,—oh, the smell of the cows
and the new mown hay, after being in the cage with 22
unburied Germans. Such heavenly country and seclusion.
However, the spirit being willing, I have asked to go upon
a machine-gun course among the poms-poms at Bailleul.

Do you know, I had not seen a corpus vile since I was
fifteen, at the Morgue, and dreamed of it for weeks afterwards. I guess you could not show me much new now in that
line. I had to bury five K.R.R.'s one afternoon in a shell-
hole in full view of the Germans. I longed to signal that we
were making a sepulchre and not a fort. However, we got it
done somehow, and read the burial service. That same evening we collected 28 British rifles in a little wood in front of
my trenches, mostly tightly clasped by their late owners.

Only one other incident, after 7 days bully beef, we felt
we *must* have lobsters and white wine, my usual luncheon

before the Varsity tennis match, and very invigorating ; so we sent an unwilling party of three to the only shop standing in Wipers :—hours later one returned, saying that one comrade had been gassed and the other sunstruck, but bearing four tins and four bottles.

My servant is ex-footman to Lady Beecham. The other day he was getting me some afternoon tea, when a " crump " crumped most effectually the dug-out in which he reposes 18 hours out of the 24. I have forbidden him to mention his ' providential escape ' to me again, under pain of being returned to duty. . . . Darling Julian is so constantly beside me, and laughs so debonairly at my qualms and hesitations. I pray for one tenth of his courage. All love to everyone.

———

St. Jean la Bièye,

[To His Mother]   *July 20th, 1915*

We are for the reserve trenches on the ramparts of Y to-morrow, quite comfortable, I believe, though full of insecs. There is fine bathing, one general shop, and unique opportunities to study the ruins. You cannot imagine how tawdry unvenerable ruins are, fragments of chests of drawers and house-maids' cupboards, instead of skeleton oriel windows. It looks like a spring uncleaning. . . . The Tiptree jam is awfully good. I like the strawberry and blackberry best. Do send a few good novels. I have never read ' *Clayhanger* ' or ' *Hilda Lessways,*' and send some of Thomas Hardy's that I have not read. I adored ' *Bealby,*' and Rupert Brooke's poems. What a fiery poignant spirit, and how unassuaged by this life ; I do not remember anything so nakedly personal since Catullus. It don't appear he was ever in love, but had drained ' love's sad satiety ' to the dregs. His sonnet to the Dead is lovely, and his witty and cynical philosophising in the *Fish*, and *Mamua* :—God, how he *felt*. I am glad not to be in England now. What a sad disgraceful, unennobled, burglarious huckster among nations we are ; and we are not doing much out here to right it, whether because we cannot or because they won't let us, the Lord knows, but one suspects the latter ; but at least we are cheerful and willing, except when some glaring Harmsworthian ' cotton ' or ' coal ' catches our eye.

The lady of this farm has twelve flaxen-haired unwashen brats, I expect you would love them as much as I hate them. I asked her the other day, as it always made me giddy to count them, how many there are. ' *Douze, et pas un mort*,' she said in a tone of unfeigned regret ; so she must agree with me and Malthus. . . .

CAPTAIN THE HON. JULIAN HENRY FRANCIS GRENFELL, D.S.O.

1st Royal Dragoons

Educated Eton and Balliol College, Oxford. Regular Army, Died of wounds, France, 26 May, 1915, at the age of 27.

[To His Mother]

[Flanders]
October 24, 1914

. . . I *adore* War. It is like a big picnic without the objectlessness of a picnic. I have never been so well or so happy. Nobody grumbles at one for being dirty. I have only had my boots off once in the last 10 days, and only washed twice. We are up and standing to our rifles by 5 a.m. when doing this infantry work, and saddled up by 4.30 a.m. when with our horses. Our poor horses do not get their saddles off when we are in the trenches.

The wretched inhabitants here have got practically no

food left. It is miserable to see them leaving their houses, and tracking away, with great bundles and children in their hands. And the dogs and cats left in the deserted villages are piteous . . .

———————

[Flanders]

[TO HIS PARENTS] *November 3rd, 1914*

. . . I have not washed for a week, or had my boots off for a fortnight. . . . It is all *the* best fun. I have never never felt so well, or so happy, or enjoyed anything so much. It just suits my stolid health, and stolid nerves, and barbaric disposition. The fighting-excitement vitalizes everything, every sight and word and action. One loves one's fellow man so much more when one is bent on killing him. And picnic-ing in the open day and night (we never see a roof now) is the real method of existence.

There are loads of straw to bed-down on, and one sleeps like a log, and wakes up with the dew on one's face. . . . The Germans shell the trenches with shrapnel all day and all night : and the Reserves and ground in the rear with Jack Johnsons, which at last one gets to love as old friends. You hear them coming for miles, and everyone imitates the noise ; then they burst with a plump, and make a great hole in the ground, doing no damage unless they happen to fall into your trench or on to your hat. They burst pretty nearly straight upwards. One landed within ten yards of me the other day, and only knocked me over and my horse. We both got up and looked at each other and laughed. . . .

We took a German Officer and some men prisoners in a wood the other day. One felt hatred for them as one thought of our dead ; and as the Officer came by me, I scowled at him, and the men were cursing him. The Officer looked me in the face and saluted me as he passed ; and I have never seen a man look so proud and resolute and smart and confident, in his hour of bitterness. It made me feel terribly ashamed of myself. . . .

[Flanders]

[To His Parents]   *November 18th, 1914*

. . . They had us out again for 48 hours trenches while I was writing the above. About the shells, after a day of them, one's nerves are really absolutely beat down. I can understand now why our infantry have to retreat sometimes ; a sight which came as a shock to me at first, after being brought up in the belief that the English infantry cannot retreat.

These last two days we had quite a different kind of trench, in a dripping sodden wood, with the German trench in some places 40 yards ahead. . . . We had been worried by snipers all along, and I had always been asking for leave to go out and have a try myself. Well, on Tuesday the 16th, the day before yesterday, they gave me leave. Only after great difficulty. They told me to take a section with me, and I said I would sooner cut my throat and have done with it. So they let me go alone. Off I crawled through sodden clay and trenches, going about a yard a minute, and listening and looking as I thought it was not possible to look and to listen. I went out to the right of our lines, where the 10th were, and where the Germans were nearest. I took about 30 minutes to do 30 yards ; then I saw the Hun trench, and I waited there a long time, but could see or hear nothing. It was about 10 yards from me. Then I heard some Germans talking, and saw one put his head up over some bushes, about 10 yards behind the trench. I could not get a shot at him, I was too low down, and of course I could not get up. So I crawled on again very slowly to the parapet of their trench. I peered through their loop-hole and saw nobody in the trench. Then the German behind me put up his head again. He was laughing and talking. I saw his teeth glistening against my foresight, and I pulled the trigger very slowly. He just grunted, and crumpled up. . . . I went out again in the afternoon in front of our bit of the line. I waited there for an hour, but saw nobody. . . . I reported the trench empty. The next day, just before dawn, I crawled out there again, and found it empty again. Then a single German came through the woods toward the trench. I saw him 50 yards off. He was coming along upright and careless, making a great noise. I heard him before I saw him. I let him get within 25 yards, and shot him in the heart. He never made a sound. Nothing for 10 minutes, and then there was a noise and talking, and a lot of them came along through the wood . . . I counted about 20, and there were more coming. They halted in front, and I picked out the one I thought was the officer, or sergeant. He stood facing the other way, and I had a steady shot at him behind the shoulder. He went down, and that was all I saw. I went back at a sort of galloping crawl to our lines, and sent a message to the 10th that the Germans were moving up their way in some numbers.[1] Half an hour afterwards, they attacked the 10th and our right, in massed formation, advancing slowly to within 10 yards of the trenches. We simply mowed them down. It was rather horrible. . . .

SECOND LIEUTENANT DONALD WILLIAM ALERS HANKEY
Royal Warwickshire Regiment

Educated Rugby, Woolwich, and Corpus Christi College, Oxford. Author of *A Student in Arms*. Killed in action, France, 12 October, 1916, at the age of 31.

[To His Sister]   [France]
Dear Hilda,   *July 12, 1916*

I am wondering very much whether you will receive " *A Diary* " in four parts. It is very much founded on fact,

------

[1] For this reconnaissance he received the D.S.O.

though slightly altered in parts. You will probably be surprised at a certain change in tone ; but remember that my previous articles were written in England, while this was written on the spot, and also that although I have once before seen a battle, I have never before seen the day after a battle. At the same time, thinking it over, I am not at all sure that my argument was not quite wrong. " It is a sweet and honourable thing to die for one's country," and even if one is mangled and mutilated in the process, one does not know much about it. It is, however, not "sweet" nor can it ever be a source of satisfaction, to have experienced the blood lust, to have killed for one's country and gloried in it. Yet that is an experience which comes to almost every survivor at one time or other. I can imagine nothing more horrible than suddenly to feel the primitive passion for slaughter let loose in one, and to know that one was more than at liberty to give it full rein.

Yet that is what makes the good soldier in a charge. It is that, more than anything perhaps, which brings home what an abominable thing war is. I am not and never shall be a good soldier. I am too subjective and too slow to be either daring or resourceful. At the same time I am not more afraid than other men and in some ways my nerves are better.

I confess, however, that though I am not afraid, I never before felt such a distaste for the whole business.

<hr />

[To the same]   1st R. War. R. [France]
Dear Hilda,   *Sept. 23, 1916*

. . . We are still at peace ; though I am hoping that we may get a scrap before the winter. It would be very horrible to slide squalidly into the winter without any excitement at all.

From all accounts things are going very well now in spite of the Hun having collected all the guns, etc., that he can on the threatened part of the Front.

How they do hate us ! Every day in French and English papers alike you see the signs of it. It is difficult to believe that the war will heal the nations. I should not be surprised if, when we are old, we see a repetition of this war. I have little doubt that it will take most of our lifetime (if we survive the war) for the belligerent nations to recover their strength. But I have little doubt that if, as seems likely, we beat the Hun pretty badly, he will start the moment peace is signed to prepare for his revenge. A depressing thought, isn't it ?

Also, I doubt if we shall have such a horror of war as lots of people seem to think. The rising generation won't know what we know, and we shall forget much that is bad. When a soldier can write that the brotherhood of the trench will be " a wistful radiant memory " now, what shall we be writing twenty years hence !

———

LIEUTENANT MELVILLE HASTINGS

52nd Battalion, Canadian Expeditionary Force

Schoolmaster, Wycliffe College, 1901–1907. Subsequently settled in Canada. Died of wounds, France, 3 October, 1918, at the age of about 40.

[TO THE HEADMASTER OF WYCLIFFE COLLEGE]
At the Front [France], *1917*

I see that many stay-at-homes want to keep the Anglo-German wound raw even after the peace of Berlin, 1917. The returned German prisoners will never second the motion. There are thousands of them round here. They are well fed and well clad and seem as happy as sandboys. Never once yet have I seen any British soldier attempt to ridicule or annoy any prisoner, nay, rather, he shows him all consideration. This is saying much, for we are all sorts and conditions of men, and the German prisoner knows it.

The art of remembering consists largely in discerning what to forget, and to the will belongs the undeniable power to erase the unworthy, and the acid to etch in what is worth retaining. Last night I heard a youngster offer to do another's gas guard rather than awaken him out of a very weary sleep. What I heard has been etched in and preserved with a cover of thick glass. A couple of mornings ago I reached out for my pot of jam. It was jamless. May the sun never shine on his rice garden ! No, that is a mistake. I meant I will forget it.

I write this outside a German dug-out wrecked by one of our sixty-pounders. The explosion has thrown five men lifeless down the stairway. Their boy officer, a young Absalom, is suspended head downwards by one of his Bluchers from two viced beams in the roof. Get the harrowing details out of the mind ; remember only the faithful service.

It seems to me that so many of our journals urge the remembering of the worthless, the forgetting of the worth remembering. " Remember the *Lusitania*, remember Nurse Cavell." Rather keep them out of the mind. Heaven consists largely in thinking of mothers and wives and children and other things that are thus beautiful. Get the habit. Increase Heaven by thinking of the homely, fat but selfless Frau and the lad who hangs from the ceiling by his foot. Hell consists largely in thinking of our own nastiness. We cannot forget them even when forgiven, and so this Hell survives, but other people's nastiness we can forget quite easily. Forget the *Lusitanias*, the Louvains—there are paid servants of the State who will attend to these.

Kipling has it that " East is East and West is West and never the twain shall meet." Nowadays it is fashionable to put Germany in the place of the East. We are at war and must go on until Justice shall be triumphant. I hope, however, that humanity will not for ever sanction these " Wallace Lines," war-jaundiced and fear-bred. All the world over a boy is a boy and a mother is a mother. One there was Who after thirty years of thinking appealed to *all* mankind, and not in vain.

German food and British food, examine them closely,

they are the same. The same in terms of stomach, of ears, of eyes or of the immortal soul. A week since I was lying out in no man's land. A little German dog trotted up and licked my British face. I pulled his German ears and stroked his German back. He wagged his German tail. My little friend abolished no man's land, and so in time can we.

At the Front [France],
Autumn, 1917

[To the same]

Quite frequently, in raids and attacks, British soldiers meet Germans whom they have known before the war. A bird cage facing us in Sanctuary Wood was at regular intervals occupied by an expert sniper who had served with one of our number as a waiter in Broadway, New York. His cage was only about twenty yards away. He killed one or two of us every day. In the intervals he engaged with us in racy conversation. Near Wulvergem I found on a corpse a pay book which showed the man to have been a chemist in Leipzig. On several toilet boxes belonging to my sister, who before the war was a student at Leipzig University, I had often seen this man's name.

It is not to be wondered at that many a Fritz, who has lived amongst us for years, bears us far from bitter feelings. When a very green soldier, I was sent out at Armentieres to cover a party engaged in cutting down a patch of seeding chicory a few yards in front of our own wire. Being ordered to advance a hundred yards Fritzwards, I had paced but eighty odd, when, to my astonishment, I found myself securely entangled in the wire of what was evidently an unlocated listening post. My rifle, wrenched from my hands, evidently collided with a screw stake, and a flare shot up *instanter*. Not fifteen yards away, sticking out from a hole sunk into the turf, were a rifle and the head and shoulders of a man. Of course I " froze " stiff. Seeing, however, no movement of the rifle, I began to think—though such seemed impossible—that I was undiscovered. It was impossible. He had seen me plainly. Perhaps he was a sportsman, and scorned to wing a defenceless man. He laughed heartily, called out " Hallo, Johnny Bull, you silly old ——," and sank into the earth. Yours truly likewised, plus rifle, but minus half a yard of tunic, and nearly a pair of pants. A very similar experience befell my friend a Captain of Canadian Infantry. Scouting alone in No Man's Land— a most unwise proceeding, by the way—he walked on to the levelled rifle of a sniper. Halting the Captain, the sniper ordered him to hands up and step back five paces. In the couple of minutes of conversation that ensued it appeared that my friend was in the hands of a Saxon, an Oxford graduate, and a man who—despite repeated requests not to be used on the British Front—had been sent against us. My friend was right-abouted and ordered to count fifty. At fifty-one he found himself alone and free. On the Roll of Honour of Oxford University is the name of a German who fell in defence of his fatherland. I have often wondered whether this hero and my friend's captor are different men, or just one and the same.

Behind the lines we use humanity of every hue, from heliotrope to mud and water. Even in the trench regiments colour strains are numerous. Some days ago in Belgium I saw three Chinese walking arm in arm with four French girls, and another carrying a bouncing boy with curls like a Teddy bear and a face which Day, Martin and Co. could not have made more black. The same night I saw two Jamaican negroes win 200 francs from a Canadian sapper, and two Japanese cheat a Russian out of 5 francs at cards. I was myself called " Bo " by a Chink, and offered a cocktail by two Canadian Indians, drunk to the wide, wide world. Whatever are we coming to, when these darned foreigners are allowed all the white man's privileges ? In Canada, thank God, we have no black question, and we mean to have no Yellow one, but what about Britain equatorwards ? All these blacks and yellows will require hats two sizes larger when they return home. They never come near us when we are characteristically British, but they associate with us in our vices, and the dominant race is ominously unpedestalled. They may be good trench diggers and road repairers, but Britain, I fear, is laying up in pickle a toughish rod for her own broad back.

LIEUTENANT-COLONEL JOHN PLUNKETT VERNEY HAWKSLEY, D.S.O.
R.F.A.

Educated Shrewsbury and Woolwich. Regular Army. Killed in action France, 8 August, 1916, at the age of 39.

[Flanders]

[To Lord D——]   *October 23rd, 1914*

I don't think I can be betraying any confidence in saying that we have taken a railway journey and are now in Belgium ; not all of us, but I, personally, am. I was glad to leave the Aisne ; the place was getting very smelly. The first thing we did on detraining was to drive in German advanced troops ; which we did after sharp fighting, in which the artillery were of very little assistance, as it was a very foggy day. Now we are opposite each other, and unless we can break through somewhere the position will be similar to that on the Aisne, where no one could advance. This country is much more enclosed than that was, and difficult to observe. Our obvious observing station was the tower of a huge and beautiful château. The Germans allowed us to direct our fire from it for two days when I commanded the battery ; but the third day, when my Major was in charge, they had him out of it by putting shell after shell into it. The tower is still standing, and I hope to go presently and have a squint out of it. Meanwhile, we have to observe what we can from the top of a haystack— not nearly so good as the tower, and we have a subaltern, reporting on our fire, practically in the infantry firing-line at the end of a telephone. The night before last he had an experience. During that day the Germans had been attacking at the part of the line opposite *us*. We had not been able to get many messages, as our wires were cut. Just after dark he turned up at the guns on a motor-cycle and gave us some very useful information ; then returned to the convent, whence he had been observing, 200 yards in rear of our trenches, which were 500 yards in rear of the German front line. There he lay down for the night. At dawn he was woken up by heavy firing and shouting. He got up to go to his telephone, but found the convent surrounded with Germans, and had three shots fired at him at twenty yards, which missed him, and he dodged behind a friendly wall. Presently he found a German officer coming towards him. The officer saluted ; Macleod saluted. The officer bowed ; Macleod bowed ; and then they all bowed to each other. My subaltern then was searched, his military equipment taken from him, and his revolver bullets examined, presumably to see whether they were expanding bullets or not. His private property was given back to him. Then he and other prisoners were marshalled in the courtyard and put under escort of about twelve men and given some of the English rations which were captured in the convent. Someone (either ourselves or the Germans) began shelling the convent, and they were put in the cellars. After an hour or so of this someone shouted in English, ' Hands up.' This was a party of East Lancashires, which had made a counter-attack, retaken the convent, and taken about 100 prisoners as well. So my subaltern was released. He had the satisfaction of taking his own glasses back from the neck of the N.C.O. who was escorting him. We thought he had had a bit of a shock, so another subaltern has gone down to do the job ; they are all keen on doing it. A few days ago I had a long talk with Colonel ——. He had just returned from Antwerp ; he had not waited for much of the bombardment. He said that he had returned to his old profession on one occasion there, and made a speech to some Belgian soldiers, who, he thought, had evacuated a fort prematurely, and persuaded them to return. Very soon after he saw a shell from one of those huge 17-in. howitzers fall into the fort, which quietly collapsed like a pack of cards. He saw the Belgian army march out of Antwerp, not at all like a beaten army, but shockingly equipped ; some men in carpet slippers ! I am so glad the King has remained with his Army ; I wonder what old Leopold would have done !

LIEUTENANT ARTHUR GEORGE HEATH
Queen's Own Royal West Kent Regiment

Educated Grocers' Company's School and New College, Oxford (scholar). Fellow and Tutor of New College. Killed in action, France, 8 October, 1915, at the age of 28.

[To H. W. B. JOSEPH, FELLOW OF NEW COLLEGE]

[Flanders]

My dear Joseph,   *July 10th, 1915*

. . . Many thanks for the College gossip. I am very glad Allen and Haldane were re-elected ; I do not think we could afford to forgo the honour of their membership. The Warden's letter about the Germans seemed to me very good, and just what is wanted. The attack[1] on us was just on a par with all the other attempts people make to represent the Germans as fiends, each and all of them, just because as a nation they are behaving fiendishly. I find I have got pictures of travel too plain in my mind to think that all the kind, solid, ingenuous people I met were really child-murderers just waiting their chance. The best thing that has been said about Germany was Lloyd George's reference to the ' potato spirit.' I have been reading Belloc's ' *General*

[1] Some letters had appeared in the *Morning Post* criticizing New College for including, upon a list in Chapel of the members who had fallen fighting for their country, the names of three German officers who had been undergraduates at New College.

Sketch,' and wondered again at the extent to which a man can twist facts into the scheme he has ready for them.

Germany a barbarian intruder on a Western civilization she cannot understand, and France the upholder of the ancient tradition of the West ! I don't know whether that means Catholicism—if it does, the ancient tradition is a good deal stronger in Bavarian villages than in the Quartier Latin. I do think certainly that the French and English are fighting for what I should call toleration and decency in international relations, and England at any rate is carrying on her traditional opposition to any Power that tries to dominate the Continent. But what has this got to do with the ancient spirit of the West, and what is the good of treating the Germans as aliens to a civilization for which they have provided half the science and more than half the music ? I like the military part of the book—always excluding the silly diagrams—but the introduction seems to me what the Army calls ' hot air.' We suffer enough from it in military circles. . . .

I continue to be made very indignant by the search for scapegoats. The attack on Von Donop was especially malignant. None of those who take part in it can possibly know the facts, and it is a pure waste of time stopping to ascertain them. The exaltation of the soldier out fighting is the other craze I cannot abide. One of my brother officers has just read me a sentence or two from one of his men's letters to his home. The man is very indignant because his people took exception to the behaviour of his brother, who is also at the front and appears to have been drinking more than is good for him. ' He is out here fighting for his country and nothing should be denied him.' Similarly the local paper at Bromley objects to deserters being put in the dock. After all, it says, they have volunteered to serve their King. The sooner people realise that a man may wear khaki and still be a slacker, the quicker we shall ' get on with the war.' It is surprising really how little the men have been spoilt by the way they are treated in the Press and on the platform. But it cannot be denied that some of them feel they have done a remarkably generous thing in offering themselves to their country, and that their country ought in return to be all gratitude and very careful what sort of a life it gives them. I would rather have reluctant conscripts than self-righteous volunteers. But, as I said, it is gratifying that the Press and public have not succeeded in doing more to demoralise our soldiers, and it is some testimony to the men's natural good sense, I think. . . .

My love to you.

ARTHUR HEATH

We were watching an aeroplane being shelled yesterday, and a man remarked, " It's almost as good as a picture palace."

———————

[To His Mother]   [Flanders]
My dear Mother,   *July 11th, 1915*

It is Sunday, and though we shall be working all the same in a few hours, I feel that I should like to take the opportunity of telling you some things I've wanted to say now for a long time. You remember that I told you when I was going that nothing worried me so much as the thought of the trouble I was causing you by going away, or might cause you if I was killed. Now that death is near I feel the same. I don't think for myself that I've more than the natural instinct of self-preservation, and I certainly do not find the thought of death a great terror that weighs on me. I feel rather that, if I were killed, it would be you and those that love me that would have the real burden to bear, and I am writing this letter to explain why, after all, I do not think it should be regarded as merely a burden. It would, at least, ease my feelings to try and make the explanation. We make the division between life and death as if it were one of dates—being born at one date and dying some years after. But just as we sleep half our lives, so when we're awake, too, we know that often we're only half alive. Life,

130

in fact, is a quality rather than a quantity, and there are certain moments of real life whose value seems so great that to measure them by the clock, and find them to have lasted so many hours or minutes, must appear trivial and meaningless. Their power, indeed, is such that we cannot properly tell how long they last, for they can colour all the rest of our lives, and remain a source of strength and joy that you know not to be exhausted, even though you cannot trace exactly how it works. The first time I ever heard Brahms' *Requiem* remains with me as an instance of what I mean. Afterwards you do not look back on such events as mere past things whose position in time can be localised ; you still feel as living the power that first awoke in them. Now if such moments could be preserved, and the rest strained off, none of us could wish for anything better. . . . And just as these moments of joy or elevation may fill our own lives, so, too, they may be prolonged in the experience of our friends, and, exercising their power in those lives, may know a continual resurrection. You won't mind a personal illustration. I know that one of the ways I live in the truest sense is in the enjoyment of music. Now just as the first hearing of the *Requiem* was for me more than an event which passed away, so I would like to hope that my love of music might be for those who love and survive me more than a memory of something past, a power rather that can enhance for them the beauty of music itself. Or, again, we love the South Down country. Now I would hate to think that, if I died, the ' associations ' would make these hills ' too painful ' for you, as people sometimes say. I would like to think the opposite, that the joy I had in the Downs might not merely be remembered by you as a fact in the past, but rather be, as it were, transfused into you and give a new quality of happiness to your holidays there. . . . Will you at least try, if I am killed, not to let the things I have loved cause you pain, but rather to get increased enjoyment from the Sussex Downs or from J—— singing folk songs, because I have such joy in them, and in that way the joy I have found can continue to live.

And again, do not have all this solemn funeral music, Dead Marches, and so on, played over me as if to proclaim that all has now come to an end, and nothing better remains to those who loved one than a dignified sorrow. I would rather have the Dutch Easter Carol, where the music gives you the idea of life and joy springing up continually.

And if what I have written seems unreal and fantastic to you, at least there's one thing with which you'll agree. The will to serve now is in both of us, and you approve of what I'm doing. Now that is just one of the true and vital things that must not be, and is not, exhausted by the moment at which it is felt or expressed. My resolution can live on in yours, even if I am taken, and, in your refusal to regret what we know to have been a right decision, it can prove itself undefeated by death.

Please forgive me if I have worried you by all this talk. If we loved one another less I could not have written this, and, just because we love one another, I cannot bear to think that, if I died, I should only give you trouble and sorrow. . . .

All my love to you,
ARTHUR

———

SECOND LIEUTENANT STEPHEN HEWETT

Royal Warwickshire Regiment

Educated Downside and Balliol College, Oxford (scholar). Ireland scholar. Hockey Blue, 1914. Killed in action, France, 22 July, 1916, at the age of 23.

B.E.F.

[TO HIS SISTER]   *May 7, '16*

. . . My letters written to Mother will explain to you how it was that on May-day I found myself leaving a town near the firing-line, and walking along accompanied by my servant under Heaven's benediction and a warm sun, through jolly, quiet-looking country ploughed by careless old folk, with only the shell-holes in the road to remind you that the white streaks on the hills a mile and a half away were the front trenches of the German lines. It was all because I happened to have been detailed for a Course of Instruction in a little village miles behind the line,—instruction in one of the latest inventions of the devil's ingenuity for smashing limbs and scattering the harmless earth. A very easy course with short hours, and lovely weather : a heaven-sent rest from the trenches in the first week of May, which gives time to think the thoughts of early summer, more poignant than ever before in this time and place. Let me try and think them over again for you. . . . War is a fear-fully boring business at the best, a waste of time : but many hours as we waste on duty, there are always many hours with no duties to occupy them, and I am able to keep the spirit in me alive by constant reading. . . .

I have just had to break off in order to go to Mass in the village church. I have been able to hear Mass for the last three Sundays,—on Easter Sunday when we were at rest in billets, and last Sunday in . . . amid ruins, and with the noise of guns around, in a chapel attended by nuns with great bonnets on their heads like white wings.

However many and hard troubles may be mixed up with life, there are simple things which no one however unfortunate can be deprived of, things ridiculously simple, like spring and the other seasons, and a little field in spring (such as we have been living in here) surrounded by the tall sinuous trees of northern France and strewn with daisies and the first buttercups. My feeling is that, with all the countless troubles of the world, there is an *inevitable* balance in favour of happiness for anyone who has eyes to see and a heart to feel. And this is borne out (setting aside the fear of death) by the natural and surely not unreasonable desire of men to live. To live, to live. And with all determination to do the will of the Maker, or, as Pagans and Philosophers in their best moments put it, to live in accordance with nature (as Lucretius, Marcus Aurelius, Spinoza, teach), it is difficult for the ordinary man, who tries to make the most of " nature " as he finds it, to understand why life should have been made so naturally and innocently good to live : it is hard for him to understand the perfect happiness of a life " beyond," which is not a repetition or a continuation of the earthly life. Yet he supposes that this cannot be. The second man is of heaven, heavenly : the first man, presumably the " natural man," is of the earth, earthy. So that his earthy interests are doubtless incompatible with the heavenly,—his love of the hills and the waters (atoms like himself), of the thrill of the spring ; his ambitions for the furtherance of earthly causes, be they never so unselfish and humane ; his most unselfish loves ; his interest, for which he would lay down all else, in family, or school, or city, or country. And even if there be an element of the heavenly and therefore permanent, as there certainly is of the spiritual, in these efforts of his life on the earth, the material and the conditions of his work (apparently essential to the work itself) are bound to disappear. The faces of his friends, the stones of his house or his city, are corruptible. And as for the recompenses of his work here, and the unsought pleasures, *they* seem to him " earthy," of the nature of this particular and finite world. Now you will not convince him that certain natural pleasures are bad, or even that they are not definitely " things good in themselves " (as Plato defines). And though he may agree that a purely spiritual happiness is greater, or perhaps we should say higher, he cannot see that the natural pleasures can be surpassed, or even that there can be anything in the spiritual order at all to *correspond* with them. And if he is right, where is the justification of all these pleasant and good things in the *economy* of the spiritual order ? Especially does this question arise in the case of the artist,—who lives in the single and impersonal yearning to *express* beauty, in obedience to a command as urgent, as imperious, and apparently as *spiritual* as any impulse of saint or martyr. Yet *his* impulse is to express beauty in a material, in matter, and he works through *perception*, which is supposed to be unspiritual. Plato has said that the *Philosopher* exercises only that part of himself which is eternal, so that he can " carry on " with his philosophy in the other life : but he does not prove that the Philosopher is any better fellow than the " healthy natural man " who is worried at losing for ever all the goodness of this life here : and as for the poet, Plato treats him most unfairly—and I venture to say, unphilosophically. . . .

But the same apparent lack of economy remains. If you are a sentimentalist, you must be overwhelmed with the sense of pathos ; if you are a Philosopher, you tend to do injustice to one half of this life ; if you are a plain Stoic, a Regulus, you are acting upon a grand principle, but again a negative and one-sided one, which cannot satisfy reason, much as it exalts the imagination, nor can appeal to the common-sense demand of the ordinary multitude.

Now all these states of mind are unhappy or unsatisfying, and I think always must be—unless and until we take the analogy of human friendship, of those personal relationships which are really the best of the natural or " earthy " good things : for as Shelley says of the human spirit, " it keeps its purest happiest tone for one beloved Friend alone " —if we dwell on this phenomenon, we may find that the best way out of the temptation to pathos or pessimism in regard to the whole order of things, is to bring a personal element into our philosophy or Ethics : and just as one is best helped in a particular worldly trial by love, confidence, or admiration for some person, so to regard our efforts in life as made to please, and supported by, a person. And so the Incarnation meets at half-way the desire of the natural man, and fulfils his need. Without it there is only the pessimism of the sensualist or the melancholy of the Stoic.

As for those earthly goods—of which the renunciation, however holy, seems a waste—more especially Beauty, which with all due deference to Plato I cannot think of as convertible with or subordinate to Truth, Beauty in which, as Browning says, " you get about the best thing God creates,"—there is very little definitely laid down by the

Church and the Doctors. I do not know that even St. Augustine says any more than Plato. Yet in the absence of dogma, although the Church is to some degree careless of beauty, and places the state of celibacy and deliberate renunciation on a higher level than wedlock and the full enjoyment of innocent pleasures,—yet for my own part there does seem to be a division in life corresponding to the two things, and both states seem to me equally right and pleasing and meritorious. The artist who " lives laborious days " for the sole expression of beauty in matter—Fra Angelico the painter as opposed to the Dominican—or the man who goes about making others happy and never failing in his duty of happiness, with eyes and heart open to the goodness of the world—seem to realise a divine type for which they were created.

But whereas the wholly spiritual or religious life, renouncing these things, enjoys a good which eternity cannot take away, the artist and the good man of the world stand to lose more, and to feel greater sorrow, when they must leave this world—" This warm kind world "—" Your chilly heavens I can forego." But even they have consolations of a kind neither selfish nor unspiritual. When the mere sentimentalist sighs at death " *d'autres auront nos bois* " —for them there is nothing but joy to think that, even when they are gone, the trees will flower and the stream leap carelessly from the mountains, and that there *are others* to enjoy them, and in whose enjoyment there will be something good on earth and rejoicing in heaven. Of a good man killed in battle Vergil says

> " *Te nemus Angitiae, liquidâ te Fucinus undâ*
> *Te liquidi flevere lacus.*"

That is the voice of a Poet and a Stoic. But the Christian can say : my life passes, but the life of nature is perpetually renewed ; do you my friends " carry on " with my work of being happy, and in the thought of you there will still be happiness for me in the grave.

> *" Let the blow fall soon or late,*
> *Let what will be o'er me,*
> *Give the open heaven above,*
> *And the road before me."*

Crash ! I am back in the Trenches and a beautiful thing called an aerial torpedo shatters itself on the roof of my dug-out. . . .

———

B.E.F.

[TO MRS. ROBERTSON]   *June 2nd, 1916*

 . . . I regret to say that my chances of leave have evaporated, and it looks as if I must wait another three months or more. However, I do not mind very much : I am happy enough where I am, and well content if my first leave coincides with the end of the War. I have just heard on very good authority that well informed opinion in England has never been so optimistic as it is at this moment ; and in spite of the tremendous power which the Huns are showing all round, even now, the power which one can gauge for one's self in one's own bit of the Line, there are already indications of certain forces working under ground towards the conclusion of it all. And when it is over, what terrible shame and remorse and indignation for the survivors, and for posterity ! What a poor show the war has been !—And even granting that a life is well laid down if it contributes to our victory, what a multitude of lives have been simply wasted. And if we feel this, Lord ! what must it be for a German who thinks ! How can he keep from cursing his own country ? In some moods one thinks that this war, which is moving slowly to an end, even when ended will leave a " stain on the imagination " and a scar on the very earth. But at other times it would seem that just as some of our greatest blessings are found in memory, so there is a merciful forgetfulness in human nature, and sorrowful dark passages in life become " old, unhappy, far-off things." The enjoyable things are fortunately permanent, simple, and easy to find. The complications and disorders which we make for ourselves are little things by comparison with—

" *La paix de la grande nature.*"

We are taught laboriously to make sorrows for one another and to tear up and harass the earth, but after a single spring the traces of the past are overwhelmed by a riot of growth " which labours not," and in their place spring up the poppies of oblivion. The trenches which in February were grim and featureless tunnels of gloom, without colour or form, are already over-arched and embowered with green. You may walk from the ruins of a cottage, half hidden in springing green, and up to the Front line trenches through a labyrinth of Devonshire lanes. Before the summer comes again children will play between the trenches as in a garden, hide in strange hollows where old fragments of iron peep out from a wilderness of poppies and corn-flowers. Even in the shapeless ruins, where for the moment we are living, you may look up and see a swift dart from a cranny ; and all is well. . . .

COLONEL SIR VICTOR HORSLEY, C.B.
A.M.S.

Educated Cranbrook and London University. Professor of Pathology. University College Hospital. F.R.S. Died on active service, Mesopotamia, 16 July, 1916, at the age of 59.

[Alexandria]

[TO HIS WIFE]   *June 20* [*1915*]

. . . I had to go into Alexandria to hunt up some X-ray help, since the creators of chaos have poured 160 wounded upon us while we are getting in, and while our X-ray apparatus cannot be fixed up, as they know, till Thursday. This is the history of all the hospitals here ; and some have none at all. The public-house loafer at home is far better treated by the nation medically than the soldier who has sacrificed his life. Of course, the usual lie will be uttered, " Oh, but this is War." The net result is that the shirker and drinker benefit enormously and the unfortunate wounded are practically told to shut-up. The work as you can understand is depressing beyond words, and the more so as every effort to get better drugs and conditions is criticised and thwarted as if something unreasonable was being asked, instead of the bare essentials of medical treatment. Egypt produces nothing but raw cotton and food. Consequently when the home authorities refuse to send out X-ray plates ordered as long ago as last April, it is obvious that the drink trade has got well hold of our nation, for they know that we cannot by any manner of means get hold of these prime necessities of military surgery. One authority I heard of dared to say of X-rays that they were ' so misleading.' Of course such an infernality he would not venture to say in a meeting at home. I am not, therefore, in any condition to write you amusing or interesting letters : all my energies are devoted to trying to get our unfortunate men the merest clements of medical care. . . .

[Egypt]

[TO A FRIEND]   *February 2, 1916*

. . . If the English people choose to go on without universal suffrage for men and women, then, as Lecky points out, they will have to have wars, and as they get killed and kings and emperors don't, it does seem rather stupid of them.

My eldest son Siward, who was wounded at Neuve Chapelle, has been invalided and is at present testing steels in Armstrong's gun works. The second, Oswald, who was shot in the left shoulder in 1914, was hit in the right shoulder last August, but luckily without involving the joint. He was in charge of the bombers, and rather distinguished himself, so has been mentioned in despatches ; and is now back at Aberdeen getting a new draft to go out again. My wife joined me out here in August : and P—— in October while I was at the front in Gallipoli. They worked in the stores of a neighbouring hospital : and P—— was struck down with malignant dysentery. Fortunately she had the devoted care of an I.M.S. colleague of mine, Major McCarrison, who pulled her through splendidly : and after six weeks I got her and her mother off to Helwan near Cairo where they are rusticating and recuperating on the desert edge. Now you know all about us.

As to what we are doing, I can only say that my whole life is spent trying to get order out of chaos, trying to make the aged and incompetent realise that the British Soldier *is* a human being. ·. . . It is very difficult to explain the sense of weariness produced by the dull ' apathetic ' indifferences of the person above you in command. And what is also fatiguing is the realisation that owing to the censorship and oligarchical government the people at home are kept in a fool's paradise. I daresay it is not a fool's paradise, but they have no real conception of what is going on. What, too, is irritating is that, as of course we shall win ultimately, it is certain that the lives sacrificed will be wholly forgotten in a year or two, except by the poor relatives of those thousands who have died for absolutely nothing, and the hundred and fifty thousand who have been crippled. . . .

BRIGADIER-GENERAL PHILIP HOWELE, C.M.G.

4th Hussars

Educated Lancing and Sandhurst. Regular Army. Brigadier-General, General Staff, XIIth Corps. Killed in action, France, 7 October, 1916, at the age of 38.

[To His Wife] *3rd Nov. [1914]*

Not one moment have I had since whenever it was I last wrote. This has been our biggest battle so far—at least it's all one continuous battle really, but the last few days have been more strenuous than usual. And for certain periods things looked rocky indeed.—Now I think we're all right again. . . . Little K.C. was just about the best officer of his rank and age I've met. . . . I've never struck a man who appeared so utterly devoid of any sense of fear and who could keep so altogether cool whatever was taking place. I had to select *one* officer in the regiment for a D.S.O. the other day and left the selection more or less to the vote of all the officers.—K.C. they all planked for at once. . . . I don't know how much will ever be known, but for about 24 hours the regiment, quite alone, held the most important point in the line. . . . Somehow the fighting round the south and east got divided into two sorts of groups. . . . We filled the gap with a big reserve in rear. The fighting . . . became so serious that all the reserve got moved off north. And for 24 hours we filled the gap alone : and during that 24 hours new Germans came up in very great force and tried to rush the gap. . . . I tried to blow up the canal bridge, but the wretched things wouldn't explode. So we then wired it up and hung on to the hill on one side of the bridge and road and to the edge of a wood on the other. All the week previously (when we'd been living in and holding the village on the hill) I'd thought that there might have to be a fight on this bridge, and so by good luck I'd had some very good trenches dug by the men who happened to be at any moment free. I've never seen or heard such a hell of shell fire as they poured upon our hill and wood ! They must have had dozens of every kind of gun, both large and small. However, when the shell fire was hottest we hid behind the hill : and when the shell fire slackened to let their infantry come on to try to rush the bridge we popped up again and shot them down. All ranks behaved splendidly, for really it was a pretty severe trial. The maxim was about the middle of the little hill, in a rather prominent trench. K.C. was on the lookout there when a shell came right through his loophole and severely wounded him in half a dozen places. F—— came down to report to me : I sent up the doctor, who reported that K.C. was so bad that he'd better not be moved. By this time there was another spell of heavy shelling, so I sent F—— a written message to clear out of all the trenches and come behind the hill. I enclose his reply— the last thing he ever wrote. Just afterwards in came another shell : blew F—— literally to bits, destroyed my order, which therefore never got down to the troops : and broke poor little K.C.'s thigh. G—— (attached to us from the Indian cavalry) called for volunteers and brought down K.C. still conscious and marvellously brave—just a mangled mess but quite quietly giving directions as to how he should be carried. He lived about an hour. Of poor F—— they could find next to nothing. Meanwhile the shell fire got worse and two " Black Marias " dropped on to two trenches, each knocking out a dozen men—and then, and not till then, I realised that the order to withdraw had not got through.. This time that we withdrew the German infantry came out pretty strong and the fire from the trenches (then reoccupied) was not enough to stop them, though a great many were knocked over. Just at that moment I got this other message from the Grenadiers about a mile away on our left. Being terrified that the bridge was going to be rushed I dashed off to seek for some Frenchmen who I knew were hiding in the wood near A. Found about 200 who at first refused to budge, for the shell fire was terrific ; waving my arms, I yelled " *Allons, venons, nous avons cerné toute une compagnie d'allemands. Venez, venez nous aider les massacrer !* " —all in shocking French, but enough to be understood. That at once started them : and once started they behaved jolly well, and we drove the Germans back. Shortly after that, up galloped the 6th Cavalry Brigade—and that finished the show. . . . I write now from a trench with the hell of a hallaballoo—the French passing through our weak little outpost line to attack a village called Messines in strength, with about 100 guns supporting them. Rather a fine sight, for they are getting on very well though very slowly. Their attacks seem generally to dwindle down to nothing, but this time they are driving on hard and I hope will get there. The German Emperor is said to be the other side of the hill : and Poincaré was round the outposts on this side last night. To me it still seems more or less stalemate. I believe that the Germans have made tremendous efforts this last week : and have failed : and that they must be coming to the end of their offensive resources : and that we shall then be back more or less at the situation on the Aisne, both sides on the defensive, dug in and unable to move. It then becomes a mere question who can last out longest—a question of population and wealth and resources and temperament and grit. Unless, of course, the Russians bring off a series of dramatic coups, which I don't believe they will, especially now that they are busy with the Turks. What a time we're in for ! You and I who love excitement ought not to complain, but I do wish we could get our excitement together. . . .

———————

[France]

[To His Wife]   15.9.15

. . . I wonder if you've read the Correspondence in the *Westminster Gazette*—" Religion and the War." How I wish we could have read them and talked about them together. There have been heaps of letters and I've only had time to gallop through them. . . . It is *VILE* that all my time should be devoted to killing Germans whom I don't in the least want to kill. If all Germany could be united in one man and he and I could be shut up together just to talk things out, we could settle the war, I feel, in less than one hour. The ideal war would include long and frequent armistices during which both sides could walk across the trenches and discuss their respective points of view. We are really only fighting just because we are all so ignorant and stupid. And if diplomats were really clever such a thing as war could never be. Shall I desert and see if any of them will listen on the other side ? My little German officer was rather flabbergasted when the first question I asked him the other morning, when the escort had gone out and shut the door, and after I'd put him into a comfortable chair and given him a cigarette, was, " Now first of all do *you* really hate *me*, and if so why ? " He said he didn't. But then later, when I asked him what we could possibly do to stop all this nonsense, he had no suggestions to make. " I have my ideas " he said but somehow he couldn't express them.

Goodnight . . . and bless you.

P.

CAPTAIN SIR EDWARD HAMILTON
WESTROW HULSE, BART.
Scots Guards

Educated Eton and Balliol College, Oxford. Regular Army. Killed in action, France, 12 March, 1915, at the age of 25.

[To His Mother]   [Flanders]
My Dearest Mother,   *28/12/14*

Just returned to billets again, after the most extraordinary Christmas in the trenches you could possibly imagine. Words fail me completely in trying to describe it, but here goes !

On the 23rd we took over the trenches in the ordinary manner, relieving the Grenadiers, and during the 24th the usual firing took place, and sniping was pretty brisk. We stood to arms as usual at 6.30 a.m. on the 25th, and I noticed that there was not much shooting ; this gradually died down, and by 8 a.m. there was no shooting at all, except for a few shots on our left (Border Regt.). At 8.30 a.m. I was looking out, and saw four Germans leave their trenches and come towards us ; I told two of my men to go and meet them, *unarmed* (as the Germans were unarmed), and to see that they did not pass the halfway line. We were 350–400 yards apart at this point. My fellows were not very keen, not knowing what was up, so I went out alone, and met Barry, one of our ensigns, also coming out from another part of the line. By the time we got to them, they were $\frac{3}{4}$ of the way over, and much too near our barbed wire, so I moved them back. They were three private soldiers and a stretcher-bearer, and their spokesman started off by saying that he thought it only right to come over and wish us a happy Christmas, and trusted us implicitly to keep the truce. He came from Suffolk, where he had left his best girl and a $3\frac{1}{2}$ h.p. motor-bike ! He told me that he could not get a letter to the girl, and wanted to send one through me. I made him write out a postcard in front of me, in English, and I sent it off that night. I told him that she probably would not be a bit keen to see him again. We then entered on a long discussion on every sort of thing. I was dressed in an old stocking-cap and a man's overcoat, and they took me for a corporal, a thing which I did not discourage, as I had an eye to going as near their lines as possible. . . . I asked them what orders they had from their officers as to coming over to us, and they said *none* ; they had just come over out of goodwill.

They protested that they had no feeling of enmity towards us at all, but that everything lay with their authorities, and that being soldiers they had to obey. I believe that they were speaking the truth when they said this, and that they never wished to fire a shot again. They said that unless directly ordered, they were not going to shoot again until we did. . . . We talked about the ghastly wounds made by rifle bullets, and we both agreed that neither of us used dum-dum bullets, and that the wounds are solely inflicted by the high-velocity bullet with the sharp nose, at short range. We both agreed that it would be far better if we used the old South African round-nosed bullet, which makes a clean hole. . . .

They think that our Press is to blame in working up feeling against them by publishing false " atrocity reports." I told them of various sweet little cases which I have seen for myself, and they told me of English prisoners whom they have seen with soft-nosed bullets, and lead bullets with notches cut in the nose ; we had a heated, and at the same time, good-natured argument, and ended by hinting to each other that the other was lying !

I kept it up for half an hour, and then escorted them back as far as their barbed wire, having a jolly good look round all the time, and picking up various little bits of information which I had not had an opportunity of doing under fire ! I left instructions with them that if any of them came out later they must not come over the half-way line, and appointed a ditch as the meeting place. We parted after an exchange of Albany cigarettes and German cigars, and I went straight to H.-qrs. to report.

On my return at 10 a.m. I was surprised to hear a hell of a din going on, and not a single man left in my trenches ; they were completely denuded (against my orders), and nothing lived ! I heard strains of " *Tipperary* " floating down the breeze, swiftly followed by a tremendous burst of " *Deutschland über Alles*," and as I got to my own Coy. H.-qrs. dug-out, I saw, to my amazement, not only a crowd of about 150 British and Germans at the half-way house which I had appointed opposite my lines, but six or seven such crowds, all the way down our lines, extending towards the 8th Division on our right. I bustled out and asked if there were any German officers in my crowd, and the noise died down (as this time I was myself in my own cap and badges of rank).

I found two, but had to talk to them through an interpreter, as they could neither talk English nor French. . . . I explained to them that strict orders must be maintained as to meeting half-way, and everyone unarmed ; and we both agreed not to fire until the other did, thereby creating a complete deadlock and armistice (if strictly observed). . . .

Meanwhile Scots and Huns were fraternizing in the most genuine possible manner. Every sort of souvenir was exchanged, addresses given and received, photos of families shown, etc. One of our fellows offered a German a cigarette ; the German said, " Virginian ? " Our fellow said, " Aye, straight-cut " : the German said, " No thanks, I only smoke Turkish ! " (Sort of 10/- a 100 me !) It gave us all a good laugh.

146

A German N.C.O. with the Iron Cross,—gained, he told me, for conspicuous skill in sniping,—started his fellows off on some marching tune. When they had done I set the note for " *The Boys of Bonnie Scotland, where the heather and the bluebells grow*," and so we went on, singing everything from " *Good King Wenceslaus* " down to the ordinary Tommies' song, and ended up with " *Auld Lang Syne*," which we all, English, Scots, Irish, Prussian, Wurtembergers, etc., joined in. It was absolutely astounding, and if I had seen it on a cinematograph film I should have sworn that it was faked ! . . .

From foul rain and wet, the weather had cleared up the night before to a sharp frost, and it was a perfect day, everything white, and the silence seemed extraordinary, after the usual din. From all sides birds seemed to arrive, and we hardly ever see a bird generally. Later in the day I fed about 50 sparrows outside my dug-out, which shows how complete the silence and quiet was.

I must say that I was very much impressed with the whole scene, and also, as everyone else, astoundingly relieved by the quiet, and by being able to walk about freely. It is the first time, day or night, that we have heard no guns, or rifle-firing, since I left Havre and convalescence !

Just after we had finished " *Auld Lang Syne* " an old hare started up, and seeing so many of us about in an unwonted spot, did not know which way to go. I gave one loud " View Holloa," and one and all, British and Germans, rushed about giving chase, slipping up on the frozen plough, falling about, and after a hot two minutes we killed in the open, a German and one of our fellows falling together heavily upon the completely baffled hare. Shortly afterwards we saw four more hares, and killed one again ; both were good heavy weight and had evidently been out between the two rows of trenches for the last two months, well-fed on the cabbage patches, etc., many of which are untouched on the " no-man's land." The enemy kept one and we kept the other. It was now 11.30 a.m. and at this moment George Paynter arrived on the scene, with a hearty

" Well, my lads, a Merry Christmas to you ! This is d——d comic, isn't it ? " . . . . George told them that he thought it only right that we should show that we could desist from hostilities on a day which was so important in both countries ; and he then said, " Well, my boys, I've brought you over something to celebrate this funny show with," and he produced from his pocket a large bottle of rum (not ration rum, but the proper stuff). One large shout went up, and the nasty little spokesman uncorked it, and in a heavy, ceremonious manner, drank our healths, in the name of his " camaraden " ; the bottle was then passed on and polished off before you could say knife. . . .

During the afternoon the same extraordinary scene was enacted between the lines, and one of the enemy told me that he was longing to get back to London : I assured him that " So was I." He said that he was sick of the war, and I told him that when the truce was ended, any of his friends would be welcome in our trenches, and would be well-received, fed, and given a free passage to the Isle of Man ! Another coursing meeting took place, with no result, and at 4.30 p.m. we agreed to keep in our respective trenches, and told them that the truce was ended. They persisted, however, in saying that they were not going to fire, and as George had told us not to, unless they did, we prepared for a quiet night, but warned all sentries to be doubly on the alert.

During the day both sides had taken the opportunity of bringing up piles of wood, straw, etc., which is generally only brought up with difficulty under fire. We improved our dug-outs, roofed in new ones, and got a lot of very useful work done towards increasing our comfort. Directly it was dark, I got the whole of my Coy. on to improving and re-making our barbed-wire entanglements, all along my front, and had my scouts out in front of the working parties, to prevent any surprise ; but not a shot was fired, and we finished off a real good obstacle unmolested.

On my left was the bit of ground over which we attacked on the 18th, and here the lines are only from 85 to 100 yards apart.

The Border Regiment were occupying this section on Christmas Day, and Giles Loder, our Adjutant, went down there with a party that morning on hearing of the friendly demonstrations in front of my Coy., to see if he could come to an agreement about our dead, who were still lying out between the trenches. The trenches are so close at this point, that of course each side had to be far stricter. Well, he found an extremely pleasant and superior stamp of German officer, who arranged to bring all our dead to the half-way line. We took them over there, and buried 29 exactly half way between the two lines. Giles collected all personal effects, pay-books and identity discs, but was stopped by the Germans when he told some men to bring in the rifles ; all rifles lying on their side of the half-way line they kept carefully ! . . . .

They apparently treated our prisoners well, and did all they could for our wounded. This officer kept on pointing to our dead and saying, " *Les Braves, c'est bien dommage.*" . . .

When George heard of it he went down to that section and talked to the nice officer and gave him a scarf. That same evening a German orderly came to the half-way line, and brought a pair of warm, woolly gloves as a present in return for George.

The same night the Borderers and we were engaged in putting up big trestle obstacles, with barbed wire all over them, and connecting them, and at this same point (namely, where we were only 85 yards apart) the Germans came out and sat on their parapet, and watched us doing it, although we had informed them that the truce was ended. . . . Well, all was quiet, as I said, that night ; and next morning, while I was having breakfast, one of my N.C.O.'s came and reported that the enemy were again coming over to talk. I had given full instructions, and none of my men were allowed out of the trenches to talk to the enemy. I had also told the N.C.O. of an advanced post which I have up a ditch, to go out with two men, *unarmed* ; if any of the enemy came over, to see that they did not cross the half-way line, and to engage them in pleasant conversation. So I went out, and found the same lot as the day before ; they told me again that they had no intention of firing, and wished the truce to continue. I had instructions not to fire till the enemy did ; I told them ; and so the same comic form of temporary truce continued on the 26th, and again at 4.30 p.m. I informed them that the truce was at an end. We had sent them over some plum-puddings, and they thanked us heartily for them and retired again, the only difference being that instead of all my men being out in the " no man's zone," one N.C.O. and two men only were allowed out, and the enemy therefore sent fewer.

Again both sides had been improving their comfort during the day, and again at night I continued on my barbed wire and finished it right off. We retired for the night all quiet, and were rudely awakened at 11 p.m. A H.-qr. orderly burst into my dug-out, and handed me a message. It stated that a deserter had come into the 8th Division lines, and stated that the whole German line was going to attack at 12.15 midnight, and that we were to stand to arms immediately, and that reinforcements were being hurried up from billets in rear. I thought, at the time, that it was a d——d good joke on the part of the German deserter to deprive us of our sleep, and so it turned out to be. I stood my Coy. to arms, made a few extra dispositions, gave out all instructions, and at 11.20 p.m. George arrived. . . . Suddenly *our* guns all along the line opened a heavy fire, and all the enemy did was to reply with 9 shell (heavy howitzers), *not one of which exploded*, just on my left. Never a rifle shot was fired by either side (except right away down in the 8th Division), and at 2.30 p.m. we turned in half the men to sleep, and kept half awake on sentry.

Apparently this deserter had also reported that strong German re-inforcements had been brought up, and named a place just in rear of their lines, where, he said, two regiments were in billets, that had just been brought up. Our guns were informed, and plastered the place well when they opened fire (as I mentioned). The long and short of it was that absolutely *nixt* happened, and after a sleepless night I turned in at 4.30 a.m., and was woken again at 6.30, when we always stand to arms before daylight. I was just going to have another sleep at 8 a.m. when I found that the enemy were again coming over to talk to us (Dec. 27th). I watched my N.C.O. and two men go out from the advanced post to meet, and hearing shouts of laughter from the little party when they met, I again went out myself.

They asked me what we were up to during the night, and told me that they had stood to arms all night and thought we were going to attack them when they heard our heavy shelling ; also that our guns had done a lot of damage and knocked out a lot of their men in billets. I told them a deserter of theirs had come over to us, and that they had only him to thank for any damage done, and that we, after a sleepless night, were not best pleased with him either ! They assured me that they had heard nothing of an attack, and I fully believed them, as it is inconceivable that they would have allowed us to put up the formidable obstacles (which we had on the two previous nights) if they had contemplated an offensive movement.

Anyhow, if it had ever existed, the plan had miscarried, as no attack was developed on any part of our line, and here were these fellows still protesting that there was a truce, although I told them that it had ceased the evening before. So I kept to the same arrangement, namely, that my N.C.O. and two men should meet them half-way, and strict orders were given that no other man was to leave the lines. . . . I admit that the whole thing beat me absolutely. In the evening we were relieved by the Grenadiers, quite openly (not crawling about on all fours, as usual), and we handed on our instructions to the Grenadiers in case the enemy still wished to pay visits ! . . .

DR. ELSIE MAUD INGLIS

Commandant, Scottish Women's Hospitals

Educated Edinburgh School of Medicine for Women. Active in Women's Franchise Movement. Founder of Scottish Women's Hospitals and commanded units in Serbia and Russia. Died of illness due to war service, Newcastle, 26 November, 1917, at the age of 53.

[Reni, Rumania]
March 23, 1917

We have been awfully excited and interested in the news from Petrograd. We heard of it, probably long after you people at home knew all about it ! It is most interesting to see how everybody is on the side of the change, from Russian officers, who come to tea and beam at us, and say, " *Heresho* " (good) to the men in the wards. In any case they say we shall find the difference all over the war area. . . .

Do you know we have all been given the St. George Medal ? Prince Dolgourokoff, who is in command on this front, arrived quite unexpectedly, just after roll call. The telegram saying he was coming arrived a quarter of an hour after he left ! General Kropensky, the head of the Red Cross, rushed up, and the Prince arrived about two minutes after him. He went all over the hospital, and a member of his gilded staff told matron he was very pleased with everything. He decorated two men in the wards with St. George's Medal, and then said he wanted to see us together, and shook hands with everybody and said, " Thank you," and gave each of us a medal too ; Dr. Laird's was for service, as she had not been under fire. St. George's Medal is a silver one with " For Bravery " on its back. Our patients were awfully pleased, and impressed on us that it carried with it a pension of a rouble a month for life. We gave them all cigarettes to commemorate the occasion.

It was rather satisfactory to see how the hospital looked in its ordinary, and even I was *fairly* satisfied. I tell the unit that they must remember that they have an old maid as commandant, and must live up to it ! I cannot stand dirt, and crooked charts and crumpled sheets. One Sister, I hear, put it delightfully in a letter home : " Our C.M.O. is an idealist ! " I thought that was rather sweet ; I believe she added, " but she does appreciate good work." Certainly, I appreciate hers. She is in charge of the room for dressings, and it is one of the thoroughly satisfactory points in the hospital.

The Greek priest came yesterday to bless the hospital. We put up " Icons " in each of the four wards. The Russians are a very religious people, and it seems to appeal to some mystic sense in them. The priest just put on a stole, green and gold, and came in his long grey cloak. The two wards open out of one another, so he held the service in one, the men all saying the responses and crossing themselves. The four icons lay on the table before him, with three lighted candles at the inner corners, and he blessed water and sprinkled them, and then he sprinkled everybody in the room. The icons were fixed up in the corner of the wards, and I bought little lamps to burn in front of them, as they always have them. We are going to have the evening hymn sung every evening at six o'clock. I heard that first in Serbia from those poor Russian prisoners, who sang it regularly every evening. . . .

I have heard two delightful stories from the Sisters who have returned from Odessa. There is a great rivalry between the Armoured Car men and the British Red Cross men about the capabilities of their Sisters. (We, it appears, are the Armoured Car Sisters !) A B.R.C. man said their Sisters were so smart they got a man on to the operating-table in five minutes after the other one went off. Said an Armoured Car man : " But that's nothing. The Scottish Sisters get the second one on before the first one is *off*." The other story runs that there was some idea of the men waiting all night on a quay, and the men said, " But you don't think we are Scottish Sisters, sir, do you ? " I have no doubt that refers to Galatz, where we made them work all night.

SECOND LIEUTENANT ALAN EDWARD AFLALO JACOBS, M.C.

East Surrey Regiment

Educated St. Dunstan's College. Civil Servant. Missing, France, 7 August, 1916, at the age of 21.

[TO HIS PARENTS]   8th E. Surreys [France]
Dearest Mother & Father & Everybody,   *1 /4 /16*

Somewhere down the line, perhaps Lihons and Rosieres, there is the distant rumble of a hate being conducted with a certain amount of vigour, while one of our batteries is lazily registering on a few fifth ribs round the *Chapeau de Gendarme ;* the buzz of our sentry aeroplanes overhead completes all that serves to remind me there is a war on somewhere as I sit on a rustic French seat in a young wood, enjoying the bright spring sunshine, and when the countless wild birds occasionally cease to interest me, I add a few words to this letter, which, if it conveys nothing else, shows plainly that the British Army is suffering from a paper famine and cries for relief from home. The Somme is a sparkling streak of silver-blue amid the budding trees down in the valley, and apart from an occasional glance at my new platoon (for I have been transferred to No 6 of B Co. under my old friend Capt. Nevill) engaged in the leisurely manufacture of hurdles in the copse opposite, I have nothing to do but enjoy the spring in the country ; should Fritz turn nasty and send a few woolly bears over, I have only to dive philosophically into the commodious funk hole on my right and there continue my letter undisturbed. Just down the road is the bridge of Eclusier and the few houses of that hamlet that remain. On our side of the bridge we place the last sentry of the British Army, while a handsome Poilu in his smart steel helmet and light blue uniform stands near by on duty. The opposite bank of the river is always alive with ardent Froggies shooting the water fowl and their occasional shots ring across the water, while just beyond, the Saucy Sally, alias the Lady of the Lake, lies moored to a tree, and of a fine afternoon two shovels and this leaky punt are ample to afford an amusing time dodging occasional whizz-bangs and watching the young pikes and shoals of minnow and dace and roach ; I think I know somebody somewhere in Flanders who would duly appreciate this part of the line. In a shattered cottage of Eclusier dwells " Mrs. Pegg," a dear old French woman who persists in remaining in her native village even through the recent Hun show here, and as Lt. Pegg reminds her of her favourite grandson, we are on excellent terms and find the exchange of coal and rations for her new laid eggs a profitable bargain. . . .

There are one or two amusing stories I want to write you. The first is of my poor old prisoner Josef Adler. As little Fitzgerald of the Queen's marched him down with an escort, he suddenly realised in the streets of Suzanne that his guard were wearing rifle covers, were unloaded and their bayonets not fixed. He halted to remedy these defects, and of course poor old Joe thought his last —— birthday had arrived, and the assurance of " no shoot " from a Bairnsfather burly ginger sergeant who pointed his rifle at the poor brute while he talked, merely made matters worse. This humorous interlude was quite unintentional but Josef's tongue was afterwards most pleasantly loose at his examination. There is a wonderful court-martial in Bray to try a Lancashire Tommy charged with " conduct prejudicial to the maintenance of discipline." When his Company was on parade in the main street the aforesaid criminal made such a realistic imitation of a big shell coming that a very prim old sergeant major lay flat down in the gutter. Encouraged by this success, he repeated the noise with equally good results. The third time our ventriloquist was nabbed—I hope he gets off. Tait of the Buffs, with whom I spent my physical drill course at Tidworth, besides being an excellent fellow, is also an excellent shot ; and the other day while watching Curlu, a Hun village most foolishly not shelled because of French inhabitants, he saw four fat Fritzes digging as bold as brass in a garden.

Though it was 1500 yards range he took aim and hit one Hun just as he was completing a stroke with his pick right on the —— 27th of March. Fritz hobbled off holding it with one fist and viciously shaking the other behind him, assisted by two colleagues who appeared to suffer from cold feet. Many thanks for the letters and papers and parcels. The socks are excellent and I see you have rightly adjusted the cubic contents : you see the last pair had room for both feet all right, but it was badly distributed, for I could get both feet in one and neither in the other sock. . . .

With best love to all, I remain your loving son

ALAN

———

CAPTAIN JOHN LLEWELLYN THOMAS JONES

3rd London Regiment

Educated Llangollen County School. Member of printing firm. Killed in action, Flanders, 16 August, 1917, at the age of 22.

[TO HIS FATHER AND FAMILY] France,
My Dearest Dad, Ethel and Gwen, *4/4/17*

I have written this letter so that, in the event of anything happening to me, I do not go under without letting all you dear ones at home know how much I owe to your loving care and the little kindnesses that go to make life so pleasant and inviting.

You know what an undemonstrative nature mine is, but my love for you all is, nevertheless, strong and deep, and though I said nothing about these things before I left England, it was just because—I couldn't—my heart was too full.

One has to face the prospect of getting knocked out, as many other and probably better fellows than I have been. All I can say is that you do not grieve for me, because, although it may sound exceedingly quixotic, how better can one make one's exit from this world than fighting for the country which has sheltered and nurtured one all through life ?

War is cruel and I detest it, but since it was not possible to keep out of this without loss of prestige and perhaps worse, it behoves us all to carry it on to a successful conclusion. Of course, it entails sacrifices, but that is all in the game. I had hoped to be able to return home and take up what little responsibility lay in my power away from your shoulders, and to care for and look after the girls, but if that is not to be, I want you all to remember that though the break may seem unbearable—there are many other homes which have suffered losses. We should rather, I think, thank God that we have been a happy and united little family. I know how hard it is, and, as I write, the thought that I may not see you dear ones again in this world brings a lump to my throat and the tears to my eyes. I trust that I shall return, but . . .

All I can say to you is that I thank God for giving me the best father in the world and two very dear sisters. I cannot write to all, but send my deepest love to . . . I don't think that I can write any more, so just good-bye and God bless you all and protect you is my fervent prayer.

With all my fondest love,

Yours affectionately,
LLEW

LIEUTENANT HENRY PAUL MAINWARING JONES

Tank Corps

Educated Dulwich. Scholar-Elect of Balliol College, Oxford. Joined Army from school. Killed in action, France, 31 July, 1917, at the age of 21.

[France]

[TO HIS FATHER] *August 8th, 1916*

I am more thankful than I can say to have your permission to apply for transfer to the R.F.A. Since I wrote to you a circular has come from G.H.Q. stating that officers for the artillery are wanted urgently. . . .

As for the A.S.C., I consider that my particular branch of the service is overstocked. In itself the mere fact of the work not appealing to me (though I absolutely loathe it) would not be decisive. It is because I am convinced that I could do better work in other directions that I am longing for a transfer. Even the transport of the A.S.C. I would not object to. . . . But in my heart and soul I have always longed for the rough-and-tumble of war as for a football match. What I have seen of the war out here has not frightened me in the least, but rather made me keener than ever to take part in the fighting. It is all very well to be an " organiser of victory," but it does not appeal to me, even if I had the particular type of mind necessary for success at it. But I am not a good business man, and the details of business bore me stiff. On the other hand, it is my passionate desire to share the hardships and dangers of this war. . . .

A few words now about some personal experiences. At a certain village not far from here are a number of Boche prisoners. Every day they go out to shovel refuse into army wagons, and then unload these wagons elsewhere on to refuse heaps. It is a daily occurrence to see a Boche mount up on the box beside the English driver, and off they go—if the Boche can speak English—chatting merrily as if there had never been a war. I have even seen Tommy hand over the reins to his captive, who cheerfully takes them and drives the wagon to its destination, while the real driver sits back with folded arms. That will show you how far the British soldier cultivates the worship of Hate. It is small incidents of this kind, unofficial and even illegal though they may be, that make one realise the true secret of Britain's greatness—her magnanimity and her kindliness.

[To His Brother]

. . . Have you ever reflected on the fact that, despite the horrors of the war, it is at least a big thing? I mean to say that in it one is brought face to face with realities. The follies, selfishness, luxury and general pettiness of the vile commercial sort of existence led by nine-tenths of the people of the world in peacetime are replaced in war by a savagery that is at least more honest and outspoken. Look at it this way : in peacetime one just lives one's own little life, engaged in trivialities, worrying about one's own comfort, about money matters, and all that sort of thing—just living for one's own self. What a sordid life it is ! In war, on the other hand, even if you do get killed you only anticipate the inevitable by a few years in any case, and you have the satisfaction of knowing that you have " pegged out " in the attempt to help your country. You have, in fact, realised an ideal, which, as far as I can see, you very rarely do in ordinary life. The reason is that ordinary life runs on a commercial and selfish basis ; if you want to " get on," as the saying is, you can't keep your hands clean.

Personally, I often rejoice that the War has come my way. It has made me realise what a petty thing life is. I think that the War has given to everyone a chance to " get out of himself," as I might say. Of course, the other side of the picture is bound to occur to the imagination. But there ! I have never been one to take the more melancholy point of view when there's a silver lining in the cloud.

Certainly, speaking for myself, I can say that I have never in all my life experienced such a wild exhilaration as on the commencement of a big stunt, like the last April one for example. The excitement for the last half-hour or so before it is like nothing on earth. The only thing that compares with it are the few minutes before the start of a big school match. Well, cheer-oh !

SERGEANT-MAJOR FREDERIC HILLERSDON KEELING

Duke of Cornwall's Light Infantry

Educated Winchester and Trinity College, Cambridge (scholar).
Writer and student of economic and social questions. Killed in action,
France, 18 August, 1916, at the age of 30.

6th D.C.L.I., B.E.F.,

[To R. C. K. Ensor]   *23 December, 1915*

. . . Well, do you honestly think there is a chance that
I shall be able to celebrate *next* Christmas in peace and
safety ? It is pathetic to find how many of the Tommies
are always believing that peace is coming before some date
a month or two hence. One can see vividly how religions
are born and grow—the human craving for a comforting
doctrine is very strong.

We are in a camp of tents with a very few mud huts. By
the way, the " *Chronicle* " published some time ago some
rot from some blithering correspondent who, I suppose,
drives about comfortably in G.H.Q. motor-cars and thinks
it a wonderful thing to come under shell fire, to the effect
that all the troops are comfortably housed for the winter
in nice warm huts. That sort of thing makes men sweat
out here. I don't grumble at a tent with a coke fire (when
coke is available) even in the coldest weather ; but it is a
bloody shame to deceive the public at home and say we
are in comfortable huts when we aren't. Till the autumn
we hadn't even got tents, but generally just our waterproof
sheets as roofs for bivvy shelters. It is rather like these
blessed deputations who are taken into the trenches in some
convalescent home where they fire about one shell and two
rifle shots a day, and who spread the impression that time
hangs on our hands in the trenches. In our brigade a man
is damned lucky if he gets a dozen hours' sleep in three
days in the trenches—it's working and carrying parties
whenever it isn't sentry and listening post, and trench mor-
tars and whizz-bangs on and off all day and night in the

intervals of bombardments by crumps. I don't pretend to
have been through anything like as much as men who have
been out here eight months and never missed the trenches,
but I have been through enough to know what they have
been through. And then people think it is mud and wet
we mind ; that is nothing, absolutely nothing, compared
with the nerve-racking hell of bombardment. Of course,
people at home can imagine that more easily than the
bombardments, so that is what they talk about. I can't
think that human nature ever had to stand in any kind of
warfare in history what the modern infantryman has to
stand. The strange thing in a way is that there doesn't seem
to be any limit to what you can make human nature stand.
But I do think that after the war there will be a wave of
practical pacifism from the ex-infantrymen of Western
Europe that will sweep many barriers to progress away.
I will go on fighting as long as is necessary to get a decision
in this war and show that prepared militarism cannot
dominate the world—whatever hell may be in store for me.
But I will not hate Germans to the order of any bloody
politician, and the first thing I shall do after I am free will
be to go to Germany and create all the ties I can with German life. It is the soldiers who will be the good Pacifists—
just as every decent Pacifist should be a soldier now, whether
he is a German or an Englishman. I dislike Liebknecht
almost as much as I do the Union of Democratic Control.

What a miserable business the Cavell agitation was ! I
believe a large proportion of the men out here who think
at all share my sentiments about it. I have no sympathy
with people who want to execrate the whole German nation as much as possible. It doesn't help to win the war.
Women seem to be particularly bad in this way. I met a
lady—a ward-maid in the hospital where I was after Hooge
—whose catlike ferocity of sentiments about Germans and
Germany simply made me sick. A dose of shelling would
cure a lot of that in any one. When you are lying at rest
and hear a bombardment going on, you can't help thinking of the poor devils of infantry in the trenches on both

sides with sympathy. You are none the worse soldier or fighter for that.

———

6th D.C.L.I., B.E.F.

[To E. S. P. Haynes] *25th March, 1916*

. . . At present I am in the Divisional Camp—a sort of semi-hospital, not far from the firing-line, for the slight cases of sickness. I have had three attacks of " flu " in three weeks. I got going again twice after lying up for a day or two in the trenches, but collapsed after each effort. They say I am thoroughly run down. I am certainly more fed-up with fighting than I have ever been.

I had as near a squeak as one can have ten days ago when going down from the trenches accompanied only by a private at nine o'clock on a delightful spring morning. They were shelling quite unpleasantly all the time we were going down. We reached the outskirts of the village which we were making for safely and I thought we were all right, when suddenly a high-velocity shell burst right by us. I could see nothing for the thick smoke. Instinctively I jumped into a deep trench on the edge of which we were walking. As I jumped I heard the private—one of my best men—call out, " Oh, major ! " (short for sergeant-major) " the bastards have got me at last ! " He had been through everything with our battalion without a scratch, and I was in the devil of a funk, knowing that the cunning Boche frequently sends two shells in the same place if he suspects any one of being there. But I scrambled out of the trench as quickly as I could (having no equipment on) and found the lad lying horribly wounded in the stomach. I cut his trousers down and stopped the blood in the worst place with a large shell dressing which I had carried for months. He was so bad that I could not bear to lift him down into the trench alone, as it was so deep and I should have hurt him badly. So I took the chance of another shell doing us both in, and bellowed for stretcher-bearers—there was another regiment billeted in the village. After some minutes they arrived, and we got the lad to their dressing station after numerous halts due to damned German aeroplanes overhead. He was fetched away by the motor-ambulance, but died the same day.

That sort of thing, repeated a good many times, in addition to the nervous strain of shelling and bombardments, makes one utterly war-weary. On this particular occasion I was damned lucky. I was not touched, but found a couple of holes in my clothes, made, I think, by bits from the shell which killed the lad who was with me.

Of course, I don't want peace to be made as things are. The job must be finished off. And the thought of the French at Verdun inspires one to endure as nothing else does at the moment. But how one dreams of the end ! I used to be primarily a reformer—full of zeal for remedying this or that specific social injustice. I still am—*au fond*. But when I dream of *après la guerre* I do not think at all of the great social problems which will immediately arise. I just think of the world—this good old cheery ball of earth—as a place of exquisite beauty, adventure, joy, love, and experience. I am perfectly content with it as it is. I even almost love its defects, as one almost loves the defects of a friend or lover who satisfies one. You will not find the man from the trenches is going to hate the German to the order of the politician, and refuse to buy German goods which are obviously preferable to the British product. By God ! I can see the scene—before the peace, even during the armistice. The Infantrymen will swarm over the parapets of the trenches on both sides and will exchange every damned thing which they can spare off their persons—down to their buttons and hats and bits of their equipment—for " souvenirs."

If only one has the luck to be alive to enjoy that day ! The happiest fate of all would be to be alive and to be in the trenches.

I am not far from the original haunts where my battalion spent its first nine months out here. It is pleasant to have a change, but it is not in all ways for the better. The spring is delightful in this rolling chalk country. Every morning when I was in the front-line trenches I used to hear the larks singing soon after we stood-to about dawn. But those wretched larks made me more sad than almost anything else out here. . . . Their songs are so closely associated in my mind with peaceful summer days in gardens or pleasant landscapes in Blighty. Here one knows that the larks sing at seven and the guns begin at nine or ten. Every damned morning the Boches whizz-banged and trench-mortared the trench that I was in. For some reason they never touched the greater part of the front of our battalion. It was only one end—where I happened to be—that they worried. We had some but not a great many casualties from the shelling. But it gets on one's nerves. The humorous side of being shelled is well portrayed by that fellow Bairnsfather. Have you seen his collection of drawings " *Fragments from France* " ? They are not art, but they are extraordinary good expressions of the soldier's humour about his own rat-in-a-trap predicaments. He has a drawing called " Where did that one go to ? " when the shell has actually " blown in "—as we say —the speaker's own dugout. That is the remark you hear after every burst ; each man anxiously asks his neighbour, " Where did that one go ? " It is funny—if one's nerves have left one any sense of humour—and funnier still when you reflect that the " next one " may by *force majeure* prevent you from making any inquiry at all.

Excuse these dirty " scraps of paper "—but perhaps they are appropriate for the correspondence of one who rushed to volunteer on the inspiration caused by poor old Bethmann-Hollweg's unfortunate phrases of those hot August days of long ago. I write lying on the floor of a well-built hut which we English have taken over from the French Red Cross. The bright sunshine, blue sky, and clouds and budding trees which I can see through the window make me think of the Alps and Northern Italy. But, damn it, they are fighting even where I tramped for pleasure in the Dolomites ! Well, it will end some time and somehow. Only let it be a definite well-established peace when it does come. The Prussian monarchy must be smashed, but the German people must be given a chance to live an honourable life in the world if they will dissociate themselves from the bloody system of militarism. . . .

Have been reading Anatole France, Voltaire, and Maupassant while I have been ill. . . . Voltaire is one of the great figures of all the ages—his combination of luminous sanity and passion for human rights makes him stand out even among the great. I have always ranked him far above Rousseau.

CAPTAIN THOMAS MICHAEL KETTLE
Royal Dublin Fusiliers

Educated University College, Dublin. Barrister, Member of Parliament, and Professor of National Economics, National University, Dublin. Killed in action, France, 9 September, 1916, at the age of 32.

[France]

[To Brigadier-General Hammond]   *July* [*1916*]

. . . What has moved and impressed me most, I think, is the spirit of the men and their confidence in their commander. Courage, or rather heroism, is the commonest commonplace to them. If I live longer with them I shall begin to get near their standard.

It is an amazing experience this living on a lease renewable from hour to hour or even minute to minute. If I come through, which in my individual case is doubtful enough, I will assuredly face life in a new way. . . .

. . . There are a great many things I do not know and a great many qualities I lack, but I *can* get on with Irishmen and keep them in good temper. Moreover, the responsibility of an officer is not so great as I thought. The men expect you to be a man, they do not expect you to know everything like the ideal subaltern of the silly text-books.

I am happy too in a sort of a way that, knowing what was ahead, I had the grace—I won't say the courage—to do my duty. *You* will never know, being an instructor and old soldier, how hard it is to a man of my temperament— and, lest you should think that my nerves are exaggerating the random way in which death comes, I should say that two young officers in the lines in which we are this afternoon have already been killed. . . .

I see that —— has triumphed over sense and decency. There is a passage in Edmund's Spenser's " *View of the State of Ireland* " in which he speaks of an old prophecy to the effect that England would ultimately perish through her dealing with Ireland. I wish you would get somebody to quote that and my passage cited on the front page of my " *Open Secret of Ireland* " in a letter to the papers.

For myself I am certain that unless justice comes to Ireland, England will not win this war, and is not worthy to win it. I have always thought, too, that the tone of some of the English papers, and the attempt to transform this from a war for honour into a war for trade were unholy things. Our Irish comrades at any rate did not die that new Birminghams might arise.

Forgive the seriousness of this note and don't think we are glum. We have the reputation of being the gayest company in the battalion and I personally have spent much of my time in writing comic verse ! . . .

———

[To His Wife]   *July 19, 1916*

. . . It is a grim and awful job, and no man can feel up to it. The waste—the science of waste and bloodshed ! How my heart loathes it and yet it is God's only way to Justice. . . .

_____

July 24, 1916

. . . This is the afternoon of my second day in the fire trench. My ears are becoming a little more accustomed to the diabolism of sound, but it remains terrible beyond belief. This morning as I was shaving, the enemy began to find us and dropped aerial torpedoes, shells and a mine right on top of our dug-out. Nobody was hurt, thank God. The strain is terrible. It continues from hour to hour and minute to minute. It is indeed an ordeal to which human nature itself is hardly equal.

What impresses and moves me above all is the amazing faith, patience and courage of the men. To me it is not a sort of looking-down-on but rather a looking-up-to appreciation of them. I pray and pray and am afraid !—they go quietly and heroically on. God bless them and make me less inferior to them. . . .

_____

Aug. 10, 1916

. . . If God spares me I shall accept it as a special mission to preach love and peace for the rest of my life. If He does not, I know now in my heart that for anyone who is dead but who has loved enough, there is provided some way of piercing the veils of death and abiding close to those whom he has loved till that end which is the beginning.

I want to live, too, to use all my powers of thinking, writing and working to drive out of civilization this foul thing called war and to put in its place understanding and comradeship. . . .

_____

[France]
Sept. 8, 1916

... If I live I mean to spend the rest of my life working for perpetual peace. I have seen war and faced modern artillery, and know what an outrage it is against simple men. ...

We are moving up to-night into the battle of the Somme. The bombardment, destruction and bloodshed are beyond all imagination, nor did I ever think the valour of simple men could be quite as beautiful as that of my Dublin Fusiliers. I have had two chances of leaving them—one on sick leave and one to take a staff job. I have chosen to stay with my comrades.

I am calm and happy but desperately anxious to live. ... The big guns are coughing and smacking their shells, which sound for all the world like over-head express trains, at anything from 10 to 100 per minute on this sector ; the men are grubbing and an odd one is writing home. Somewhere the Choosers of the Slain are touching, as in our Norse story they used to touch, with invisible wands those who are to die. ...

LIEUTENANT HARRY SACKVILLE LAWSON
R.F.A.

Educated Haileybury and Peterhouse, Cambridge. Headmaster of Buxton College. Killed in action, France, 5 February, 1918, at the age of 41.

British Expeditionary Force,
[To His Former Pupils]   France,
My Dear Boys,   *July 3rd, 1917*

I wish I could be with you in person to say good-bye to you all, and to hand over my Headmastership to my successor. Instead, I'm writing from a dug-out, to the sound of guns, the sort of message I want you to have before Term ends. But although I am in a dug-out at the Front, I am picturing myself as sitting in my study at the College in the midst of surroundings of busy boyhood. I see the war potato field and the cricket pitch—the wickets casting a dark shadow in glaring contrast with the thin, white line of the block. Momentarily I think of the need of camouflage for concealing the position from the observation of hostile air-craft. Only for the moment. I'm back again in the study, and a bell, rather jaded and weary, has sounded the end of a period.

I've got one thing in particular to say to you all—just the main thing we've talked about together in its different bearings in the past—just the one important thing which keeps life sweet and clean and gives us peace of mind. It's a Christian thing, and it's a British thing. It's what the Bible teaches—it's what the Christian martyrs suffered in persecution for. It soon found root in England and began not only to fill the land, but also to spread abroad and become the heritage of the Empire. It's the story of the Crusaders, of the Reformation, of the downfall of the power of Spain, of our colonisation, of the destruction of Napoleon's might, of the abolition of slavery, and of the coming awakening of Germany. The thing is this : Playing the game for the game's sake.

Now I've had many opportunities in years gone by of having a talk with you about this, and I've always found that we've got a clear starting-off point. For whether I have been talking to a boy alone, or to a class in its class-room, or to the school met together in the New Hall, I have found opinion quite clear and quite decided as to what the game is and what the game is not. We've had a sure foundation. And the difficulty for us all consists, not in knowing what the game is, but in trying to live up to the standard of life which our knowledge of the game puts before us. Don't think that I am referring to the breaking of school rules. I am not. School rules don't live for ever, and, further, school rules suffer change. I am referring to deeper things than these, to rules which do live for ever and which do not suffer change. I am thinking of high honesty of purpose and of the word duty.

I'm going to tell you a story of something that happened at the College in days, I think, not within the memory of any of you. I pick this story because it illustrates well what I have said about school rule and deeper rule.

On a certain whole school day afternoon in the Lent Term some years ago, the Vth Form made a raid upon the IVth Form. The IVth barricaded themselves very securely in their own class-room by piling up desks and furniture against both doors. The raid was still in progress when I came along at half-past three to take the IVth in English. I passed through the IIIrd, where there were evident symptoms of excitement, and came to the door of the IVth. The door wouldn't open. But my voice acting as a kind of "Sesame," the barricade was quickly removed and I entered. The class-room was pandemonium, desks littering the place in wild confusion, and in particular concentrated against the door opposite to that through which I had entered. I held a court of enquiry—pronounced judgment—went to the study for my cane and dealt with the IVth Form ringleaders on the spot. This, mind you, for a breach of school rule. Desks are not designed to be used for splinter-proof dug-outs. Now the enquiry showed clearly that though the IVth were guilty, they were not nearly so guilty as the Vth. So peace once more reigning in the IVth, I went along to the new hall to have a talk with the Vth. I told them what had happened—what punishment had been meted out to the IVth, and I said, "You've got the IVth into a row and you are the guiltier party of the two. I have caned the principal culprits in the IVth, and I shall be in the study at five o'clock and shall be glad to cane there those of you who feel you ought to turn up."

At five o'clock seven of them arrived and received their caning. Before they left I said to them, "I'm very proud of you chaps, and I've got to thank you for the first caning I've ever enjoyed giving."

They felt they ought to turn up. They did turn up. I need
say no more. . . .

H. S. Lawson,
2nd Lieut., R.F.A., and
Headmaster of Buxton College.

LIEUTENANT PETER CLEMENT LAYARD

Suffolk Regiment

Educated Bedales School. Killed in action, France, 23 August, 1918,
at the age of 22.

[France]
[*March, 1916*]
[To His Parents]   *Wednesday, 7.55 p.m.*

. . . The people about ½ mile on our right have been
having a great bombing attack—it was wonderful to watch
all the flashes in the dark—and our artillery put over 4
17-inch shells. They are the most ghastly things imaginable.
When they exploded they shook all the ground right round
here—and they make a hole 30ft. deep and 50ft. across.
Isn't it too awful—the shell alone weighs just over a ton !

I rather hate watching these strafes in a way, because you
think of all the poor men being broken and killed—and for
what ? I don't believe even God knows.

Any faith in religion I ever had is most frightfully shaken
by things I've seen, and it's incredible that if God could
make a 17-inch shell not explode—it seems incredible that
he lets them explode ; and yet, on the other hand, I don't
know if I told you that in our horrid bombardment I
described to you, the shell which came near to me was a
dud, and that seems rather deliberate luck or something,
tho' He knows I didn't deserve it a fraction as much as the
poor splendid heroes who are killed. I hate the whole thing,
and so do we all, because it shouldn't be.

The Germans were quite nice two days ago. The battn. on our left sent out a patrol, and the Hun machine guns saw them and fired, hitting 3. They got 2 back, and in the morning they put up a notice in German : " Tho' alive when we took him into our trench, No. 1328 Pte. Summers has since died from wounds." When we saw this we put up a notice : " Danke sehr." It was rather sweet, wasn't it ? But of course that makes it worse, as it shows how unwilling everyone is to fight. We kill them because they'd kill us if we didn't and vice versâ, and if only we could come to an ordinary agreement—— But we can't. . . .

LIEUTENANT THE HON. CHARLES ALFRED LISTER
R.N.V.R.

Educated Eton and Balliol College, Oxford. Diplomatic Service. Died of wounds received at Gallipoli, 28 August, 1915, at the age of 28.

Hood Battalion, B.M.E.F.
[TO FATHER RONALD KNOX]   [*April, 1915*]

Rupert Brooke died of blood-poisoning caused by a germ called the *pneumo coccus*. He had been rather pulled down at Port Said and suffered from the sea, so the p.c. had a favourable field to work in. There was no doubt as to his fate ; he died within twenty-four hours of the ill making itself manifest. He was buried in an olive-grove hidden in a ravine thick with scrub that runs from a stony mountain down to the sea. The grave is under an olive-tree that bends over it like a weeping angel. A sad end to such dazzling purity of mind and work, clean cut, classical, and unaffected all the time like his face, unfurrowed or lined by cares. And the eaglet had begun to beat his wings and soar. Perhaps the Island of Achilles is in some respects a suitable resting-place for those bound for the plains of Troy.

.   .   .   .

Rupert's was certainly a perfect death, and a very fitting close to a fine life ; but it is rather a bitter thought that he should have seen none of the soldiering he had devoted himself to with such ardour, and that the gift made so gladly should have been accepted before Experience gave him any return. For any one with a mind alive, this war is primarily a search after the new, and appeals keenly to one's sense of curiosity. . . .

———

Blue Sisters Convent, Malta.

[TO LADY DESBOROUGH]   *June 3, 1915*

I can't write what I feel about dear Julian. The void is so terrible for me and the thought of it quite unmans me. I'd so few ties with the life I left when I went abroad—so few, that is to say, that I wanted to keep, and I always felt as sure of Julian's love as he did of mine, and so certain of seeing his dear old smile just the same. We did not often write or anything of that sort just for that reason, and now the whole thing has gone. How much worse it must be for you and yours. All of us loved him so, and I'm sure if I were back with father and D—— we should be in the depths and feel almost worse than I do now that one of our nearest and dearest has gone.

I suppose that if death meant wholly loss, all recollections would be wholly bitter ; but the consciousness that we are recalling memories of one who may still be near us makes recollection precious, an abiding realization of what is, and not a mere regret for what has ceased to be.

I suppose everybody noticed dear Julian's vitality, but I don't think they were so conscious of that great tenderness of heart that underlay it. He always showed it most with you, and with women generally it was his special charm. I think now of the way he used to take my hand if he had felt disappointed with anything I had done and then found out why I'd done it. I remember a time when he was under the impression I'd chucked Socialism for the " loaves and fishes," etc., and of course that sort of thing he couldn't abide, and he thought this for a longish while, then found out that it wasn't that after all, and took my hand in his in the most loving way.

I don't suppose many people knew of the ardent love he had for honesty of purpose and intellectual honesty, and what sacrifices he made for them, and sacrifices of peace of mind abhorrent to most Englishmen. The Englishman is a base seeker after happiness, and he will make most sacrifices of principle and admit any number of lies into his soul to secure this dear object of his. It is want of courage on its negative side, this quality—and swinish greed on its positive side. Julian in his search for truth and in his search for what he believed to be his true self caused himself no end of worry and unhappiness, and was a martyr who lit his own fires with unflinching nerve. Out stalking he always wanted to do his own work, and he was just the same in his inner life. Surely the Lady he sought with tireless faith, the Lady for whom he did and dared so much on lonely paths, will now reward him ? God, it is glorious to think of a soul so wholly devoid of the pettiness and humbug, the cynicism and dis-honesty, of so much that we see. There is a story in one of Miss Kingsley's books of a West African medicine-man who found himself at death's door. He applied all his herbs and spells and conducted all his well-worn rites before his idols, and with his friend's intercessions, without any effect. At last he wearied of his hocus-pocus, and took his idols and charms down to the seashore and flung them into the surf, and he said, " Now I will be a man and meet my God alone." Julian from the time I knew him had flung away his idols and had met God. His intense moral courage distin-guished him even more than his physical bravery from the common men—and his physical bravery was remarkable enough, whether he was hunting, boxing, or whatever he was at.

I think he found his true self on what we all knew would be the scene of his glory, and it is some melancholy satisfaction that his services received recognition. What must make you still happier must be the glorious glowing tone of those letters of his, and the knowledge that his last few months were crowded hours of glorious life, stronger than death in that they abide. I shall never forget how much they heartened me when I came to see you to get your kind offices for this show. The recollection of them will be a constant strength. No one wrote of the war like that or talked of it that way, and so many went from leave or after healing wounds as a duty, but without joy. Julian, apart from the physical delight he had in combat, felt keenly, I am sure, that he was doing something worth while, the thing most worth while in the world, and looked on death and the passing beyond as a final burst into glory. He was rather Franciscan in his love of all things that are, and in his absence of fear of all God's creatures—death included.

He stood for something very precious to me—for an England of my dreams made of honest, brave, and tender men, and his life and death have surely done something towards the realization of that England. Julian had so many friends who felt for him as they felt for no one else, and a fierce light still beats on the scene of his passing, and others are left to whom he may leave his sword and a portion of his skill.

You must have known all this splendour of Julian's life far better than I did, so I don't know why I should write all this. But I am so sad myself that I must say something to you, and because you knew how very fond I was of Julian.

One can seek comfort at this time in the consciousness of the greatness of our dead, and the work they have left behind them, and the love we have borne them : and such comfort is surely yours, apart from any larger hope.

———

PRIVATE ROGER MARSHALL LIVINGSTONE

44th Battalion, Canadian Expeditionary Force

On staff of Canadian Bank of Commerce. Died of wounds, France,
27 October, 1917, at the age of 24.

[France]

[To His Mother]   [*October, 1917*]

Mother dear, your letters worry me, worry me considerably. It is evident that you do not understand, but I shall put it to you this way : Do you realise that Christ was the first one to fall in the present war ? How ? Well simply this : The very principles for which Christ gave His life are identically those principles for which Britain is to-day giving her life-blood. It is an old struggle, and Christ Himself was the first martyr to the cause. We are fighting for principles. Right against might. Would the world be worth living in if might and might alone prevailed ?

Therefore, Mother, rather than pray that Harry and I should never be sent to the front, pray that we shall acquit ourselves like men and be strong, for we are on duty primarily for God. Don't feel badly if you hear that we have been specially detailed for dangerous work. Rather look on it as an honour and a special privilege that we should be chosen for special duty in upholding the cause for which Christ laid down His life. If you pray for our return, and only for our return, it is selfishness. Other mothers have been called on to endure greater sacrifices than any we can endure in this war.

Pray for victory for right ; pray that we shall be able to do our duty faithfully, and if we fall in the cause of Christ, remember mother dear, that ' greater love hath no man than this, that he lay down his life for his friends.'

Personally, I don't want to go back except with honour and a clear conscience of having done my duty. Life under any other circumstances after the war would not be worth while.

LIEUTENANT THE HON. ERIC FOX PITT LUBBOCK, M.C.

R.F.C.

Educated Eton and Balliol College, Oxford. Joined Army while an undergraduate. Killed in action, Flanders, 11 March, 1917, at the age of 23.

[France]

[TO HIS MOTHER]   *15th April, 1915*

... Although rainy days are very long and often numerous they give place to fine ones sooner or later. The hard thing is to keep a sense of proportion.

But don't you sometimes feel that we should be glad to think that we who are living and suffering and dying now are really all playing a great part in the advancement of human nature. I am sure that this war will do a lot to make nations realise that the laws of Christianity which we have for so long tried to apply to private life apply also to public life. We have excused public sins, arrogance in nations, etc., which we would not tolerate in private people. Those laws of right and wrong which we have applied to individuals have not been applied to nations. But now we are applying them.

An individual pledged to defend a friend would not receive any sympathy if he allowed his friend to be attacked and did not defend him, and so England being pledged to defend Belgium, defended her when attacked. Germany was the most ruthless offender because she attacked. When that great fact is realised by all nations a step will have been taken to advance our world. And we should feel proud that we are suffering for that step and sweating blood to help the world, as One once sweated blood before to save it.

Of course, that idea does not make the suffering less awful, but it is another way of looking at it. Also we cannot help being thankful that we were chosen, and not another generation, to do this work and pay this price, and also that England was sufficiently enlightened to do what she is doing rather than to choose as others did, the easier broader road.

I am very well. They are taking away all my staff except 3 to-morrow and sending me 42 new men, so that I shall have an awful time keeping the work going. They have also sent me a clerk but I prefer to do all my figures myself so that if anything goes wrong it's my fault. Otherwise one feels if only I'd not been lazy enough to let that fool do it, it would have been alright. Of course, I do make mistakes, though not nearly as many as I did at first. . . .

———————

[France]

[TO HIS MOTHER]   *10 /11 /15*

One is here confronted almost daily with the possibility of Death, and when one looks forward to the next few months the possibility becomes really a probability. I am therefore sitting down now to write to you briefly a few words which in the event of my death I hope may help to comfort you and cheer you. That is my purpose in writing, for as my object in life is to comfort and help you, so it is my last hope, if I should be taken from you, that I may not cause you too great a grief. The thoughts which I here intend to write are those which I have had on occasions when it seemed that my life was about to be cut short. Also I know that if in my last hour I am conscious, my chief consolation will be to feel that these thoughts may reach you. I shall therefore simply write down my ideas about it all and I hope thereby to enable you to feel that although I may be taken away yet that fact is not all grief.

Now one of the questions one asks oneself about it all is, Do I fear death ? and I have, I think, convinced myself that I do not.

My reasons for this I will show later. Of course, it is the natural instinct of a human being to avoid Death in all possible ways. " Life every man holds dear ! " Yes, and every animal of God's holds this great gift dear, but whereas an animal only holds life dear by instinct, it is, I think, our especial privilege to hold life dear for reasons.

Now my reasons are two (1) love and ambition, (2) that I know my death would cause pain to you and I don't want to do that. My love is firstly love for you, secondly love for others, and thirdly love for the world in general. I love you all, my brothers, my sisters, my friends. My love for you all makes me long for life because with it I hope to be able to help you all and to add to your happiness. And my love for Dad makes me want to live because I hope perhaps in some small way I might carry on one of his great works and in so doing honor him. My love for the world in general makes me hope that before I go I may be able to make it in some way (however small) just a bit better than I found it.

Ambition I should perhaps better call interest, it is simply the desire to learn something more of this wonderful and beautiful world before I leave it.

And the other reason, which is more the cause of my dreading death than anything, is why I am writing now. To fear or dread death for its own sake is absolutely against all reason, and I want to point out to you that you must not grieve too much if I die. . . .

Suppose now that you went off to sleep at 10 one night and woke up at 8 next morning having had no dreams or consciousness at all, would that not seem to you a blessed 10 hours ? Now Death at its very worst is that—absolute blank, and therefore why fear it ?

But I do not believe death is that. I believe it is something very different.

You and I know very well that there is what we call right and wrong. We also know that if there is right there must be reward for right doing, and if there is wrong there must be punishment. Now in this world that is not always so, for many are happier and ' better off ' as we call it for doing wrong. Now if this world were the end then our wonderful consciousness, and our knowledge of right and wrong is altogether vanity, and life is a hopeless failure. If this world is the final end, this imperfect world with all its sorrows, passions and griefs, if this is the best we can attain to, then the great Giver of Life is but a torturer, and if you love me then you will rejoice that I have left so miserable an existence and lost so painful a consciousness before I suffer any more. But the very fact that we do know and believe in doing right, in kindness, and in love, the very fact of love itself, seems to prove that this world is not the end. It proves to my mind that there is a something which gave us knowledge and power and which will bring us to the full understanding of purity, of love, of God.

Then we can feel that

> ' *Death is a path that must be trod*
> *If man would ever pass to God.*'

If then I leave this world to enter a fuller and better and happier life, need you grieve for me that I do so ? Oh ! let your love for me conquer pain and bless the chance that brings me to Eternal Joy.

What I have meant to say is that either Death is the end or not the end. That it should be the end is inconceivable, and if it is not the end then that which comes after must be better and higher than this world.

I do not attempt to imagine what is after death. There are many many things which baffle one when one thinks of them, but this seems to me the most impossible of all problems to solve. Just as a child has no idea of what life is really like, so can we have no idea of after life. But this I do believe, that this world is our nursery and that we are being trained by it to make us fit for another and a better life.

Of course, I know all this is not going to relieve you of the first pangs of parting. You will say I might have been spared for some time yet to help and comfort you. Yes ! and I hope I may be spared. We mortals have such deep feelings in the world that it is inevitable that we should have pain at parting. But I hope that you will let me help you even if I am not alive, by believing as I do that we cannot judge for ourselves, and that we cannot here on earth see anything in its true proportion. Is not the sorrow of a child when it loses its doll a very real and great grief? And yet, although it is not much use saying so to the child, we know that it doesn't much matter. So Mummy if you lose me try not to let it be too great a blow to you, try and conquer your own sorrow and to live cheerfully. You have great work before you in caring for M—— and in bringing him up to be the great and good man he is going to be. And you have got to help U——, who although she is so wonderfully strong and good, needs help to bring up her children, and help which you more than anyone else can give. Live for them cheerfully. . . .

———

[France]

[TO HIS BROTHER]   *10 /11 /15*

To my —— I love very dearly as a real and loving brother I write just a line now in case I am taken away from him.

I do hope, ——, that your life will be one of peace and happiness and if you attain to half the things which I picture for you, you will indeed be a great and clever man.

Let me just offer you one word of advice, ——, which is the maxim I found helped me most in life—' Visit the fatherless and widows in their affliction and keep yourself unspotted from the world,' that is to say, make your object in life to help, comfort and love, and avoid always such things as are vile. For a thousand virtues do not atone for one vice, and a man who has sinned in any of the big vices, committed any unclean act, although he may repent all his life, is not the same as a man who has kept himself ' unspotted from the world.' Help Mum and look after her. Do not let her grieve too much, try and keep her interested. I hope you will never see this letter.

———

MISS MARGUERITE McARTHUR
Y.M.C.A.

Educated Newnham College, Cambridge. Died while on service in
France, 12 February, 1919, at the age of 26.

[France]
May 26th, 1918

. . . We were sitting peacefully in the salon, writing letters,
and had planned to go early to bed, when we heard the
sound of guns, and realised that a raid was on. It was soon
after ten, and almost at once we heard the loud sound of
German engines, apparently overhead. The French maid
was upstairs, but when the guns grew very noisy we called
her down, and after a while went into the front room,
opened all the windows, put up the shutters, and waited.
For two hours or more pandemonium reigned. The crash
of bombs shook the house, guns thundered incessantly,
machine-guns clattered, we heard shrapnel pattering on
the roofs, and the sudden shiver of masses of broken glass.
Twice at least the crash seemed to be just over the house,
and I remember thinking that we should not get through
with our lives. There was nothing we could do—part of
the time we played the piano—afterwards a soldier told
me he heard " *Chanson Triste* " as he dashed past the house ;
and we sang " *John Peel,*" I remember, and " *The Marseil-
laise,*" and " *Nearer, my God, to Thee.*" We knew they were
trying for the station, which is pretty close to us. Once,
when a bomb fell with tremendous violence, the shutters
burst open, and there was a crash of broken tiles and glass.
We did not know whether the house was hit or not. I do
not remember feeling really very nervous. The big crashes
made us jump, and my heart was in my mouth once or
twice, but I did not feel afraid of what seemed likely to
happen. I scribbled a note home and put it in another
room, in the hope that it might escape if we did not. It
seemed as if the guns and bombs would never stop. Once
I went into the bedroom, and saw searchlights sweeping

the sky, and we could hear the loud deep whirr of the engines very distinctly.

At last there was a lull. In a few moments we heard voices in the street, and we opened the door and went out—I, in a dressing-gown, picking our way over a road littered with broken glass and plaster. Someone said there was a bomb in the *Place*, so we ran in and put on coats, and went quickly along. It was a wonderful night—brilliant moon and stars, clear and still, and most wonderfully peaceful after the long clamour of the raid. . . .

At the Hut the raid was the only subject of conversation. The men seemed to feel an urgent necessity to speak of it to someone. I began to understand how bad it had been, and what an escape we had had, when one after another told us that they had never experienced anything so bad up the line, where you had some idea where the shells were falling, and places in which you could take shelter. It must have been an awful time in the camps and hospitals. . . . In one tent every man was killed except one who was standing up ! There was no shelter anywhere. All the men could do was wait for bombs to fall, and run the risk of death and wounds from our own shrapnel. . . . At the hospitals men worked rescuing the wounded, carrying stretchers through a hail of shrapnel, with bombs bursting close by. Two of the interpreters bound up a badly-wounded corporal, fetched a stretcher, and got him to hospital. On the way a bomb burst close to them. One interpreter, who was standing at the door of the German prisoners' ward, was blown across the hut by an explosion which tore the door off. A marquee was fired by a direct hit. Six men cut the cords, so that the whole thing collapsed, smothering the flames, and somehow rescued the men who were inside. One man, whose companion was hit as they hurried to the work of rescue, bound him up, half-carried him into a ward, and then spent the rest of his time walking calmly about through it all, lending a hand where he could, quieting the patients, and helping the nurses. At the 1st Canadian General Hospital the most awful havoc was wrought, though it is said that flares were sent up to show what it was. Bombs fell in the men's lines, killing 60 and wounding many more of the personnel. The nurses' rest hut was blown in, one sister being killed outright and two mortally wounded. Their club was riddled with shrapnel. Yet amidst the horror of it all shone the glory of great courage. Light-duty patients risked their lives to drag the orderlies from the burning huts—32 of them died in the attempt. The nurses and M.O.s stuck to their posts, though knowing that it would be impossible to save their patients, great numbers of whom were helpless femur cases. The nurses who were wounded showed the greatest heroism in the face of mortal pain, and begged those who were doing the little that was possible to leave them and care for the men. The nurses could not say enough of the heroism and splendid work of the men, and the men were full of the courage shown by the women. One said to a patient, who was crying out in terror : " Just look at Sister. When she shows fear you can cry out, but not till then." They spoke, too, of the Ambulance Girls—" the pluckiest of the lot "—out in the thick of it, picking up wounded—pressing through the rail-tunnel, which was crowded with men seeking shelter—carrying on their work regardless of imminent danger. And the men's anxiety for the women they knew was wonderful. Everywhere they were asking : " Are the Y.M. ladies all right ? " Some came to the hut at 2 in the morning to reassure themselves. Several told me that they could hardly restrain themselves from breaking bounds, and coming into the town to ask after our safety. . . .

Everyone had the " wind up " badly. There was talk of the Boches' intention of wiping out the Base—of gas bombs to be dropped that night. . . . There was threatening talk of reprisals on the German prisoners if the Boche came over again, and the interpreters and guards had an anxious night wondering how they could protect their charges if the crowd outside the barbed wire lost its head and broke through. Three German officers from a raider were brought in. One was dead, the others wounded. Very little information could be got from them, except that there were 36 machines, that it was so wonderfully clear that they could see cars on the roads and figures in the streets and on the beach, and that it was impossible for them to tell which were hospitals, since they had no distinguishing marks. Amongst our men the prevailing feeling seemed to be that we should not have hospitals so close to the two legitimate objectives, the railway line and a big infantry depot. . . .

LIEUTENANT G. D'O. MACLEAR
M.C.
I.A.R.O.

Educated King's School, Canterbury, and St. John's College, Oxford. Indian Educational Service. Died in London from effects of wounds received in Mesopotamia, 25 January, 1919, at the age of 31.

[Mesopotamia]

[To P. C. PLOWDEN]   [*Spring, 1917*]

. . . A battle is not in the least as I had imagined it. It is not nearly so terrifying. One becomes so accustomed to bullets flying somewhere near that after the first few minutes one begins to imagine oneself exempt. We were sent in late, after we had done a lot of marching and digging and very probably weariness had blunted the sense of fear Also we had no H.E. among us and H.E. is to my mind peculiarly horrible. . . . It was a very spectacular little battle. Gun flashes and a tremendous uproar on the left and Ramadie —or the Turkish dumps in Ramadie—blazing straight in front. A regular Barnum and Bailey finale. After the Turk had failed to break away our brigade attacked and went straight thro'. The Turks surrendered except in one or two places as soon as we got near their trenches.

I went over as we were charging the front trench. I saw the Turks bolting and had just executed an exceptionally clean-cut miss with my revolver when what felt like a small planet struck me in the neck and I crumpled up. . . .

I haven't now too clear a recollection of my sensations during the five or ten minutes which elapsed between the launching of the attack and my collapse. When we charged and the Turk bolted I felt naturally intense exhilaration but behind there lurked the thought " how beastly if he turns and fights it out." Most of them looked so offensively muscular ; I think it was that reflection that made me take a pot-shot at a bunch of three. I am glad now it was so scandalous a miss. . . .

<hr>

SECOND LIEUTENANT ROBERT WALLACE McCONNELL
King's Own (Royal Lancaster) Regiment

Educated Queen's University, Belfast. Joined Army while an under-graduate. Killed in action, Mesopotamia, 9 April, 1916, at the age of 20.

[En route for Gallipoli,
[TO HIS FATHER]   *late 1915*]

. . . The men are all topping fellows. But one has to let them know who is master. First an officer has to be an officer, and then he may become a man. I have just censored the letters of my men. By Jove ! if you could read some of those letters, they would do you good. The tenderness of those great, rough fellows is wonderful. I love them all for it. Last night was the most beautiful night I ever saw. We loitered about the deck till the wee sma' hours. The moon was all but full, and wake of the ship glistened white in the darkness. It reminded me very much of the 5th Act in the ' *Merchant of Venice*.' It was too beautiful for words, but just a tiny little bit sad. It was a funny feeling when we all lapsed into silence, and we all knew that each one of us was thinking of home. . . . The other night two chaps came into my cabin, and we sat and read. We read

186

Browning and Tennyson and ended up by reading the 52nd and 53rd chapters of Isaiah. They are splendid. It's strange that beauty and loveliness seem to wake up in darkness and sadness. Not that I am sad. Far from it. I am quite contented and happy. None of you are ever out of my mind. But I do not allow thoughts even of *you* to make me discontented or unhappy, and I want you to be able to say the same of me. Remember that God is equally near to both of us. On Sunday I sat down to Communion with four other officers. It was a quiet little service. We went through the good old service and sang the old Communion Psalms. It did me good. . . .

LIEUTENANT-COLONEL JOHN McCRAE
Canadian Army Medical Service

Educated Toronto University. Physician. Author of *In Flanders Fields*. Died on active service, France, 28 January, 1918, at the age of 45.

[TO HIS MOTHER]   France, *May 17th, 1915*

The farther we get away from Ypres the more we learn of the enormous power the Germans put in to push us over. Lord only knows how many men they had, and how many they lost. I wish I could embody on paper some of the varied sensations of that seventeen days. All the gunners down this way passed us all sorts of kudos over it. Our guns—those behind us, from which we had occasional prematures—have a peculiar bang-sound added to the sharp crack of discharge. The French 75 has a sharp wood-block-chop sound, and the shell goes over with a peculiar whine—not unlike a cat, but beginning with n-thus-neouw. The big fellows, 3000 yards or more behind, sounded exactly like our own, but the flash came three or four seconds before the sound. Of the German shells—the field guns come with a great velocity—no warning—just whizz-bang ; white smoke, nearly always air bursts. The next size, probably 5-inch howitzers, have a perceptible time of approach, an increasing whine, and a great burst on the percussion— dirt in all directions. And even if a shell hit on the front of the canal bank, and one were on the back of the bank, five, eight, or ten seconds later one would hear a belated shirr, and curved pieces of shell would light—probably parabolic curves or boomerangs. These shells have a great back kick ; from the field gun shrapnel we got nothing behind the shell —all the pieces go forward. From the howitzers, the danger is almost as great behind as in front if they burst on percussion. Then the large shrapnel—air burst—have a double explosion, as if a giant shook a wet sail for two flaps ; first a dark green burst of smoke ; then a lighter yellow burst goes out from the centre, forwards. I do not understand the why of it.

Then the 10-inch shells : a deliberate whirring course— a deafening explosion—black smoke, and earth 70 or 80 feet in the air. These always burst on percussion. The constant noise of our own guns is really worse on the nerves than the shell ; there is the deafening noise, and the constant shirr of shells going overhead. . . .

The road thirty yards behind us was a nightmare to me. I saw all the tragedies of war enacted there. A wagon, or a bunch of horses, or a stray man, or a couple of men, would get there just in time for a shell. One would see the absolute knock-out, and the obviously lightly wounded crawling off on hands and knees ; or worse yet, at night, one would hear the tragedy—' that horse scream '—or the man's moan. All our own wagons had to come there (one every half hour in smart action), be emptied, and the ammunition carried over by hand. Do you wonder that the road got on our nerves ? On this road, too, was the house where we took our meals. It was hit several times, windows all blown in by nearby shells, but one end remained for us.

Seventeen days of Hades ! At the end of the first day if any one had told us we had to spend seventeen days there, we would have folded our hands and said it could not be done. On the fifteenth day we got orders to go out, but that was countermanded in two hours. To the last we could scarcely believe we were actually to get out. The real audacity of the position was its safety ; the Germans knew to a foot where we were. I think I told you of some of the ' you must stick it out ' messages we got from our (French) General—they put it up to us. It is a wonder to me that we slept when, and how, we did. If we had not slept and eaten as well as possible we could not have lasted. And while we were doing this, the London office of a Canadian newspaper cabled home ' Canadian Artillery in reserve.' Such is fame !

LIEUTENANT J. WOODALL MARSHALL, M.C.
Northumberland Fusiliers

Educated Oakham School, and in Germany. Law student. Enlisted in French Foreign Legion. Subsequently transferred to British Army. Killed in action, France, 1 July, 1916.

[TO HIS MOTHER]
[France, *Autumn, 1914*]

I have been in many places and have had strange experiences, but never in all my life have I struck anything so wonderfully romantic and extraordinary as the French Foreign Legion. I am, after three days experience as a recruit, not at all put out by the actuality. The Legion is the strangest thing ever thought of by the mind of man. In my room, which is comfortable, there is myself, an Irishman, my next neighbour is an American, and the other inhabitants include an ex-officer in the army of the So. American Republic, who came specially over from South America for the war, and is my greatest friend, a Dutch solicitor, a Russian Jew, three Cossacks, two Italians, a student from a Russian University, an Englishman who has always been resident in Paris and who can hardly speak English, a Spaniard, and other mysterious individuals whose identity is absolutely hid.

I have only signed on for the duration of the war, probably six months, but of course there are many old Legionaries who have been years in the Regiment, notably an Englishman, who has been seventeen years in the Legion, a gentleman and a thoroughly decent fellow. Of course these old hands are all disappointed men, who have joined the Legion through all sorts of reasons—scandal, disappointments in love, and anything that might drive a man to despair. Also there are the adventurers to whom the Legion has appealed through its romantic conditions. And the wonderful thing is that all these strange men coming from all over the world have knit themselves so much together that they are as one great family. Everyone is " my comrade," " my good friend." These words enter into every phrase. " Let me have a light, my good comrade," " Have a cigarette, my friend." It is wonderful, this life in the Legion.

I have told you of the inhabitants of my room. The Legion includes men of every rank, rich and poor, but all under the same flag, ' for honour,' and all, as I have said, of one great family. We have counts and Jewish pedlars, millionaires and paupers, officers from foreign armies and deserters from all countries. I should not be a bit surprised if we could supply a bishop. If the electric light goes wrong, an electrician comes forward. If a man hurts himself in the field of exercise, there is not any need to send for the regimental doctor. You can always for a sou get a tailor to mend your clothes or an ex-barber to give you a shave ; an ex-cigarette maker will show you how to make a cigarette, and an old clothes merchant will tell you the exact value of your civilian clothes. But if I were to attempt to describe all the professions and occupations of the various legionaries I would exceed the amount of paper at my disposal and should probably be late for barracks to-night.

I may, just as a sample of nationalities, give you a dozen

or so out of the way people who are represented in the Legion. A Persian, a Japanese, a small bevy of Cossacks, a representative of every South American Republic, a full-blooded negro, a few dozen half-blooded worthies of every mixture imaginable. Montenegrins and the Balkan races generally and, well, almost every race under the sun, even an Esquimo. And the wonderful thing is that all these races have so taken upon themselves the doctrines of the Legion that everything runs as smoothly and as calmly as a first-class hotel. It is a standing rule that no one shall put anyone else to any extra trouble and no one shall interfere with anyone else's business. Thus if a man were to take a bayonet and announce his intention of running himself through no one would interfere with him or advise him not to. But the orderly of his room would probably ask him, in the nicest manner possible, as a good comrade, not to do it in the room, as it would make a mess which he would have to clear up. Nobody thinks of asking anybody else his private life or the why or wherefore of his entry into the Legion. There is a complete absence of swearing. A complete calm, every idea is to save anybody else trouble. Everything is shared in common.

On second thoughts I should almost liken the Legion to an extremely strict but well conducted monastery, except, of course, the complete absence of any religious exercises, though, mentioning the different religions, they are not wanting—Catholics, Protestants, Jews, Mohammedans, members of the Russian Orthodox Church, and heaven knows what else. What the fighting qualities of the Legion, in a war like this, are, is a matter of conjecture, but I could not have greater confidence in the bravery and self-sacrifice of my comrades if I were in the finest crack corps any country could possess. I think I have dwelt enough on the peculiar qualities of my regiment, and you will, I think, understand that some of them might not shine in a drawing room, though, as to the latter some of them would shine uncommonly well. As a whole, they are quite capable of sending representatives to either a palace or a workhouse and those representatives would not feel the slightest bit out of place.

We cater for a very decent music hall display, possessing as we do, Vitas, ' the strongest man in the world,' who, by the way, has a rival in the Legion itself, a conjurer and a Japanese juggler. The American representative could give a very good ragtime exhibition, while I have no doubt the Cossacks would oblige with an example of rough riding. As for sentimental and comic songs, well, there would be an embarrassment of riches.

Our uniform is that of the ordinary French soldier—a blue tunic, overcoat turned over from the knees, a red képi, red trousers, with the exception of the distinctive addition of a blue sash which every Legionary wears, and is the only soldier in the French Army so habited. As for the life, it is not hard for me. I have always walked a good deal for pleasure, and marching is the great speciality of the Legion and I do not find it beyond me, though many I dare say would find it hard. To sum up, life is a strenuous but quite happy one. . . .

———

CAPTAIN WILLIAM JOHN MASON
Gloucestershire Regiment

Educated St. Olave's School. Lecturer at Bristol University. Killed in action, France, 3 July, 1916, at the age of 27.

[France,
Autumn, 1915]

. . . I don't know how anyone can ' glory ' in war except perhaps during the actual heat of an attack, then you cease to be yourself, and are released from all ordinary cares and associations. I know we marched on September 25th with tremendous enthusiasm. Many of us felt we might never come back ; but what would that matter if only the British could be marching through La Bassée that evening ?

But in war in its quieter aspects there can be no possibility of ' glory.' Then there is time for thought and philosophy to reassert their sway over the enthusiasms and question their validity and value. And what can you think then except of the crass stupidity of mankind in waging war.

The suffering of men at the Front, of the wounded whose flesh and bodies are torn in a way you cannot conceive ; the sorrow of those at home who hear of casualties among their dear ones and the ever present anxiety for those who are not casualties. And all that is being piled up day after day in France, England, Germany, Bulgaria and Turkey ! What a cruel and mad diversion of human activity ! Food indeed for pessimism if ever there was. . . .

PRIVATE WILLIAM RANDALL CLUNAS MILL
R.A.M.C.

Educated Glasgow Academy and Glasgow University. Killed in action, Flanders, 28 May, 1918, at the age of 24.

Up the Line, near Gaza.

[To His Parents]   *Sunday, October 28th, 1917*

. . . The weather last night must furnish the chief subject of this letter, for at last the rains have fallen, and the floods come and beaten upon our houses, so that they fell in. In fact, we had a great night of it.

Know first of all that on the surface we have only a few tents for the patients, and that the rest of us dwell in dugouts and bivvies in the sides of the gullies. Now, a night or two earlier two chance shells from the Turks had burst among the tents, whereupon those in Authority got the wind up, and ordered the removal of the patients to dugouts in the gully. Yesterday was cloudy and gusty, with scarcely a blink of sunshine in the 12 hours. The wind blew over the dry brown hills, raising huge clouds of dust all over the thirsty land. The clouds were very low, the general aspect of things extremely threatening, and it was very obviously going to rain before long. After an ominously red and black angry sunset the sky grew more gloomy than ever. To the north and east huge inky-black clouds were piled up, and were soon illuminated by very vivid violet flashes of wildfire which ran backwards and forward along the edge of the bank of cloud, and there was heavy thunder rumbling a few miles off. Shortly after nine o'clock, when the wildfire was so dazzling that it gave you a headache, the first few heavy drops fell. In a minute the whole thing was on us. We were prepared for rain, but the succeeding two hours made short work of our preparations. The dug-out S. and I occupied had been dug with tremendous trouble by the ambulance before us, to the depth of eight feet or so—an advantage certainly, when shells are coming over, but the possibility of bad weather had been overlooked ; in fact, as we were not long in finding out, this particular dug-out filled the duty of a general drainage centre for the slopes of the little side gully. In two minutes a tiny rivulet began to pour in down our steps, and would not be daunted. Soon it was like a mountain torrent, and came flooding into our floor, and over our blankets. We could not hear each other speaking for the row on the water-proof roof. It was, however, a time for *deeds*, not *words*. We shoved the most valuable articles of our kits outside, threw a waterproof sheet over them, and then, leaving the rest of our belongings floating about on the rising tide, we struggled out against the torrent that was rushing through what was once our door, and made for shelter. The rain was coming down like hail, and the sides of the gully were streaming. Another torrent was rushing along where the dry bed of the " Wadi " had been. We made for a substantial dug-out with sandbagged and corrugated iron roof. Other people had arrived before us, and " standing room only " was the order, so we stood, and prepared to stand for the rest of the night. But it was not so to be. A suspicious sound came from the back of the dug-out, a light was produced, and lo ! another torrent descending through a breach in the back wall. In about ten seconds we were again flooded out. . . . The rain lasted for 2 hours or so, and I think we had between one inch and a quarter and an inch and three quarters in that time. The clay-ey slopes were almost impassable, and where the water lay for any time, you sank in mud up to your knees. Eventually we all got stowed away into the tents, and I had a good sleep ; half of me on an empty " *fantassie* " and the other half on a Field Medical Pannier, an island in the 4 inch deep sea in the dressing tent.

If we were amused at the Variety Entertainment overnight, our good humour next morning knew no bounds. This was due in part to the beautiful morning, and to the extraordinary change in the landscape. All the dull browns and greys had changed to greens and yellows. The trees were glistening ; there was no dust, and the freshness and sweetness of the country, and of the air, were a great delight. The sky was very blue with huge white billowy clouds, " *On dirait un jour de printemps.*" But the place was a sight, and our dug-out was unanimously voted the chef d'oeuvre. The whole gully, and the banks, were seamed with deep cracks and crevices. Once I said in a letter that I did not see how the rainfall *could* cause the thousands of gullies and wadis and ravines that cross and re-cross in this 'ere promised land. After last night's demonstration my wonder is that there is any *Holy Land* left at all. Alas for our much vaunted camp ! Where are now its pathways, and its parapets ? Where are its neat dug-outs, and its trim bivvies ?— That mass of sodden canvas was the orderly room, and that lake, on whose surface float innumerable bandages and bottles, and scraps of lint, was our dressing tent. Truly the rain can say with Caesar, " I came, I saw, and I jolly well did them in." We knew that a considerable amount of our personal stock would be, so to speak, in liquidation, but we were not prepared for the reality. As we neared our little street we saw a large crowd standing on a mound, evidently greatly amused at something below them. . . .

Our dug-out had been transformed into a pond, and its surface was almost covered with books, papers, clothing, loaves, jam tins, gas masks, a camera, boxes, and odds and ends of every description. We waded in encouraged by admiring cheers from an ever growing crowd of Officers and men, and fished out the rest of our stuff, amid the clicking of innumerable cameras. At last we got everything out, and repairing to the top of the ridge, we spread the whole show out to dry in the sun, and a brave display it was. Everything from blankets to razor blades.

We have had a great discussion as to whether the wild-fire was brighter than it was . . . at Cape Helles, and whether the rain here was heavier than the rainstorm we had at Mudros.—I think it was—for the two hours it lasted. . . .

SECOND LIEUTENANT GLYN RHYS MORGAN
Royal Welch Fusiliers

Educated Pontypridd Intermediate School. Joined Army from school. Recommended for a posthumous V.C. Killed in action, Flanders, 1 August, 1917, at the age of 21.

[To His Father. *He was killed two days later*]

B.E.F.
France.
30 /7 /17

My dear Dad,

This letter is being written on the eve of our ' going over the top ' in a big attack.

It is only because I know by this time what are the odds against returning unhurt that I write it. It will only be sent in the event of my being killed in action. You, I know, my dear Dad, will bear the shock as bravely as you have always borne the strain of my being out here ; yet I should like, if possible, to help you to carry on with as stout a heart as I hope to ' jump the bags.'

I believe I have told you before that I do not fear Death itself; the Beyond has no terrors for me. I am quite content to die for the cause for which I have given up nearly three years of my life, and I only hope that I may meet Death with as brave a front as I have seen other men do before.

My one regret is that the opportunity has been denied me to repay you to the best of my ability for the lavish kindness and devotedness which you have always shewn me. I had hoped to do so in the struggle of Life. Now, however, it may be that I have done so in the struggle between Life and Death, between England and Germany, Liberty and Slavery. In any case, I shall have done my duty in my little way.

Well, Dad, please carry on with a good heart, then I shall be quite content. Goodbye, dearest of fathers, goodbye E—— and G——. May you all reap the benefits of this great war and keep cheery and happy through life.

Your affectionate son and brother,

GLYN

SERGEANT ERNEST BOUGHTON NOTTINGHAM, D.C.M.

15th London Regiment

Stockbroker's clerk. D.C.M. and *Croix de Guerre*. Died of wounds, France, 7 June, 1917, at the age of 40.

[TO F. J. PAGE]　　　　　　Northern France.
Dear Fred,　　　　　　　　*August 20th, 1915*

A pleasant tree shaded town in Northern France lay behind, and rich pastoral country unfolded itself to the eyes of the soldier walking steadily the road which sloped easily from the town towards the little hamlet which was his destination.

Crops, half out, half standing, were all ablaze in the last

glow of late afternoon. On all sides the ground rose gently with heavily wooded ridges except in one direction. The configuration of the country was that of a basin—an amber basin cunningly splashed with tones of green and brown and red—rich and vivid are the fields of France at the harvest time. But the wayfarer was nearly oblivious to the beauty around him, for he had just come from that in the town which had projected him into an almost forgotten world.

Three months work in trenches, with participation in a battle, were behind him ; and before that nearly nine months of training and preparation, a hard, keen, vigorous life more and more devoid of introspection. Only seldom had the scent of a rose beautiful in the wild profuse garden of some shelled skeleton of a cottage—or the lark's rapture at fresh May dawnings—serene above the trenches—taken him back to a distant past of emotion and sentiment.

He recalled, as he walked in the quiet and spacious evening, the many days spent between narrow clay or chalk sides of trenches—the uncounted marchings here and there —the heavy fatigues of carrying and digging—of lack of sleep. There were discomforts of wet and cold, heat and flies and all manner of unclean parasites.

There was the novelty of a hundred bivouacs in barns, schools, stables, woods and meadows, and houses in abandoned villages.

Memorable too the snatched hours of sleep in the trenches. Perhaps on a narrow firing ledge, between sentry duties— or in a dug-out. He saw again one such—a long narrow, chamber hewn out of the chalk by the French originally, with ceil[ing] of pine pit props. In it were extended some fifteen men. Along the walls were niches made to hold candles, and across the narrow entrance sacking and a waterproof sheet kept the reflection of light from the enemy some few hundred yards away. Rifles and such parts of the equipment as could be discarded lined the walls. At the further end was one who had been a scholar reading the *Odyssey*, best of all campaigning books in his opinion.

Some slept, most were at cards. Everything in that life made for hardness, for starkness. Language was divested of its graces and ornaments. Many had not spoken to a woman, or seen one,—save, when on short relief, those of the village estaminets—for many months. An almost universal slang was spoken. Its expressions were sometimes apt and amusing, but in many examples quite primitive— vulgarly sexual, altogether unlovely. Men, kept from things they craved, fashioned of them terms of abuse or endearment ; wholly irrelevant and meaningless, except as denoting deprivations—for the most part to be entirely forgotten under normal conditions.

There were sterner recollections than these—of murderous bombardments, of pitiful mutilated bodies, of agonised cries by day and night. There was the place of innumerable little burying places—their neat crosses and flowering plots— their heroic inscription " Killed in Action." Again, the bracing to fare forth for duty ; the studied indifference to whatever might befall the individual, so only that the business in hand went forward. He had seen from a flank [a] charge against odds and had had the wild longing to flesh bayonet in foe, driving him headlong.

There were vigils by night and crawlings thro' long grass, listening, in the no man's land that lies between the lines. He lay again out from the end of a disused trench and watched in the darkness the flash of cannon and bomb as our Allies strove tigerishly to clear the labyrinth. Ah ! the exultation of the roar of the bombardment veritable ! Hour on hour's ceaseless rolling reverberation !

There is a sudden silence. That is the moment of the assault. Up and over, fierce, yelling,—stark to conquer—to kill, or to be killed.

.   .   .   .

He came back to life behind the trenches during rest intervals, with its recreation in the way of sports, its relaxations and minor dissipations of drinking and gambling. The grave man or boy of the firing line possibly flippant, blasphemous, unheedful, boisterous, as may be, but always good fellow, always *bon camarade*. No reproach here, just release from strain.—After this fashion had been his environment for many months.

The sun was now behind the tops of the trees on a green ridge, and the glamour of the half light succeeded the brilliance of the afternoon.

At the church of the town in which the soldier had been wandering—that church whose huge square tower can be seen from afar—a reminder at least of other professions than that of arms—he had been greatly moved by the service. It happened to be a Saint's Day, and there had been much music. Great is the fascination of the French congregation's response to a Litany. After long deprivation from beauty of tone, doubly thrilling sounded the reed-like quality of the voices, three clearly defined tones predominating. The high altar had been ablaze with light, and the priest's voice came detached, remote, other-worldly.

What glory of stained glass—the sunlight projecting fantastic patterns in glowing colours of inexpressible beauty on mellowed stone of arch and column.

Many were the worshippers, and he felt the atmosphere earnest—supplicating.

Then a famous intermezzo had been sung—exquisitely sung by an artist—perhaps a famous voice—on leave like himself. And at the close part of a majestic organ sonata had been played.

Poignant the contrast between the soft world of artistic susceptibility and that present life of armed camp, of bomb and bayonet.

The khaki clad figure is now near his destination, and the lights of the village shine soft between the stooked sheaves. From the estaminets come shouts, and the clink of glasses. He passes a sentry standing solid and stiff in the gloaming, and with that re-enters, as it were, a kingdom standing four square—firm and definite in knowledge and practice. We leave him wondering how far one manifestation of life is the necessary corollary of another—and as to why the heroic and splendid qualities of war and of warriors

cannot be retained in the civil life of communities, with
the joy and happiness of art added.

Much love to yourself, to J—— and the Babe.

Thine,

E. N.

———

[To Charles Williams]   France
My dear Charles,   *Monday, 27 /3 /16*

. . . I will tell you a story. In the long ward, a cheerful
contented undertone of conversation. Two fires burning and
the occupants lying comfortably on mattresses or stretchers.
Fed, warm, cosy. Far from shells, bullets, bombs, min[nies],
gas.—There's the rain again. It beats furiously on the skin
window-panes and on the low roof. Up there, in uncom-
pleted lines (the enemy seized first and second some month
or more ago,—not from us) the boys stand in mud and
water thro' the night—there had been much snow and the
rain completes its evaporation into water. Silent the sentries on the fire steps, peering across 'no man's land.'—
The reliefs not yet on duty stand or crouch in their appointed bays. A peg of wood will help suspend a ground
sheet against the dripping clay wall and a man may flatten
himself under this looking like part of the trench. Rain,
pitiless rain, soaking and numbing.—And so to wear the
night away.—Blessed the tot of rum, which unlocks quickly
a man's reserves and allows him to ' carry on ' for the
necessary hours But a man is not in advanced lines all the
time, and in rotation, he comes back to ' support ' lines
where are ' dug-outs,' sometimes good, sometimes mere
crowded holes in the wet clay. Anyhow the night passes,
even the worse ones, and the morning sip of rum energizes
for breakfast making. Happy the section with a little kind-
ling wood.—

Breakfast—magic rite, it makes the world a paradise again!!
Since I became corporal of the T.M.B. I've missed some
discomfort, but I know all about it. Once again, marvel at

the reserves which every man carries which make endurance passably easy once one is ' up against it.' But here, in the warm with my three blankets I lie and listen to the rain, and see the trenches knee-deep in parts.—I feel uncomfortable ! (and yet enjoy the extreme luxury), now the light begins to fade and I must conclude.

I hope you'll be satisfied if I write as I can—about things in my mind, and you write your letters just as you do. I need not tell you how I enjoy the play of your nimble mind, even tho' my experiences here and my reading of events, seem to have hardened me against many tendencies you— what is that favourite word of A. J. Balfour's ? Some day, God willing, we'll talk about things again.—As you say, I know there's another world than this hard, cheerful objective life we lead—I feel it momentarily (and feel sad) at the sound of a train, or a church bell, or the scent and sight of a flower, or the green of a hedge. But not now in the ecstasy of a lark.—That is inseparably connected with " stand to " in trenches.—So often from Festubert onwards have I heard him singing joyously in the early dawn. I spoke of the hardening of experience. Here's an instance. All the innumerable stories of stay-at-home writers about the genius of place—I've just come from where fifty thousand bodies lie, bones and barbed wire everywhere, skeletons bleached if one takes a walk over the frightfully contested and blown up hill.—Boots and bones protruding from one's dug-out walls, and yet—one is merry there.—At the midnight hour one sees, nor expects to see, nothing of wraiths, or of the spirits of countless brave ones who met there a violent death !——

Yours,
ERNEST

CAPTAIN THE HON. ROBERT STAFFORD ARTHUR PALMER
Hampshire Regiment

Educated Winchester and University College, Oxford (scholar). President of the Oxford Union. Barrister. Killed in action, Mesopotamia, 21 January, 1916, at the age of 27.

Amarah [Mesopotamia],

[TO MISS ELEANOR BALFOUR]   *September 24, 1915*

. . . As for the future, I think it would be a mistake to expect this war to produce a revolution in human nature, and equally wrong to think nothing has been achieved if it doesn't. What I hope is that it will mark a ‚distinct stage towards a more Christian conception of international relations. I'm afraid that for a long time to come there will be those who will want to wage war and will have to be crushed with their own weapons. But I think this insane and devilish cult of war will be a thing of the past. War will only remain as an unpleasant means to an end. The next stage will be, one hopes, the gradual realization that the ends for which one wages war are generally selfish ; and anyway that law is preferable to force as a method of settling disputes. As to whether national ideals can be Christian ideals, in the strict sense they can't very well : because so large a part of the Christian idea lies in self-suppression and self-denial, which of course can only find its worth in individual conduct and its meaning in the belief that this life is but a preparation for a future life ; whereas national life is a thing of this world and therefore the law of its being must be self-development and self-interest. The Prussians interpret this crudely as mere self-assertion and the will to power. The Christianizing of international relations will be brought about by insisting on the contrary interpretation— that our highest self-development and interest is to be attained by respecting the interests and encouraging the development of others. The root fallacy to be eradicated, of course, is that one Power's gain is another's loss : a fallacy which has dominated diplomacy and is the negation of law. I think we are perceptibly breaking away from it ; the great obstacle to better thinking now is the existence of so many backward peoples incapable (as we think) of seeking their own salvation. Personally, I don't see how we can expect the Christianizing process to make decisive headway until the incapables are partitioned out among the capables. Meanwhile, let us hope that each new war will be more unpopular and less respectable than the last. . . .

CORPORAL JAMES PARR
16th London Regiment

Educated Highgate School. Wounded and missing, France, 1 July, 1916, at the age of 27.

[France]

[To His Family]   *March 20th, 1916*

Oh ! this Army ! At times I feel I could scream and put straws in my hair and I probably should if I didn't laugh. We are so messed about and badgered from pillar to post that I hardly know which way to turn ; but it's all so childish and farcical that you can't help laughing at it when you can spare the time from swearing ! I told you that we expected to move from the valley and looked forward to a short march of 3 or 4 miles ; but they sprang another 17 miles on us. It's really extraordinary how the rumour of these things runs through the battalion. I was lying on the grass, writing on the previous afternoon—sun shining, birds singing, " everything in the garden lovely "—when a man passed and remarked " Compris 17 miles to-morrow." " Nonsense, where did you hear it ? " " Oh, Price (the adjutant) told the chaps who were playing football not to exert themselves, as we had to do at least 17 miles to-morrow." " I don't believe it—tell it to the marines." But the nasty seed of unrest was planted and the sun didn't seem to shine so brightly. Then someone else strolled along, " Heard that we're moving to-morrow ? 20 miles, the signallers say." And so on, until by the time I reached my billet everybody had it in varying forms although the powers that be made no sign until the order for an emergency sick parade in the evening settled the question in favour of a long march. You've no idea of what a rush it is to get off in the morning of a long march. Reveille 5.30, blankets to be rolled in bundles of 10 and stacked at a certain place by 6, washing bowls, spades, lamps to be collected from the barns and taken somewhere else by 6.30 (L /Cpl. Parr to be responsible for this). Breakfast 6.30, barns to be thoroughly cleaned and tidied by 6.45, battalion parades ready for marching at 7—and then is generally kept waiting for an hour before it starts. (L /Cpl. Parr spent half an hour looking for a measly bowl, irredeemably perjuring his soul in the process.) Well, we started at last. I've never dropped out of a march or avoided one since I joined the Army but they nearly did it on me this time. To begin with, I had not been feeling up to the mark all the time I had been in the valley—the sudden change from the heights and frost to the valley and heat I suppose—and I had a blister on my heel, so I started with the expectation of going till I dropped—and you don't get much sympathy for dropping out, you're generally only blamed for not going sick before the march. And quite right too ; your dropping out is only a nuisance to the battalion and spoils the marching reputation. Still, I didn't think I should finish that march. It was boiling hot and mostly uphill in the morning, climbing up out of the valley, struggling on from one halt to another, very often just as much as some of us could do. We march for 50 minutes and halt for 10, regular as clockwork. The halt just pulls you round and the first 20 of the 50 minutes go fairly easily, then time begins to drag and the last 10 mins. are done by sheer physical force. On and on, till it feels as if your neck muscles were being pulled out with pincers and your boots were soled with red hot iron. You push your cap to the back of your head and the

Colonel, riding down the column, calls out " Put your cap on straight, that corporal there ! " And all the time you have to smile and joke, because the others are joking round you (when they aren't swearing) and you know that many of them are worse than you. That boy marching alongside you—it is his birthday and he's just 19—has got a swollen joint in his foot from frost bite last winter and dreads the halts almost as much as the marching because it means the pain of starting afresh ; and that bugler in the platoon in front, who is having his pack carried by an officer, is sure to fall out about the tenth mile, for he is flat footed and that is his limit. The dinner halt is very near now, thank God —only one more hill(and a nasty one) to be negotiated. I have seen nothing of the country, as my eyes have been fixed for the most part on the heels of the man in front. A final struggle up the hill and just on the crest, the longed for whistle. Just in time, as most of the men were baked and the column was beginning to waver and sag. Then that blessed hour's rest and tea ! Oh, what should we do without our tea here ! A million blessings on the head of Sir Walter Raleigh or Isaac Newton or whoever it was that discovered its gorgeous refreshing properties. I was too tired to eat more than a mouthful but just lay and basked in the waves of fatigue that passed through and out of me. Then boots and putties off, and a change of socks and when we took up our pilgrimage again, I felt a new man. Rather a tottery new man, as my feet were a bit sore, but one among many similar. It was miraculous the transformation caused by the rest and the tea—it was 1 o'clock when we halted and we had had nothing since a very hurried breakfast at 6.30 and our spirits were further raised by the name of our destination on a signpost with the magic figures " 4 K." Of course, signposts in France are very similar in their encouraging lies to those in England, and 4 K. usually means 6, but it looked good and bucked us up tremendously. About a mile from " home," my left leg began to give—I strained a little muscle in my thigh very slightly, but enough to play the devil with my leg in my tired condition. Still,

C Co. were singing at the back of us and we managed to raise a song to beat them ; and then the village in sight and then the quartermaster waiting to guide to billets and then the usual barn—never so welcome—and down on the straw to lie for an hour till I felt I could stand again. I swear I couldn't have done another 100 yards. Then the orderly sergeant " Sorry, old man but you'll have to do the guard to-night, Jones has gone sick." That meant sleeping in boots and equipment but I didn't mind anything. I was there and there were eggs for tea—my first job to make friends with the farm people. They are very obliging and have rather taken to us, especially to a man called Wood and myself, as we can keep our ends up in French. . . . Rough and ready sort of people, of course, but very kind and not spoilt by soldiers as yet. I don't think any English have been here for some time.

We have of course been marching parallel to the line, northwards, and are no nearer than our last halt. But now comes the reason for my opening sentence—here, behind the line, on active service, we carry on all the little details of ceremonial as if we were the Guards in the piping times of peace. The guards are no longer the simple affairs of the past 18 months—just a parade of the men in drill order, a casual inspection by the company orderly officer and the word to the incoming corporal of the guard from the out-going ditto " Carry on with the usual rigmarole, old man." Nowadays, the guards parade in full marching order with pack, boots cleaned, mackintoshes to show under ground sheet in top of pack (an impossibility, by the way, if the pack is packed according to regulations), the fire picket for the night parade in belt and side arms—necessitating the taking to pieces of their equipment—all are inspected by the company orderly officer, and then marched to the orderly-room, where they are inspected again by the Adjutant and Batt. Sgt. Major ; the bugle band meanwhile marches up and down playing furiously until " retreat," when the guards are marched off to their respective guard-rooms, where they duly present arms to the old guard and set to partners down the middle and up again !—the whole business taking about ¾hr. It really looks very fine, as about 100 men take part every night and the Colonel turns up and the B.S.M. hands out birds to his heart's content ; but, it's only a little French village and we can hear the guns in the distance. And the constant badgering about that it means to the men and corporals, the cleaning up that has to be done, the packing and unpacking of packs, the alteration of equipment—it's enough to turn one's hair grey. And this is only one of countless regulations that are piled on our devoted heads every day—in fact, the other night when orders came round to me (I'm orderly corporal this week) there were such stacks and stacks of rules as to dress and billets and discipline and behaviour and saluting, that they'd quite overlooked the times for parade for the day's drills, which one would have thought was the most important thing of the lot ! . . . Oh, well, as I say, it's lucky the humorous side strikes us—the reading of orders is generally accompanied by shouts of laughter from the platoon and we all turn up each night to see the show. . . .

———

[France]
[TO HIS SISTER]   *June 19th, 1916*

. . . As you know from my card, we left the line three days ago and are back where we were before we went in, doing the night digging fatigue again and occasionally some day ones. However, we clear out altogether in a day or two and go back to our last resting place for a breather—after that, *je ne sais quoi*. It is quite on the cards that we shall move to another part of the line or go right back again till we are wanted for some other job. You see we are a kind of flying division to be used anywhere that is necessary and have come up here chiefly to get these new trenches dug.

And some fierce work it was (and is) too ! I've never seen the battalion worked so hard as when we were in the trenches. Day and night they were at it in constant relays. It was work until a man dropped and then that meant someone else doing a double shift. But the boys kept smiling on the whole and stuck it well, though they were very very tired. I was almost ashamed of myself as I did not do a hand's turn for all that seven days. As I told you, my job was to form part of the covering defensive screen, which meant taking up my position with the gun and two men in the advanced trench nearest the Germans and sticking there for 24 hours, supported by half a platoon with an officer and signaller on the telephone at hand. It was a bit of a strain and the monotony was terrible. B. after sitting there for *18 hours doing nothing*, suddenly arose and said to one of his team, " For Christ's sake turn your face away ! I'm sick of looking at it ! "

. . . C. had a very narrow escape which I must tell you of, though I don't usually dwell on the casualty side of the picture do I ? He, with half the platoon, was supporting B. and the gun in the advanced trench (my day off) when the Huns started trench-mortaring. They're hellish things —so big that you can see them coming through the air— and to give you some idea of the explosive they contain— one of our *bombs* contains a few *ounces* of aminol ; these trench-mortars contain *20 lbs* ! They will blow a whole traverse in as easily as breaking an egg shell but their effect is so local that if you are in the next traverse, you will probably escape scot-free, barring the concussion. So, as you can see them, you stand a sporting chance of dodging them. Anyway, one of these damned things came over into a traverse on the right where three of our men were posted (all Gallipoli " attached " men). C., hearing the explosion, rushed to the spot to see if he could do anything and met one poor devil crawling down the trench. The other two were past help, so C. started to drag this chap into comparative safety. He had got along a traverse or two when he looked up and saw another mortar coming over right at him. He dropped the man and ran (and he blames himself for this)—I think he deserves a D.C.M. for what he did—it was a question only of one life or two if he'd stayed with him. The mortar dropped just behind him, blew him from one end of the traverse to the other, tore his shrapnel helmet off his head and buried it in the clay, the same with his respirator from his shoulder and also buried his rifle. The shock to his nerves must have been terrible but he got up and went back to look for the wounded man, only to find that he had been buried under the earth. Then he went for more help. They dug the man out and he lived till the next day, but he would have never recovered from his original injuries. They sent C. back to the village but he wouldn't go sick and was put in charge of a digging party within a few hours. And this boy (he's only 21) if there had been no war, would have remained in England, an ordinary tennis party and ball room nut. Don't tell me war does no good. Someone said to me the other day " And after all, what's the use of all this ? We lose money, we lose the best years of our lives, we run the risk of losing our lives altogether, at any rate of being incapacitated. And what do we gain ? We could live and love and work somewhere in the world whether Germany or England won. What's the use of it all ? " What do we gain ? I think we gain the one thing that every man has wanted from his boyhood up —opportunity. Opportunity to show what he is made of. Opportunity to show *himself* what he's made of, to show that he can be the hero he's always wanted to be from the time when he first made up his mind to be a pirate when he grew up. He may not always know that he wanted it, but to my mind it was the thing missing—the thing that made us at times discontented, moody and unsatisfied. What do we gain ? We stand to gain everything and to lose—only our lives. A paltry exchange, if we leave behind a memory that is good. There is a machine gun of ours which fires " Pom-tiddley-om-pom, Pom-pom "—a quaint idea to think that you might " go out " to a senseless catch-tune played on a lethal weapon ! Did I ever tell you that up at Ypres we used to sing and whistle the " *Policeman's Holiday* " at stand-to and fire our rifles—crack—crack ! to emphasise the last two notes ? . . .

. . . Oh ! I must tell you again of my washout ——. He is the absolute limit and I loathe him. He's horribly " windy," selfish, boring and snobbish. Of course, when he heard of that trench-mortar business up near the post we were relieving that night, he promptly went sick with a chill. A chill ! Ye gods ! Also of course he got M. & D. (medicine and duty) so had to carry on and the chill disappeared like magic. He sits down all day and does not attempt to help in any way except when I tell him to do things. When I ask him to give a hand in cleaning the gun, he says " I'll do my part " and his part to his mind consists in taking one small portion of the gun about 20 yds. away from the rest of the men, cleaning it very slowly, returning it and going away. He can't forget that once he's been a —— sergeant. He has a stupid, vacant supercilious face that makes me long to hit him. In fact he's driven me so near insanity that I've spoken to Mr. —— about having him removed from the team, but that —— is afraid to do unless the washout offers to come off and I don't think he'll do that, as although he's terrified to death of the gun, he's still more afraid of work and can see that the gun-team at any rate have a decent dug-out up the line and get off a lot of fatigues there. To add to my troubles, ——, my No. 1, got a bit of shell in his shoulder the other day so I've lost my best man pro. tem.,—but I'll shift that snivelling snob out somehow if I die for it. . . .

CAPTAIN THE HON. COLWYN ERASMUS ARNOLD PHILIPPS

Royal Horse Guards

Educated Eton and Sandhurst. Regular Army. Killed in action, Flanders, 13 May, 1915, at the age of 27.

[Flanders]

[To His Mother] *November 13, 1914*

I got a letter from you, E——, and D—— yesterday ; this is the first news I have had from home. . . . We are taking part in a most amazing battle : we are holding a V that sticks out into the German lines ; the result is that we have two fronts facing different ways and shells come from all directions ; this means that we can't get our horses away, but by amazing luck they have not been shelled yet. We have any amount of horses and very little for them to do ; all our fighting is in these beastly trenches, forty-eight hours at a time and up to your knees in water. It is not cold but horrid wet ; we have any amount of food, but occasional small packets of chocolate, tinned tongue, potted meat, etc.—not sardines or anything messy—are welcome. I hope you got my letter asking for walking boots, size eight, hobnailed—otherwise I am fairly well off for everything. The first thing we learn here is to forget about ' Glory.' Your regiment is no good when it is dead, and your job is to retire rather than to be wiped out ; only you must warn troops on your flanks : do it quietly and do it in time. . . . We have a new gun, a 9.2 Howitzer—they call it ' mother ' —that has for the first time coped with the Germans. But the truth is that these high angle guns are useless against each other, but all right against houses or men (worse luck). We get some pretty good fun all the same and repeat every joke a hundred times. Last night we were sleeping in a lean-to behind a barn full of men. As I was crawling over the men I stepped on a face, and a weary voice muttered, ' This is a blooming fine game played slow.' And after a very long march a man was heard saying to his very rough horse, ' You're no blooming Rolls Royce, I give you my word.' In our mess we never allow any mention of anything depressing ; it is awful to go into some other mess and hear nothing but ' Do you remember poor So-and-so ? ' Another thing we learn is to avoid ' brave men,' the ass who ' does not mind bullets,' walks about and only draws fire that knocks over better men than himself. You might also send me some paper and envelopes. Mark the boots ' uniform, urgent.' We expected a devil of a fight to-day, but the Germans seem to have wearied a bit, and things look like calming down a bit. I do most earnestly hope we do not advance ; there seems no point in gaining a few miles of Belgium at the cost of countless lives, as we have no chance of really beating the Germans here, and if we hold on the Russians may win for us. Personally I am full of confidence that, given a fair trench and plenty of ammunition, nothing can shift our squadron unless a Black Maria happens to do us in, as no trench is any good against them ; we think nothing of shrapnel now, if we can get trenches—it is beastly in the open.

We are given the day off, now I am going to wash—I have not even washed my hands for three days.

LIEUTENANT ROBERT HACKNEY PICKERING
R.F.A.

In service of Bank of New South Wales. Killed in action, France, 30 November, 1917, at the age of 25.

[TO HIS BROTHER]   Trenches [Flanders],
Sweet Mac,   *1 Sep.* [*1915*]

... We are in a most extraordinary position here in this trench—we have Huns on both sides of us—it runs up into their position through this famous wood. We were there in July last but the position was very different then. The trenches we then held were about 100 yards in front of us. They were lost in a famous flammenwerfer attack and are now untenable to either side. They are now only occupied by the heaps of dead men who lost them and are practically blown to b. . . . To our left some of the lost ground was regained and further trenches taken but immediately to our left through the wood is a ridge untenable to either side—it is simply ploughed up with thousands of shell craters —a great mine crater and thousands of dead. The undergrowth of this wood is very thick and the Huns could creep right up to our trench to throw bombs or surprise us—to provide against that we have a screen of listening patrols and bombers concealed in the scrub, they patrol our old trenches and the untenanted ridge—the Hun patrols do the same—directly any alarm is given the bombers lie down and join the huge army of stinking unburied dead. Rats by the thousands get food here—they go into a man at one place, they come out at another—the shrubs are littered with dead men and the rats which feed on them often make a noise and cause alarms. Both sides have been piling up guns and strengthening their artillery in this locality for 10 months and really a man who fights against the Turks cannot understand the dreadful weight of metal in here. Nearly all recent attacks on both sides have been here at the tip of the salient and all the guns are trained on it. The shell fire never ceases and at intervals regular bombardments take place for hours on end—to put the wind up the other party. This morning early we were in an absolute inferno for a long time and we get that kind of thing about every other day. You get perhaps 5 /700 guns going on both sides together, and the number of shells of all calibres that come over are numbered in tens of thousands. It's remarkable how one can live through such an inferno. It nearly drives you mad. Conditions are getting worse and worse for the poor infantry who man the trenches—it is simply an artillery duel. . . .

For God's sake don't conjure up visions of our old happy

days to me old man—it seems wicked to think of such things when perhaps 10,000 or more men have been killed in this wretched hole within a square mile in the last four months —these woods were lovely once—now the trees are all bare and straafed and blackened, they lie broken against one another, they lie on dead men squashing them. It must have been a place like say Burnham B. once. I have seen on the trees the names and initials of many lovers cut side by side with the dates appended. How little did those happy sweethearts imagine the desolation and death that now reigns here—the neighbourhood is a stinking cemetery. If the dead are buried at all they are buried in tens, twenties, hundreds together—they are lucky to be buried at all.

Love and good luck old chap to yourself and B—— — don't go asking for trouble—keep your head if you can and if you are in trenches no matter how heavily they are shelled —don't leave them for the open behind. I've seen a Batt. almost wiped out through leaving their trenches like that —they send over a curtain of shrapnel like hail at once and you have no chance.

Good-bye old man

loving bro. Bob

LIEUTENANT BERNARD PITT

Border Regiment

Schoolmaster and Tutor at Working-Men's College. Killed in action, France, 30 April, 1916, at the age of 35.

[To Lionel Jacob]   [France]
Dear Lionel Jacob,   *March 31st, 1916*

How is the College doing in these hard times ? It hardly seems credible that it still exists, with so many of its tutors and students away ; and yet, I so often feel that the reality is Education and Fraternity, while all this horror of war is a transient appearance of the impossible. Such a glance into the chaos that man can make, unless love is his guiding principle, is indeed a terrifying experience. I am now in a hilly wooded region, like the skirts of the Kentish Downs, with copses full of anemones and delicate periwinkles, and the sapling hazels and willows tasselled and downy with catkins and buds. A mile away is a village, shattered and wasted, and beyond that a sight more shocking than the ruin of human work, a ghastly wood where the broken trunks and splintered branches take on weird and diabolical forms. It is the Bois de Souchez. The ground round about is poisoned with human relics, limbs and bundles of clothes filled with rotten flesh, and even those poor remains of men which pious hands have buried are daily disinterred by plunging shells. S—— itself is merely a heap of bricks and stones, and it reeks to heaven of mortality. Do you wonder that, reading Wordsworth this afternoon in a clearing of the unpolluted woodlands, and marking the lovely faded colours on the wings of hibernated butterflies, and their soft motions, I felt a disgust, even to sickness, of the appalling wickedness of war. Sometimes one has great need of a strength which is not in one's power to use, but is a grace of God.

I have so far escaped injury, and have seen very heavy fighting in different parts of our line. I was recommended for the Military Cross, but my usual bad luck intervened to relegate me to " mentioned in despatches " only. Now I am in command of a Trench Mortar Battery, and I find the work as interesting as any war-making can be. You know we all long for the war to end, whether by peace, or by that furious slaughter which must lead to peace. Verdun, no doubt, has shortened the war by months.

Well, I long to get back to the Working Men's College, and, I hope, in less than a year. I was able to get a few minutes there in February, with my old class.

My kindest regards to yourself, and best wishes to the College.

Yours sincerely,

BERNARD PITT

LIEUTENANT ERNEST E. POLACK
Gloucestershire Regiment
Educated Clifton and St. John's College, Cambridge (scholar). Killed in action, France, 17 July, 1916, at the age of 23.

[TO THE REV. J. F. STERN]

D Company,
14 Batt. Gloster Reg.,
144th Infantry Brigade,
48 (South Midland) Division,
British Expeditionary Force.

Dear Mr. Stern, *Friday, 21st May [1915]*

I claim the prestige of a very slight personal acquaintanceship to let you know how deeply I sympathise with you in the great sorrow that has befallen you. The loss of Leonard Stern makes a gap in my life which can never be filled again. He was to me what no other young man ever was—not only my greatest friend, but an influence for good throughout my Cambridge days, for which I can never be sufficiently grateful. He combined in the most remarkable manner a great personal attractiveness, an irresistible sense of humour, and a very strong sense of duty—in fact I am not exaggerating when I say that to me he always appeared as something not far distant from the ideal Jewish young man. Please understand that I mean every word I am writing. I honestly loved him ; and now that he has gone, doing his duty,

> " *The idea of his life shall sweetly creep*
> *Into my study of imagination,*
> *And every lovely organ of his life*
> *Shall come apparelled in more precious spirit,*
> *More moving—delicate and full of life*
> *Into the eye and prospect of my soul,*
> *Than when he lived indeed.*"

—As Shakespeare says.—

May the Almighty comfort you in your great sorrow !

Yours sincerely,

E. E. POLACK. 2nd Lieut.

[France]

My dear Mother & Father,   *30 /6 /16*

This is not an easy letter to write, and I have long re-
frained from writing it ; but now that the Advance seems
more than a remote possibility, and is in fact due to start
to-morrow, I had better realise at once that I may not get
through it. In fact, I consider it very unlikely that I shall
get through it whole. Death has no terrors for me in itself,
for (like Cleopatra) " I have immortal longings in me."
The prospect of pain naturally appals me somewhat, and
I am taking morphia in with me to battle.

We are in Corps Reserve behind Hebuterne, and, should
all go well, will not be called upon until the second night
and then shall probably be resisting a German counter-
attack somewhere near Beaumont-Hamel. But our services
may be required at any moment.

I have little to leave except my Love and Gratitude. . . .

For the rest—" If 'tis not now, 'twill be to come." Our
cause is a good one and I believe I am doing right in fighting. To you—Mother and Father—I owe all. The thought
of you two—and of my brothers—will inspire me to the end.
I often wish Albert was with me and miss him dreadfully.

Good-bye !

> " *If we shall meet again, why then we'll smile ;*
> *If not—why then this parting was well made.*"
> (*Julius Caesar*).

‏¹חי לי ולא אוא‎

Your loving son,

ERNEST

I will ask Mr. Ramsay (our Chaplain) to send you this
if I fall.

------

¹ " The Lord is on my side ; I will not fear " : Psalm cxviii. 6.

CAPTAIN GEOFFREY BLEMELL POLLARD

R. F. A.

Educated King's College School, St. Paul's, and Woolwich. Regular Army. Killed in action, France, 24 October, 1914, at the age of 26.

On Active Service
[France]

Dear Mrs Hughes,   *October 19th [1914]*

Two more parcels reached me last night, one addressed by you and one by Vivien. Thank you all very much indeed for sending them : everything was very useful, and the battery officers and men were overjoyed. The men are particularly pleased with the writing materials, and I expect I shall have an awful time this afternoon reading through all the letters they will write as a result ! It is always with mixed feelings that I personally view the arrival of fresh paper, because the soldiers write such awful things in their letters, mostly rot, or else a repetition of a few remarks which they could quite easily put on a postcard, and I have to read them all through ! But it certainly makes them happy, and that is the great thing. As a matter of fact, the artillery have had a fairly easy time lately, though the infantry have had a lot to do. Supplies and presents have come in regularly, so we haven't much to complain of. If we could only get more and better forage for the horses the whole battery would be very contented, horses and all.

From reading all these letters lately, I have got some idea of how certain things get into the English papers in spite of the Press Bureau. Only yesterday I found that one of my gunners had written a most complete account of how we had taken a village the previous day and of what we found there, and not a single word of it was true. If that had escaped the censor, as a good many letters must have, it would probably have reached the English papers as news straight from the front. I need hardly tell you how annoyed the officers, at any rate, of our army here are to read obviously untrue tales in the papers. Most of the " tales of survivors " are fairy stories, written by some fellow who was wounded, or who lost his regiment, and promptly gave out that it was cut up. That's one of the curious things about Thomas A. He loves to tell you that his unit has taken an awful knock, and always writes home to say that his regiment was in a very tight place indeed if a few bullets whistled fifty feet over his head. And yet under fire there's no doubt that he is almost criminally unconcerned. So many fellows forget that their lives and strength belong to their country.

The inhabitants here are a puzzle. Many of them have, of course, gone back ; but they often crowd up again right into the firing line at the very first advance on our part, and they are a perpetual nuisance to us. Of those that have remained throughout the majority have suffered exceedingly little, far less than I expected (the Germans not even having burnt what forage they didn't require before they left), but they seem quite callous as to whether they have Germans, French, or English living with them, and spend most of the day rushing up and down worrying about a few potatoes and a couple of bundles of wood, or something which seems to me quite trivial in proportion to what losses they might have suffered or be suffering. None of them are starving, and though naturally a large quantity of forage is consumed by any army that is here, the people have lost so many animals from various causes that the forage would be no use to them. Meanwhile, I am being continually sent for to argue with inhabitants over quite trifling matters, and I find it awfully tiring, as they are very excited, talk very bad French, and of course are quite unorganized and all come rushing up, saying that wood, etc., is being taken, quantity unknown, destination ditto, and what do I propose to do about it ? Almost always it's some other unit, and nine times out of ten, if the quantity is worth considering, an officer is there who can tell him whose wood, etc., it really is. And all this in addition to my fighting duties. This is an aspect of war I confess I hadn't anticipated.

I am very sorry that Jim's chief doesn't see eye to eye with him about the war. There's no doubt this is a crisis, and although I've no doubt that we are going to win in the end, the sooner the end comes the better for all concerned. This sort of war is such a strain that we who have been here from the start cannot stand it indefinitely, and we shall want relieving and reinforcing until we have done our job and finished off the bad men. It's absolutely certainly a war of " attrition," as somebody said here the other day, and we have got to stick it longer than the other side and go on producing men, money, and material until they cry quits, and that's all about it, as far as I can see.

Good-bye, and much love to your family in all its delightful branches that I know.

Yours ever,

GEOFFREY POLLARD

SECOND LIEUTENANT JOHN LINDSAY RAPOPORT
The Rifle Brigade
Educated Tonbridge and New College, Oxford. Missing, France, 28 May, 1918, at the age of 24.

[France]

2. v. 18

. . . I've just got two letters from you . . . so everything is " *couleur de rose.*" . . . My love for you seems to increase every day. Darling, we were absolutely meant for one another, because you say that my love for you makes you better and stronger, and you don't know how you've influenced me. Yesterday we travelled all day and I was pretty tired after so much knocking about since I came to France. On top of that a " pukka " captain joined us and I had to give up the command of my company after just getting things going. I was quite depressed, but I think

I can say I've put up with the petty annoyance quite well—because I just thought of you.

Darling, I feel quite sure I am coming back all right, and I see that your faith is equally strong. I don't worry in the least, and I'm so thankful you don't. I feel sure God would never have let us love each other as we do if he was going to get rid of me. I just pray not to go into danger foolishly. I'm sure you'll like to know this. I can honestly say that my faith in God has increased no end now, and I can put up with much more, cheerfully, now than ever I could before. And it's all because *my* —— loves me so much and so wonderfully and because I love her as much, and I thank God so for giving you to me.

When first we meet again, won't both our hearts be awfully jumpy—just when the train comes into the station ? !

————

[France]
6. v. 18

The mail has just come in and I've got 14 letters ! Among them, my darling, were 5 from you. So you can imagine what I feel like. I got the very first one of all tonight, the one you sent to me at Havre. They've been awfully slack in forwarding it. . . . Darling, you were splendid when you saw me off at Waterloo. You just typified the women of England by your attitude, everything for us men, and you have your dark times to yourselves so as not to depress us. . . . You mean so much to me, you have no idea how much. Life without you would be absolutely empty. I wonder how ever I got on before. As a matter of fact I am full of love and for the last 2 or 3 years I've had a longing to pour it out on someone, and I've always lived in the hope of doing so—that kept me going. Now I've got someone on whom I can and *have* lavished *all* my love. ——, my darling, I love and adore you from the bottom of my heart. You wait till I come home—you will get some kisses then, and I shall hold you tight—you know how, my darling, don't you ? . . .

I am so glad we both are alike on the question of friends. Of course I want you to carry on with your men friends just as if I didn't exist. One thing I am sure of as that I exist, that is that I have all your heart and all your love. So I just want you to enjoy yourself—I love you so much. Have a topping time on the river and at shows, etc., with your friends, won't you. I asked W. W. to write to me still though we were engaged—just as friends, and I will write to —— too. I feel very sorry for your friends. Just impress on them that you can be chums just as before. I know it isn't quite the same, but I should like it, because I know what a help you'd be to any man. Just thank your friends for their good wishes, will you ? Oh, ——, the more I think of it, the more I realise how lucky I am in having you for my *own* darling wife-to-be. Oh, hasn't God been good to me—far more than I deserve.

[France]
17. v. 18

I've just got an overwhelming wave of love over me for my own sweet girlie, just like when one's sea bathing a big wave comes right over you sometimes and just overwhelms you. . . .

You are absolutely all the world to me. I'm always happy now, my darling, and that's saying a good deal because there are a good many petty annoyances out here. . . . We came out of the line last night or early this morning. It was lovely getting into the country with the may blossom smelling lovely and fresh after the foul atmosphere of trenches and dug-outs. . . .

This is quite a nice village with civilians in it. There is a Y.M.C.A. for the men and I can hear a piano playing—the sort of things they play at a cinema, and sort of way they play them there, so of course I just love it. You know why ! !

. . . Do pray hard for your Linnet that he may always do his duty out here—one is so apt to get slack. . . . There are few things more calculated to make one demoralised than the form of trench warfare we are at present engaged in here. I do so want to remain keen and good, but it's awfully hard. If my —— prays for her boy, I feel somehow that God will listen to her prayers an awful lot. . . .

———

SECOND LIEUTENANT WILLIAM HENRY RATCLIFFE

South Staffordshire Regiment

Student of Chemistry. Killed in action, France, 1 July, 1916, at the age of 19.

[France]

[TO HIS PARENTS]   *June, 1916*

. . . Another Sunday has arrived, and so far is not any more like a Sunday than the last. According to orders there was a church parade this morning but it was cancelled, but may come off later in the day, and so I have been throwing bombs this morning.

If the people in England who try to abolish the day of rest could come out here they would feel the need of it. Apart from the time afforded for spiritual recreation, a day of rest would be something to look forward to, and would break the monotony of life, and the monotony and dull routine is the chief objection to this life. Of course everyone understands the impossibility of giving the A.S.C. and the men actually in the trenches a day's rest ; but why a battalion which is out of the trenches for a rest can't stop forming fours and sloping arms for one day I don't know.

I was reading a story in one of the magazines that you sent out which was trying to prove that this war had a good effect on men's minds and made them more religious than they were before. Whilst I was in Jersey I really thought that this was the case, and I believe I wrote and told you so, and mentioned what Ian Hamilton wrote about the matter. But now that I am out here, I must confess that I almost altogether disagree with Ian Hamilton, and think that war has an almost degrading effect on the minds of soldiers.

What is there out here to raise a man's mind out of the rut ? Everywhere one sees preparations for murder ; nearly every person one sees is a filthy, dirty man with some implement of destruction about his person. The countryside and the beauties of nature, which, as you know, always have a beneficial effect on a man, are all spoilt by the dust and mud of motor lorries and by huge camps.

Everywhere the work of God is spoiled by the hand of man. One looks at a sunset and for a moment thinks that that at least is unsophisticated, but an aeroplane flies across, and puff ! puff ! and the whole scene is spoilt by clouds of shrapnel smoke !

So you can understand that men who are at war really become more bestial than when at peace, despite popular opinion to the contrary. . . .

MAJOR WILLIAM HOEY KEARNEY REDMOND
Royal Irish Regiment

Nationalist M.P. for East Clare. Joined Army at outbreak of war. Killed in action, France, 7 June, 1917, at the age of 56.

[France,
[TO SIR ARTHUR CONAN DOYLE]   *Spring, 1917*]

. . . There a great many Irishmen to-day who feel that out of this war we should try to build up a new Ireland. The trouble is, men are so timid about meeting each other half-way. It would be a fine memorial to the men who have died so splendidly if we could, over their graves, build up a bridge between the North and South.

I have been thinking a lot about this lately in France—no one could help doing so when one finds that the two sections from Ireland are actually side by side holding the trenches ! No words could do justice to the splendid action of the new Irish soldiers. They never have flinched, they never give any trouble, and they are steady and sober.

Had poor Kettle lived he would have given the world a wonderful account of things out here. I saw a good deal of Kettle, and we had many talks of the unity we both hoped would come out of the war. I have been an extreme Nationalist all my life, and if others as extreme, perhaps, on the other side will only come half-way, then I believe, impossible as it may seem, we should be able to hit upon a plan to satisfy the Irish sentiment and the Imperial sentiment at one and the same time. . . .

RALPH BONFOY ROOPER
Red Cross

Educated Charterhouse and New College, Oxford (scholar). Posthumously awarded *Croix de Guerre avec Palme*. Killed while on ambulance service, France, 29 May, 1918, at the age of 23.

S.S. [Section Sanitaire] Anglaise 20
[France]
[TO SPENCER HURST]   *November 30, 1917*

. . . It seems my brother was doing some ludicrously heroic thing ; trying to draw on himself the fire which was pressing too hard an observing machine, and charging down to help the other chap before his flight had time to back him up. We have had a splendid letter from one of his " subs " who was in his flight ; but as he says, he was too occupied in fighting to be able to see exactly what happened to Trev. Both he and the chaplain write letters obviously sincere : with a lack of the stock phrases of comfort and praise which make one realize that they too miss him a lot.

And I have hardly read M——'s letter ; it is so horribly tragic that I can't finish it dry-eyed. She daren't go and see his dog . . . but hopes to be up to it tomorrow. . . . And in the middle of her really heart broken grieving, after she has been trying to find some comfort in the fact that we shall know where the grave is, and be able to go and see it, she has the courage to write " But we don't grudge our Trev, do we darling ? . . ." Spencer, I *do*—I grudge him most frightfully to this idiotic damnable business. You know he and I used to quarrel frightfully ; and up to quite a short time ago I used to think he would waste all his splendid gifts of courage and health and good fellowship. Well, it had all changed lately, and he had become so much steadier and more thoughtful ; and though he was still a boy, one could see the promise in him of a really noble man. And now—he is killed before the flowering time—my dear, I *do* grudge his unused powers, and all the unfulfilled hopes of life and activity and happiness. " Life is a banquet spread ; I cannot stay for the feast." . . .

PRIVATE ISAAC ROSENBERG
King's Own (Royal Lancaster) Regiment

Slade School student. Poet and painter. Killed in action, France, 1 April, 1918, at the age of 27.

[France,
[To LAURENCE BINYON] *1916*]

It is far, very far, to the British Museum from here (situated as I am, Siberia is no further and certainly no colder), but not too far for that tiny mite of myself, my letter, to reach there. Winter has found its way into the trenches at last, but I will assure you, and leave to your imagination, the transport of delight with which we welcomed its coming. Winter is not the least of the horrors of war. I am determined that this war, with all its powers for devastation, shall not master my poeting ; that is, if I am lucky enough to come through all right. I will not leave a corner of my consciousness covered up, but saturate myself with the strange and extraordinary new conditions of this life, and it will all refine itself into poetry later on. I have thoughts of a play round our Jewish hero, Judas Maccabeas. I have much real material here, and also there is some parallel in the savagery of the invaders then to this war. I am not decided whether truth of period is a good quality or a negative one. Flaubert's ' *Salammbo* ' proves, perhaps, that it is good. It decided the tone of the work, though it makes it hard to give the human side and make it more living. However, it is impossible now to work and difficult even to think of poetry, one is so cramped intellectually.

LIEUTENANT LESLIE YORATH SANDERS
R.E.

Educated St. Olave's Grammar School and Trinity College, Cambridge (scholar). Killed in action, France, 10 March, 1917, at the age of 24.

[France]
December 22nd, 1916

. . . You see, in modern warfare the actual troops themselves count for less and less. Given the right sort of officers, you can make almost any physically efficient human material perform almost any task. If they are naturally brave, they need little but leading ; but with stern discipline and driving, timorous troops can be made to do just as well. The difference lies in the planning. War, as the French wage it, is an exact science. The flight of a shell is calculable, more or less ; that is to say, it can be affirmed with certainty that it will not fall short of one mark nor over another. The amount of damage a shell will do is similarly calculable, within limits. The rate of fire of a battery is known—within limits. So also other factors, if not exactly calculable, can be known from experience ; on the average of large numbers, they are constant. The amount of shelling required to demoralize a battalion, i.e., to kill or disable a certain proportion of its effectives, and reduce the remainder to a condition of helpless fear, is known approximately from experience, and does not vary much with different troops. The amount of water required by troops engaged in fighting is known. The approximate casualties in the water-carriers, with a given method of supply, and therefore the proportion of water which will not be delivered, can be estimated beforehand. For troops advancing in a given formation under given conditions of ground and obstacles, supporting fire and counter-battery work, the proportion of casualties per yard of ground covered can be foretold within limits, and therefore the number of men who must start in order to deliver a given number of bayonets in the enemy's trench can be calculated. The length of time it takes a certain number of men to put a trench pounded by barrage fire into a state of defence is again known—within limits. And so on, *ad infinitum*. Successful Generalship means, therefore, in the first place, a clear envisagement of the object to be obtained. It demands, next, an elaborate consideration of the means necessary to produce the desired effect, in which it is possible to calculate with precision the minimum which *might* be successful and the maximum which *must* be successful. And it is then the business of good Generalship to provide that maximum —or else give up the attempt altogether. Now, all this the French did very coolly and thoroughly. They are not afraid to pay the price. In war you must always pay for whatever advantage you gain. You must always expend munitions ; you must always undertake labour, hardships, and extreme discomfort ; you must almost always sacrifice life. It is for the good General, first to obtain the mysterious thing called initiative ; then to invent a scheme ; and after that—not merely hope that the preparations will cost the enemy more than his own side, but make certain that the damage to the enemy will in any case be worth the maximum cost ; or else drop that scheme altogether. It is as simple as that, and also it is the mightiest task that can be presented to the human intellect.

Well, I think I have rather let my pen run away with me. But the historians are right in filling their pages with the records of war. It is the most interesting of human phenomena.

———

[France]
Sunday, March 4th, 1917

Just a few lines of greeting from France—only a few lines, for it grows late ; but I know how welcome the postman's knock is when there is even a note from this quarter of the world.

I'm still pretty busy. Last night we were up till 1.30 this morning, to be Irish ; but since N—— has come back there is not the same urgent pressure of work. This afternoon I managed to get out for a walk of three or four miles. It was a glorious afternoon—cold still (it's not been over five degrees since the beginning of January), but brilliantly sunny. And this part of France is as yet singularly unscathed by war. The fields are ploughed up to a marvellously short distance from the lines, mostly by women, only they don't wear breeches and have their photographs in the papers. It was an unlovely country to begin with ; but the shell-holes don't show up until you are close to them, and there is little visible of war-like preparation, and the place is at least green—so, by comparison, it's quite beautiful.

We saw the most thrilling fight in the air I've yet witnessed. The first we noticed of it was the running crack of

Archies somewhere near. When we were out before they always used shrapnel against aeroplanes, the report of which is only a " pouf " ; but now they've found H.E. more effective, and air-burst H.E. gives a most resounding detonation. We looked for the target, and there was a Bosche plane impudently skimming along scarcely 500 feet up. There was a high wind, and he came slantwise almost over us—the shells bursting almost over our heads. Then from somewhere one of ours came driving up, and the machines swung round in giddy spirals, manœuvring for position. Far away two more of our machines came racing to join the fray, and then the fight swirled far down wind, and grew small in the distance.

There's one thing air fighting has done—it has brought back something of the old delight of battle to war. Do you remember that episode in—I think it is " *The Crown of Wild Olives*"—where Ruskin confesses his two thoughts of war ? The practical, that war is an evil to be avoided at all costs ; and the other, forced on him by his study of history, that there is no noble state or nation that is not frequently at war, and that in peace, if it be long-continued, even a noble nation degenerates in moral fibre. And his conclusion of the matter is that war under certain conditions is an eminently good thing. " Under certain conditions "—namely, that the arbitrament should not be of the accumulation of the means of destruction either side is able to compass, but a test of individual or collective valour, of personal skill in the management of one's weapons. That is what aerial warfare means at present. There, in the swift battle that flashed by us this afternoon, two men staked their lives upon their own skill and judgement ; creatures of glorious power, freed from the trammels of earth, whirlwind—charioted in the eye of death. And in that there is nothing mean.

———

LANCE-CORPORAL GEORGE ELTON SEDDING

Norfolk Regiment

Educated Radley. Art metal-worker. Died of wounds received in action,
France, 23 October, 1915, at the age of 33.

[France]

[TO THE REV. R. HYDE] *September 24th [1915]*

We had a little shelling yesterday, for a quarter of an
hour or so. No damage, but one or two came fairly near. It
is like the tentative touches of a blindfolded man, who
reaches out and clutches with empty hands at what he
fondly hopes is reality. Thinking he is on the right track he
rushes forward in his eagerness, only to realize his mistake.
So the gunners range and search you out with their shells.
First, one bursts over 1,000 yards away. The next within
500. Then two or three are placed only 100 yards off; while
all the time you feel under a sort of mesmeric influence.
Where will the next one land? Suddenly there is an explosion and a cloud of smoke 50 yards off. Now we are in for it,
you think! But, no, the touch is only tentative, and you
experience a feeling of relief as the following report occurs in
a field 200 yards the other side of you—and this happens
to be their last shot for the present.

The earth vibrates with the gusty thunder of a savage
assault far away on the flank. In the West a gold and purple
glow shines amidst the blackness of the trees. In the East the
brightness of the moon, veiled with a wisp of luminous
cloud, through which the light filters and turns to silver the
little clouds which surround it. . . . The evening star shines
steadily below in the dull opal of the sky, while above the
moon, the heavens are still a delicate sapphire, with a few
white fleecy clouds. Here and there the bright and cheerful
sparkle of a small star catches the eye. Meanwhile the air is
filled with the vibrant sound of bullets thudding on the
sand-bag parapets. These ricochet off with varied noises—
some with a high ringing note, others with the deep and

232

savage hum of an angry hornet ; while one hears on every side the quiet sound of men's voices, and the dull clatter of their boots on the floor-boards of the trenches. Now there comes a deeper report, as a rifle-grenade explodes, scattering its deadly discharge on all sides.

Night falls : the bullets pass at fewer intervals. We shoulder our packs with exclamations at their weight, and push off along the narrow communication-trench with staggering gait, as our haversack or rifle catches against the sides. Every now and then a bullet hisses by, or flicks through the trees and bushes at a speed which fairly makes you gasp, and wonder what it would feel like to be in its path. At last you get out of range, to all intents and purposes, and by the time you reach your destination, are too hot for words, and heave off the shoulder-straps of your equipment with the energy of a final effort. After a minute's ' breather ' you feel fit again, unpacking and hanging up your belongings over the floor-space you are to occupy. You spread out your ground-sheet, place your pack for a pillow, roll yourself in your blanket, and with your overcoat well up around your head, drop off into a dreamless sleep.

LIEUTENANT-COMMANDER PATRICK HOUSTON SHAW-STEWART
R.N.V.R.

Educated Eton and Balliol College, Oxford (scholar). Fellow of All Souls. Banker. Killed in action, France, 30 December, 1917, at the age of 29.

[*From a letter describing the voyage of the Royal Naval Division to Gallipoli, February-March, 1915*]

. . . The cruise of the Hood Battalion in the *Grantully Castle* falls naturally into two parts with an interlude. We sailed from Avonmouth (with the Anson Battalion also on board), on February 28, 1915, arrived in Mudros harbour (Lemnos) on March 11, passed a fortnight of inactivity there, diversified by training ashore, various wild rumours, and one mysterious early morning " feint " journey by the Gallipoli coast, sailed for Egypt about March 24, reached Port Said about 27th, and landed next day. . . .

In the first stage we suffered from two disadvantages : overcrowding and lack of Charles. The Anson were exceedingly pleasant shipmates, but both they and we agreed that the *Grantully Castle* was not constructed for two battalions and envied the luck (or skill) of the Howe—the third battalion of our Brigade—in developing meningitis just before embarkation and thus securing a magnificent ship all to themselves. Our men were terribly crowded ; the Fleet Reserve men took it as Fleet Reserve men would, while the recruits were for some time too sick to notice it. . . . I had the fortune to share a cabin with Denis Browne, most delightful of companions and most good-natured and unselfish of mankind. There were also comic difficulties in the way of Individual Instruction of Platoons : no one who has not tried it knows what it is like to take a " strong " platoon as a semaphore signalling class in the space afforded by about two yards of casing and the deck corresponding thereto, or how irresistibly interesting in such circumstances—to professor and student alike—are the activities of one's next door neighbours. I, for instance, on these occasions was between Johnny Dodge, and Rupert Brooke, and my platoon's development must have sadly suffered from the magnetic influence exercised on me by the gently penetrating Americanisms, and tireless oratorical resources, of the one, and the rich fancies of the other garbed in curt and telling prose. I have said that at that period we lacked Charles ; he made, however, a meteoric appearance on the day we spent at Malta, greatly impressing our naval eyes with his Jodhpore breeches, and, during our stay in Mudros harbour, he was hard by on the dignified *Franconia*, so that dinners could be exchanged, and one day he bicycled with Arthur Asquith and me to Kastro—a notable day, in the course of which Arthur Asquith tried on the inhabitants his Arabic, Charles his Turkish, and I my rudimentary Greek, and I was once more reminded to my delight of Charles's habit, immortalised by Ronald Knox in the phrase " descending obliquely from his bicycle." Finally, when we arrived at Port Said, Charles displayed unmistakable signs of wishing to exchange his position of Divisional Interpreter for a platoon in the Hood. Rupert, Arthur Asquith, and I left him in the moment of victory installed in that exceedingly sandy camp, and went joyously off for forty-eight hours leave in Cairo, where we luxuriated in almost forgotten comforts and explored with mastery, thanks to Arthur's Arabic, and where Rupert scored his usual success. When we returned to Port Said, " A " Company was full, commanded by Freyberg, with Nelson second, the four platoons being led by Johnny Dodge and myself, Charles and Rupert, in that order. Seldom can two neighbouring platoons of the Army, New or Old, have been more notably led. No sooner were we complete, no sooner had Charles begun to apply his troop-leading lore to his naval bipeds, and to fill the camp with his superb parade voice, than we were reduced. The day after we came back from Cairo I got a touch of the sun, which began as a violent headache and then shifted the scene of its ravages downwards, and retired sick to the Casino Hotel. Two days later I was joined by Rupert, who had the same complaint but worse, with high fever ; he was put in my room because the hotel was full, and because I thought I was well, but I relapsed slightly and in the end we shared that room for a week, completely starved (with one or two adventures in eggs and the little sham soles of the Mediterranean, which brought about relapse and repentance), and weak as kittens, disabilities which did not prevent me from enjoying it greatly. This enjoyment was perhaps not diminished by the thought of the wind-swept camp, where one of our stokers remarked that the continual absorption of particles of sand was rapidly forming in his interior a tomb-stone, the removal of which would, he felt, present a problem. . . .

Rupert and I were trundled on board the *Grantully Castle* when the battalion pushed off rather hastily about April 11, this time meaning business. Our protestations of fitness were true in my case but not in Rupert's, although after two or three days in his cabin he began to get up and go about, officially well but really pulled down. On this voyage the Hood had the *Grantully* to themselves, which vastly improved every one's temper and enjoyment. It further enabled a rearrangement of tables in the dining-saloon, and a table was formed consisting of Charles, Rupert, Arthur Asquith, Denis Browne, Cleg Kelly, Johnny Dodge, and myself, under the presidency of one of the ship's officers, who was occasionally, I think, a little surprised at our conversation. I subsequently happened to hear that this table was known to the others as "the Latin Club"; I do not know what piece of pedantry on whose part was responsible for the title. Certainly some noteworthy conversations were held there; it seemed always somehow to happen that we were left there at dinner among the patient stewards, long after everyone else had gone, experimenting on the rather limited repertory of the ship's vintages, and amusing one another none too silently. I wish I could recapture something of the subject-matter : it ranged from the little ways of Byzantine emperors to the correct way of dealing with Turkish prisoners ; music, in spite of organised opposition by such Philistines as myself, could not be altogether denied its place ; and Johnny Dodge, from time to time, by his radiant devotion to business, forced us to consider such stern matters as iron rations and Column of Blobs. We all read *Duffer's Drift*, we painted our holsters green to go with our webbing—green as our war experience —we were convinced that the campaign would most unfortunately be ended in a month by the R.N.D. occupying the entire Gallipoli peninsula and setting its foot on the neck of the Turks ; we were very wise indeed. But always, whatever the matter in hand, Charles and Rupert delighted each other and the rest of us ; they also walked on deck together, and I suspect talked of less hilarious and more permanently significant things. Meanwhile, Cleg Kelly and Denis Browne, encouraged by Charles, stealthily approached the ship's piano and softly, though not always too softly for some of our seniors (I do not speak of myself), who found the space confined, coaxed from it surprising melodies ; the subs of " A " Company diced for night watches, and Charles, Rupert, and Johnny Dodge (in fact, all except me), were exceedingly unselfish in this delicate connection ; and about April 17 we anchored in the southern bay of Scyros, that smelt to heaven of thyme.

Here, next day, Charles and I wandered all over the south half of the island in brilliant sunshine and sweet smelling air : we were fed on milk and goat's cheese by a magnificent islander—whom we identified with Eumaeus—in his completely Homeric steading, were rowed back to our ship by another sturdy Greek fisherman and his still sturdier wife, and were greeted over the ship's side with slight sarcasm by Rupert, who had taken our watches and suffered endless boredom to enable us to overstay our scheduled time without dire consequences. Here we floundered about on precipitous perfumed hill-sides packed with spring flowers and sharp stones, in the throes of Battalion and Divisional Field Days more bewildering, unexpected, and exhausting than any we had previously dreed on the Dorsetshire downs, till Rupert, who would not be left behind, felt tired and went to bed early while we still sat and smoked and talked after dinner. Here, one day after, we knew that the germ of pneumonia had attacked him, weak as he was, in the lip, and I was frightened to see him so motionless and fevered just before he was shifted—lowered over the side in a couch from the *Grantully* to a French hospital ship—and here, after one day more, Charles commanded the burial-party and I the firing-party, when we buried him among the olives of Scyros the night before we sailed for the Peninsula. . . .

. . . I think you have a good war-temperament—sane, humorous, enduring, and pugnacious : only you miss the real mainspring of my phlegm and success in life, which is incuriosity. I am really not exercised about the issues of life and death—was I, five years ago ? not much, I think—and am settling down to good solid practical subjects like Political Philosophy and the works of Samuel Butler. Still, I will tell you so much ; one thing I am sure of, and one thing makes me angry. I am sure that there is nothing to be looked for from the dead, either by the world in general or by me in particular, for the simple reason that whatever there is or is not, there is manifestly an end of consciousness, of the memories and associations of such and such a mind in such and such a body : and anything short of that is no. use to me, or to " this " world. And the thing that makes me angry is that people should lose, gain, intensify, or in any way differentiate their religion or irreligion because (*a*) a great many people have been killed ; (*b*) some one they like (1) has been killed, or (2) may be. It isn't the silliness, if you take me, so much as the stupidity that I mind. Now on this delicate subject (delicate because it's no use treading on the toes of people who've just lost their lover or their son), you seem to me to begin admirably (though I rather suspect your peace-time Nature-worship, reserved, as you state it, for great occasions), but to tail off badly into a weak attitude on the Mons question (on which you seem to me to resemble an excellent top-hat Christian who once told me she had no objection to saying the Apostles' Creed, because what it really meant was that self-sacrifice is beautiful), and worse still on the postures of the dead. Accept a little first-hand evidence from a poor devil of a *piou-piou* (who sees much more of the dead than the gunners do) like myself, who assure you the phenomenon has entirely escaped my notice. I have seen them in all sorts of queer positions, probably having been in pain at the time of their dissolution, but never remarked the prayerful attitude, nor the Turks (for that matter) turned towards Mecca. . . .

LIEUTENANT HENRY LAMONT SIMPSON

SIMPSON

Lancashire Fusiliers

Educated Pembroke College, Cambridge. Poet (*Moods and Tenses*, published posthumously, 1919). Killed in action, France, 29 August, 1918, at the age of 21.

The more I see of men, the more I love them. . . . A common song (even now and then a dirty song) can make one glad and sad beyond words, because one has heard men singing it times out of number. In all seriousness, the cheap popular songs of the last few years can move me infinitely more than the divinest music, because of the men I have heard sing them. This is not merely a sentimental lingering over dead friendships and individual passions— that element is very small. The main thing is a love for, a passionate faith in, my fellow men. . . . I believe with all my heart that man is, in the main, a lovable, and, at bottom, a good creature. (Curse the word good ! but you know what I mean—worthy, sterling, right, true, real.) He sings dirty songs and swears, and is altogether a sensual drunken brute at times ; but get to know him, start by loving him, believe in him through thick and thin, and you will not go un-rewarded.

I am aware that this is chaotic, illogical, and possibly, to the worldly wise, BOSH. But it is a belief that was struggling in me even at school, that flowered forth in the Army in England, and that bore fruit in France. It is a part of me, the best part of me, and right or wrong I shall stick to it. (The right or wrong is for your benefit—I *know* I am right.) And because I believe this, furiously, I *want* to write—to let everybody know it ; and for the first time in my life I absolutely cannot write a line. I have not yet arrived at ' recollecting in tranquillity ' I am too much sizzling with belief to be coherent. . . .

SECOND LIEUTENANT FRANCIS SAXON SNELL

Royal Berkshire Regiment

Educated Felsted and King's College, Cambridge. Private tutor.
Killed in action, France, 11 July, 1916, at the age of 29.

[France,

[TO HIS WIFE]   *Summer, 1916*]

. . . I have to deal with men whose response to noble
impulses has been strong enough to make them give up
their homes and everything they value, from motives that
must be almost wholly unselfish. Nothing is more remarkable than the absence of hatred or lust of battle in these
fellows, whose one hope is to go back to " Blighty " " after
the duration "—or before if it is possible even with a
wound ;—in spite of all they are full of courage and cheerfulness. They are so intensely human. I can tell you I
break all rules impressed on me in lectures at the Inns of
Court and elsewhere as regards the proper deportment of
an officer before his men.

One must not be weak or vulgar, or toadying, or showing off, or sickly sentimental of course, but neither would
one be those things with one's own social and military equals.

One may stand in relation to these men as a father or an
elder brother, in some cases ; but such relations exist between commissioned officers also. And quite as often the
boot is on the other foot, even as officers and men. Nothing
is more fatuous than the old military precept, that the
officer must by every subterfuge keep up an appearance of
omniscience, and that if he is " caught out " or reveals his
ignorance on any point, his hold over his men will be gone.

Any sort of bluff of that kind will be detected by these
men in an instant and they will despise you for it :—and
serve you right too ! They know what you are worth, and
if you are fit to lead them they will follow you. But even if
not, and you are honest, and sympathetic, and do your
best,—your level best—they'll lead you.

I think many, I hope most of them like me, and I am getting much more confident in grasping situations and organising what has to be done. . . .

R. and F. are such ripping fellows, and yet they look upon the " Bosch " as just so much unutterable vermin ; they have no sort of pity or compunction for them ; the more they kill the better. Once L. came into our mess, and he said in his open boyish way, "And you know there was a rather rotten story about that raid last night " (it was a raid on the German trenches). "What was that?" said R. and F. " Why," said L., "they captured a German officer, and were taking him back to our lines, and he had his hands tied behind his back, and a chance bullet hit one of the men forming his escort, and so they turned on him and killed him."

" I don't see anything rotten about that," said R. (and F. backed him up). " More Bosch you kill the better."

" But," expostulated little L., "he was a *prisoner*; and it was only a stray bullet that hit his escort, and his hands were tied behind his back ; and he could not defend himself ; and they simply killed him just as he was." " And a damned good job too," says R.

It's rather awful that, you know, for it means this ;—that not only hard cruel uncharitable men like some we have met—but even lots of awfully nice chaps, have simply put the Germans outside the range of all human sympathies whatever ; not in the heat of anger, but deliberately, in their calm considered moments.

There is no question whatever about a man like R. being affected by, or of his catching feelings from, the crowd of other people. And there must be thousands and thousands like him. . . .

———

CAPTAIN CHARLES HAMILTON SORLEY

Suffolk Regiment

Educated Marlborough. Scholar-Elect of University College, Oxford.
Joined Army from school. Killed in action, Flanders, 13 October, 1915,
at the age of 20.

[Flanders]

[TO ARTHUR WATTS]   *1 June, 1915*

Having begun in ink I continue in pencil. *Schottische Sparsamkeit.* You aren't worth ink. Besides ink hardly gives that impression of strenuous campaigning I am wishful to produce.

Also, this is a little hamlet, smelling pleasantly of manure. I have never felt more restful. We arrived at dawn : white dawn across the plane trees and coming through the fields of rye. After two hours in an oily ship and then in a grimy train, the " war area " was a haven of relief. These French trains shriek so : there is no sight more desolating than abandoned engines passing up and down the lines, hooting in their loneliness. There is something eerie in a railway by night.

But this is perfect. The other officers have heard the heavy guns and perhaps I shall soon. They make perfect cider in this valley ; still, like them. There are clouds of dust along the roads, and in the leaves : but the dust here is native and caressing and pure, not like the dust of Aldershot, gritted and fouled by motors and thousands of feet. 'Tis a very Limbo lake : set between the tireless railways behind and twenty miles in front the fighting. Drink its cider and paddle in its rushy streams : and see if you care whether you die to-morrow. It brings out a new part of one's self, the loiterer, neither scorning nor desiring delights, gliding listlessly through the minutes from meal-time to meal-time, like the stream through the rushes : or stagnant and smooth like their cider, unfathomably gold : beautiful and calm without mental fear. And in four-score hours we will pull up our braces and fight. These hours will have slipt over me, and I shall march hotly to the firing-line, by turn critic, actor, hero, coward and soldier of fortune : perhaps even for a moment Christian, humble, with " Thy will be done." Then shock, combustion, the emergence of one of these : death or life : and then return to the old rigmarole. I imagine that this, while it may or may not knock about your body, will make very little difference to you otherwise.

A speedy relief from Chatham. There is vibration in the air when you hear " The Battalion will move across the water on . . ."

The moon won't rise till late, but there is such placid weariness in all the bearing earth, that I must go out to see. I have not been " *auf dem Lande* " for many years : *man muss den Augenblick geniessen.*

Leb' wohl. I think often of you and Jena : where I was first on my own and found freedom. *Leb' wohl.*

[Flanders]

[To ARTHUR WATTS]   *16 June, 1915*

. . . In a job like this, one lives in times a year ago—and a year hence, alternately. *Keine Nachricht.* A large amount of organized disorderliness, killing the spirit. A vagueness and a dullness everywhere ; an unromantic sitting still 100 yards from Brother Bosch. . . . None of that feeling of confidence, offensiveness, " personal ascendency," with which the reports so delight our people at home. Mutual helplessness and lassitude, as when two boxers who have battered each other crouch dancing two paces from each other, waiting for the other to hit. Improvised organization, with its red hat, has muddled out romance. It is not the strong god of the Germans—that makes their Prussian *Beamter* so bloody and their fight against fearful odds so successful. Our organization is like a nasty fat old frowsy cook dressed up in her mistress's clothes : fussy, unpopular, and up-start : trailing the scent of the scullery behind her. In periods of rest we are billeted in a town of sewage farms, mean streets, and starving cats : delightful population : but an air of late June weariness. For Spring again ! This is not Hell as I hoped, but Limbo Lake with green growths on the water, full of minnows.

So one lives in a year ago—and a year hence. What are your feet doing a year hence ? . . . I am sometimes in Mexico, selling cloth : or in Russia, doing Lord knows what : in Serbia or in the Balkans : in England, never. England remains the dream, the background : it is the memory and the ideal. Sorley is the Gaelic for wanderer. I have had a conventional education : Oxford would have corked it. But this has freed the spirit, glory be. Give me *The Odyssey*, and I return the New Testament to store. Physically as well as spiritually, give me the road.

Only sometimes the horrible question of bread and butter shadows the dream : it has shadowed many, I should think. It must be tackled. But I always seek to avoid the awkward, by postponing it.

You figure in these dreams as the pioneer-sergeant. Perhaps *you* are the Odysseus, I am but one of the dog-like ἑταῖροι, ... But however that may be, our lives will be πολύπλαγκτοι, though our paths may be different. And we will be buried by the sea——

> " *Timon will make his everlasting mansion*
> *Upon the beached verge of a salt flood,*
> *Which twice a day with his embossèd froth*
> *The turbulent surge shall cover.*"

. . . I will write later—when the drains are not so close : and let me hear from you meanwhile. Since starting this letter I begin to scent romance in night patrolling.

[TO HIS FATHER]

. . . We are now at the end of a few days rest, a kilometre
behind the lines. Except for the farmyard noises (new style)
it might almost be the little village that first took us to its
arms six weeks ago. It has been a fine day, following on a
day's rain, so that the earth smells like spring. I have just
managed to break off a long conversation with the farmer
in charge, a tall thin stooping man with sad eyes, in trouble
about his land : les Anglais stole his peas, trod down his
corn and robbed his young potatoes : he told it as a father
telling of infanticide. There may have been 15 francs worth
of damage done ; he will never get compensation out of
those shifty Belgian burgomasters ; but it was not exactly
the 15 francs but the invasion of the soil that had been his
for forty years, in which the weather was his only enemy,
that gave him a kind of Niobe's dignity to his complaint.

Meanwhile there is the usual evening sluggishness. Close
by, a quick-firer is pounding away its allowance of a dozen
shells a day. It is like a cow coughing. Eastward there begins a sound (all sounds begin at sundown and continue
intermittently till midnight, reaching their zenith at about
9 p.m. and then dying away as sleepiness claims their
makers)—a sound like a motor-cycle race—thousands of
motor-cycles tearing round and round a track, with cut-
outs out ; it is really a pair of machine-guns firing. And
now one sound awakes another. The old cow coughing has
started the motor-bikes : and now at intervals of a few
minutes come express trains in our direction : you can hear
them rushing towards us ; they pass going straight for the
town behind us ; and you hear them begin to slow down
as they reach the town : they will soon stop : but no, every
time, just before they reach it, is a tremendous railway
accident. At least, it must be a railway accident, there is
so much noise, and you can see the dust that the wreckage
scatters. Sometimes the train behind comes very close, but
it too smashes into the wreckage of its fore-runners. A tremendous cloud of dust, and then the groans. So many trains

and accidents start the cow coughing again : only another cow this time, somewhere behind us, a tremendous-sized cow, θαυμάσιον ὅσον, with awful whooping-cough. It must be a buffalo : this cough must burst its sides. And now someone starts sliding down the stairs on a tin tray, to soften the heart of the cow, make it laugh and cure its cough. The din he makes is appalling. He is beating the tray with a broom now, every two minutes a stroke : he has certainly stopped the cow by this time, probably killed it. He will leave off soon (thanks to the " shell tragedy ") : We know he cannot last.

It is now almost dark : come out and see the fireworks. While waiting for them to begin you can notice how pale and white the ground is in the summer twilight : no wonder with all this whooping-cough about. And the motor-cycles : notice how all these races have at least a hundred entries : there is never a single cycle going. And why are there no birds going back to roost ? Where is the lark ? I have not heard him all to-day. He must have got whooping-cough as well, or be staying at home through fear of the cow. I think it will rain to-morrow, but there have been no swallows circling low, striking their breasts on the full ears of corn. Anyhow, it is night now, but the circus does not close till twelve. Look ! there is the first of them ! The fireworks are beginning. Red flares shoot up high into the night, or skimming low over the ground, like the swallows that are not : and rockets bursting into stars. See how they illumine the patch of ground a mile in front. See it, it is deadly pale in their searching light : ghastly, I think, and featureless except for two big lines of eye-brows ashy white, parallel along it, raised a little from its surface. Eyebrows. Where are the eyes ? Hush, there are no eyes. What those shooting flares illumine is a mole. A long thin mole. Burrowing by day, and shoving a timorous enquiring snout above the ground by night. Look, did you see it ? No, you cannot see it from here. But were you a little nearer, you would see behind that snout a long and endless row of sharp shining teeth. The rockets catch the light from these teeth and the teeth glitter : they are silently removed from the poison-spitting gums of the mole. For the mole's gums spit fire and, they say, send something more concrete than fire darting into the night. Even when its teeth are off. But you cannot see all this from here : you can only see the rockets and then for a moment the pale ground beneath. But it is quite dark now.

And now for the fun of the fair ! You will hear soon the riding master crack his whip—why, there it is. Listen, a thousand whips are cracking, whipping the horses round the ring. At last ! The fun of the circus is begun. For the motor-cycle team race has started off again : and the whips are cracking all : and the waresman starts again, beating his loud tin tray to attract the customers : and the cows in the cattle-show start coughing, coughing : and the fire-work display is at its best : and the circus specials come one after another bearing the merry-makers back to town, all to the inevitable crash, the inevitable accident. It can't last long : these accidents are so frequent, they'll all get soon killed off, I hope. Yes, it is diminishing. The train service is cancelled (and time too) : the cows have stopped coughing : and the cycle race is done. Only the kids who have bought new whips at the fair continue to crack them : and unused rockets that lie about the ground are still sent up occasionally. But now the children are being driven off to bed : only an occasional whip crack now (perhaps the child is now the sufferer) : and the tired showmen going over the ground pick up the rocket-sticks and dead flares. At least I suppose this is what must be happening : for occasionally they still find one that has not yet gone off and send it up out of mere perversity. Else what silence !

It must be midnight now. Yes, it is midnight. But before you go to bed, bend down, put your ear against the ground. What do you hear ? " I hear an endless tapping and a tramping to and fro : both are muffled : but they come from everywhere. Tap, tap, tap : pick, pick, pick : tra-mp, tra-mp, tra-mp." So you see the circus-goers are not all gone to sleep. There is noise coming from the womb of earth, noise of men who tap and mine and dig and pace to and fro on their watch. What you have seen is the foam and froth of war : but underground is labour and throbbing and long watch. Which will one day bear their fruit. They will set the circus on fire. Then what pandemonium ! Let us hope it will not be to-morrow !

[To the Master of Marlborough]
[Flanders]
4 August, 1915

... There is really very little to say about the life here. Change of circumstances, I find, means little compared to change of company. And as one has gone out and is still with the same officers with whom one had rubbed shoulders unceasingly for the last nine months, and of whom one had acquired that extraordinarily intimate knowledge which comes of constant συνουσία, one does not notice the change : until one or two or three drop off. And one wonders why.

They are extraordinarily close, really, these friendships of circumstance, distinguished as they remain from friendships of choice. If one looks back to early September and sees what one thought of these others then : how one would never, while not disliking them, have wished to see any of them again : but that incorrigible circumstance kept us penned together, rubbed off our odd and awkward corners where we grated : developing in each a part of himself that might have remained always unsuspected, which could tread on common ground with another. Only, I think, once or twice does one stumble across that presence into whom one fits at once : to whom one could stand naked, all disclosed. But circumstance provides the second best : and I'm sure that any gathering of men will in time lead to a very close half-friendship between them all (I only say half-friendship because I wish to distinguish it from the other). So there has really been no change in coming over here ;

248

the change is to come when half of this improvised " band of brothers " are wiped away in a day. We are learning to be soldiers slowly—that is to say, adopting the soldierly attitude of complete disconnection with our job during odd hours. No shop. So when I think I should tell you " something about the trenches," I find I have neither the inclination nor the power.

This however. On our weekly march from the trenches back to our old farmhouse a mile or two behind, we leave the communication-trench for a road, hedged on one side only, with open ploughland to the right. It runs a little down hill till the road branches. Then half left up over open country goes our track, with the ground shelving away to right of us. Can you see it ? The Toll House to the First Post on Trainers Down (old finishing point of A House sweats) on a small scale. There is something in the way that at the end of the hedge the road leaps up to the left into the beyond that puts me in mind of Trainers Down (as C House called it). It is what that turn into unhedged country and that leap promises, not what it achieves, that makes the likeness. It is nothing when you get up, no wildness, no openings. But there it remains to cheer me on our relief. . . .

I hear that a *very* select group of public schools will by this time be enjoying the Camp " somewhere in England." May they not take it too seriously ! Seein' as 'ow the training is washed out as soon as you turn that narrow street corner at Boulogne, where some watcher with a lantern is always up for the English troops arriving, with a " *Bon courage* " for every man.

A year ago to-day—but that way madness lies.

———

[Flanders]
[To Arthur Watts]   *26 August, 1915*

Your letter arrived and awoke the now drifting ME to consciousness. I had understood and acquiesced in your

249

silence. The re-creation of that self which one is to a friend is an effort : repaying if it succeeds, but not to be forced. Wherefore, were it not for the dangers dancing attendance on the adjourning type of mind—which a year's military training has not been able to efface from him—I should not be writing to you now. For it is just after breakfast—and you know what breakfast is : putter to sleep of all mental energy and discontent : charmer, sedative, leveller : maker of Britons. I should wait till after tea when the undiscriminating sun has shown his back—a fine back—on the world, and one's self by the aid of tea has thrown off the mental sleep of heat. But after tea I am on duty. So with bacon in my throat and my brain like a poached egg I will try to do you justice.

On the whole—except for the subtle distinction that I *am* at the front, you not (merely a nominal distinction for the present)—I am disposed to envy you. I am moving slowly to and fro over an unblessed stretch of plain—a fly on a bald man's head. You are at least among rich surroundings, like the head of hair of your half-Slav. I wonder how long it takes the King's Pawn, who so proudly initiates the game of chess, to realise that he is a pawn. Same with us. We are finding out that we play the unimportant if necessary part. At present a dam, untested, whose présence not whose action stops the stream from approaching : and then—a mere handle to steel : dealers of death which we are not allowed to plan. But I have complained enough before of the minion state of the " damned foot." It is something to have no responsibility—an inglorious ease of mind. . . .

But out in front at night in that no-man's land and long grave-yard there is a freedom and a spur. Rustling of the grasses and grave tap-tapping of distant workers : the tension and silence of encounter, when one struggles in the dark for moral victory over the enemy patrol : the wail of the exploded bomb and the animal cries of wounded men. Then death and the horrible thankfulness when one sees that the next man is dead : " We won't have to *carry* him in under fire, thank God ; dragging will do " : hauling in of the great resistless body in the dark, the smashed head rattling : the relief, the relief that the thing has ceased to groan : that the bullet or bomb that made the man an animal has now made the animal a corpse. One is hardened by now : purged of all false pity : perhaps more selfish than before. The spiritual and the animal get so much more sharply divided in hours of encounter, taking possession of the body by swift turns. . . .

[Flanders]

[To ARTHUR WATTS]   5 October, 1915

Just a line—albeit on military ruled paper. It is the eve of our crowning hour.

I am bleached with chalk and grown hairy. And I think exultantly and sweetly of the one or two or three out-standingly admirable meals of my life. One in Yorkshire, in an inn upon the moors, with a fire of logs and ale and tea and every sort of Yorkshire bakery, especially bears me company. And yet another in Mecklenburg-Schwerin (where they are very English) in a farmhouse utterly at peace in broad fields sloping to the sea. I remember a tureen of champagne in the middle of the table, to which we helped ourselves with ladles ! I remember my hunger after three hours ride over the country : and the fishing-town of Wismar lying like an English town on the sea. In that great old farmhouse where I dined at 3 p.m. as the May day began to cool, fruit of sea and of land joined hands together, fish fresh caught and ducks fresh killed : it was a wedding of the elements. It was perhaps the greatest meal I have had ever, for everything we ate had been alive that morning—the champagne was alive yet. We feasted like kings till the sun sank, for it was impossible to overeat. 'Twas Homeric and its memory fills many hungry hours.

I was interested in your tale of meeting Wells. Yet a man

to whom every private incident is legitimate " copy " I cannot understand.

I can see you amongst your staff of warrior non-combatants : and (with you) both wish you, and wish you not, rid of them. To be able to prove oneself no coward to oneself, will be great, if it comes off : but suppose one finds oneself fail in the test ? I dread my own censorious self in the coming conflict—I also have great physical dread of pain. Still, a good edge is given to the sword here. And one learns to be a servant. The soul is disciplined. So much for me. But the good it would do in your case is that it would discipline your liver. The first thing of man is health. And I wish it you for your happiness, though somehow I seem to know you more closely when you are fighting a well-fought battle with ill-health.

Adieu ! or (chances three to one in favour of the pleasanter alternative) *auf wiedersehen* ! Pray that I ride my frisky nerves with a cool and steady hand when the time arrives. And you don't know how much I long for our next meeting—more even than for the afore-mentioned meal !

CAPTAIN EVELYN HERBERT LIGHTFOOT SOUTHWELL
The Rifle Brigade

Educated Eton and Magdalen College, Oxford. Assistant Master, Shrewsbury. Killed in action, France, 15 September, 1916, at the age of 30.

B.E.F.

[TO HIS MOTHER]   *Feb. 27, 1916*

To-day was Sunday. And there was Celebration in the school here, and we knelt at the familiar desks in the familiar room all hung with maps, and I remembered that I was a schoolmaster too : and I saw the familiar blackboard ; also I reflected that I could not write on it so beautifully as the (doubtless) dear old painstaking master of the little village. And I thought of you all, and wondered whether you knew I was doing so. Only last night one of my officers produced the " *Golden Treasury*," and I turned up " *The Blessed Damozel* " of Rossetti, and came at once across the passage where the two are praying, widely separated, as we are :—

> " *Are not two prayers a perfect strength ?*
> *And shall I feel afraid ?* "

And I said ' Thank you,' and I closed the book, and I thought of my home.

———

B.E.F.
July 16, 1916

[TO A FRIEND]

If I could write the sort of letter which I know I ought to try and send you, I should be the happiest man alive, in spite of everything. For it seems, somehow, that you must be in the very centre of the pain that goes with every word of the news ; since to be in the New House all the time without our Man. . . .

I don't think, Man, that it will be clever to try and belittle the calamity. One wonders, sometimes, whether the ' Loss is common to the race ' attitude is any good, and I am pretty sure it isn't. Too many priceless things have happened ever since Broadlands ; and to pretend to drop (even to the small degree which might be possible) this memory, is surely a loss rather than a gain. There was never a man really like ours, and I think the answer must be : ' So much the better for the men that owned him ; still better, the more they remember.'

Oh Man dear, I am sticking down all this philosophy, and I do hope it's all right : I try to offer *something*, for what it's worth, and please don't be angry if the ring is a bit hollow :

the tune is a bit shaky, but it *is* the right tune ; of that I am sure. What you want is a great strong man, with a faith like the foundations of all the hills ; and if I, evidently, Heaven knows, am not fit to kiss the feet of such a man as that, much less to be the kind of real support I would give everything to be, yet I thank God all day and every day that, if ever two men answered that description, I believe they are in that house with you now. Do let them talk about the Man, and what they really think is the explanation of it all ; if I were to be shot to-morrow, I would leave you that as my very last message. You mustn't try and carry it off alone : I know what that's like. Dear me, Man, a heavy letter ; I almost wonder if the Man's smiling over my shoulder. So clumsy and so voluble, isn't it ? But not wrong, Man ; no.

B.E.F.

[To Dr. C. A. Alington] *Aug. 2, 1916*

. . . And so the term is over, and I know—how well !—what that last week has been like. I suppose they came round, as they always do, to say good-bye, though with more regret than ever—alas !—when they came to you ; and there would be the last Sunday evening Chapel, and your address (I await it eagerly) ; and the almost conscious look of ' Good-bye ' on the face of the Breiddens,[1] which (even before I came away) used to send one's heart into one's mouth ; and some of us would be thinking how we paced the School Yard, years ago, on just such a Summer night ; and the younger amongst us would be wondering how the place could carry on during another year, when this and that place was empty—having not learnt yet from experience that a school is the only immortal thing on earth, and the only thing about which all the platitudes are true and all the longings undying.

[1] The Welsh hills nearest to Shrewsbury:

It is not like that in the Army—at least, I think, not to the same extent. Not but that the number of adorable days here is not incalculable ; but it is not quite the same story. . . .

Well, well, this had better go now. Let me have your address in Chapel won't you ? Later on, perhaps, I will send you some news, should there be any. At present we are happy enough in this existence, wondering a little, but generally too tired and contented for more than wonder ; and, perhaps luckily, we are not allowed too much time for that, either. In fact, now I come to think of it, I doubt if I've done any of that for some time now. It seems a trifle futile, considering how very little there is to be wondered at, and how many better men have contrived to get through with no wondering at all. But I would like to see your address, all the same.

LIEUTENANT ADRIAN CONSETT STEPHEN, M.C.
R.F.A.

Educated Sydney University, New South Wales. Killed in action, Flanders, 14 March, 1918.

[France,
July, 1916]

What about the gun—My Lord the Gun !

He lives in a lair that takes a month to build. Six men slave for him day and night. He has his whims and his humours. In a good temper he shoots like a dream, when hot and sulky and steaming, he jams sometimes or jibs, and then men pet him, bathe him down, stroke him with cloths, and fuss around with oil cans, till with a roar he leaps into action again. His snout tilts upwards, sniffing the air, his lips slobber with smoke and flame.

All night men sleep around him, and further behind the line an army toil to feed him with long rows of glistening shells. Men and gun are one and indivisible. My Lord the

Gun has come into his own, and his kingdom to-day is large—it is the world.

The great day " Z " has been postponed. To-morrow is " Y1 " day, and the next " Y2 " day, and then " Z " day.

" Y1 " and " Y2." Nothing new, just a repetition of the other days, just marking time—that's all. On the eve of Day " Z " we dined together at the RX, and cracked our last bottle. Although the LX are doing counter battery work on " Z " day, I decided to go to the O.P.T. in order to be on the spot, in case of a counter attack, and in case the guns had to be switched on to the trenches. I walked over to the LX with F—— and we told the men about the morrow.

Day " Z." The assault was to begin at " Zero time." All the programme of the day as regards bombardment, &c. had been arranged from zero time. Zero time was 7.30 a.m. At 6.20 the guns opened, and I made my way to O.P.T. with a telephonist. I passed through a ruined village on my way—not a soul to be seen—streets empty, billets cleared. At the O.P. I found H—— of D /241 who was also observing for counter attacks.

The bombardment roar was terrific. The ear-splitting bark of the 18 pounders, the cough of the howitzers, the boom of the heavy guns, swelled into a jerky roar that was flung from horizon to horizon, as thunder is tossed from mountain to mountain. It was wonderful music—the mightiest I have ever heard. It seemed to throb, throb into our very veins, beating up and down and yet never quite reaching a climax, but always keeping one's nerves on the thrill. And then at last, ten minutes before zero, the guns opened their lungs. The climax had been reached. One felt inclined to laugh with the fierce exhilaration of it. After all, it was our voice, the voice of a whole Empire at war. At zero I looked out of the O.P. The din had quietened a little. What I saw made me cry out, so that the others, telephonists and all, ran up to me. It was smoke and gas. For a mile stretching away from me, the trench was belching forth dense columns of white, greenish, and orange smoke. It rose curling and twisting, blotting everything from view, and then swept, a solid rampart, over the German lines. For more than an hour this continued, and I could see nothing. Sometimes the smoke was streaked with a scarlet star as a shell burst among it, and sometimes a smoke candle would be hurled high into the air, spluttering and making a cloud of its own far above the rest. It seemed impossible that men could withstand this awful onslaught—even if it were only smoke. And yet a machine gun played steadily all the time from the German front line. What fighters they are ! He swept the O.P., cutting twigs from above our heads, and splashing mud out of our sandbags. Somewhere to the right of that smoke the Infantry were advancing. I could see nothing. Reports and rumours came dancing down the wires.

" Our Infantry have taken the front line without resistance."

" Prisoners are coming in."

" Enemy giving themselves up in hundreds."

" Infantry have crossed the Serre Ridge."

" Beaumont Hamel is ours."

" More prisoners reported."

This continued until 11.30 when the smoke cleared, and I looked out upon the invisible battle ! Far as I could see not a soldier could be seen, not a movement of any sort. Could it be that we held those trenches. Had we captured Serre ? Once the village had been hidden by thick trees and hedges, now it stood bare and shattered, the trees leafless, as though a comb had been dragged through them.

The Germans were shelling their own trenches, that was all the sign of change I noticed.

I tried to observe while F—— ranged on hostile batteries, but the smoke was too confusing, and flying pieces and bullets made it a difficult matter. In the afternoon the Germans launched a counter attack immediately opposite our O.P., but unfortunately invisible to us. Their shelling was heavy and accurate. Our O.P. swayed perilously, our wires were cut in four places, within 100 yards of the O.P. ;

a linesman of D /241 mended them, and I have mentioned him for distinction. We sat in the dug-out waiting and calculating.

The Captain from O.P.F. had a clear view of the counter attack and switched the LX on it. In fact the LX and one other battery stopped the attack. Unfortunately I could see nothing, as I had to watch another point from which attacks had been expected.

The Infantry were cut to pieces, they came running back between the lines ; Germans stood on their parapets and shot them down. H—— and his men left soon after, but I stayed to register the guns on to —— Valley in case of a counter attack in that direction. Then about 6.30 I came away.

I met an Infantry officer. He was grey in the face and had not shaved. " Well," he said, " what do you think of it ? "

" Seems all right."

" Um, we got to their third line and were driven back ; we are barely holding our own front line—we're—we're wiped out—General's a broken man."

" But Gommecourt ? "

" Lost."

" Another Loos," I said.

" Looks it." He turned away.

I felt tired suddenly. The few yards home were miles. The world was full of stretchers and white faces, and fools who gibbered about the great advance.

But news from elsewhere was more cheery ; down south we were doing well, and the French also, and our little battle here was only one pebble in the mosaic. What did it matter ? We ourselves had been lucky ; three men slightly wounded in the RX and one sergeant in the LX—a good fellow. Later on we would join in the great advance.

The evening was quiet. For the first time in a week or more I heard the silence. It was fine, too, and warm. But our battle—our work—our hopes——!

Bunches of brown figures, lines of brown figures, stretched

out on the dried grass between the lines ! Stray shrapnel burst among them, but they did not move ; they lay still where they had fallen or dropped motionless across the wire, not far, poor fellows, on the road to Germany. That was all. Aeroplanes throbbed overhead ; observation balloons hung quietly against the sunset. " Z " day had ended.

I sat in my dug-out and had a brandy. I think it was only the knowledge of what the Infantry had gone through that kept me from weeping. It was their ordeal—not ours ; theirs the glory and the sorrow.

[France,

September, 1916]

. . . Noon on the 26th found me at the O.P. with the Captain. Zero was at 12.35, and as yet the trenches were silent and motionless. Then suddenly, at the appointed minute, the slopes of Thiepval seemed to move with small brown figures, like a field alive with rabbits, and the guns swept down on Thiepval and the country to the right of it. At first the men advanced in disordered masses, but gradually taking their own time they opened out like a stage crowd falling into their allotted places. I could see the first wave walking towards Thiepval, and then a second wave sprang up and spread out behind them, then the last wave took shape and followed up in artillery formation ; small bunches of men, with an interval between each bunch, or more often six men advancing in single file with a stretcher bearer in the rear. It was a wonderful sight. Never have I seen such a calm, methodical and perfectly ordered advance. It seemed incredible that this parade could be marching on Thiepval, the most sinister of German strongholds, yet hardly a man fell. The barrage was as perfect as it was terrible. The white smoke of shrapnel ran like a rampart along the trenches that were the first objective, as clear as though it were made of tape carefully placed and measured.

Indeed, the barrier of white smoke, broken now and again by a black puff from an enemy gun, might have been an ermine fur with its little black tufts.

From my vantage point I could even look over the barrage on to the trenches beyond, but it was hard even for a moment to drag one's eyes away from the little brown figures that were slowly but steadily drawing upon Thiepval. Sometimes a wave of men would dip and disappear into a trench only to emerge on the other side in perfect line again. Now they are into Thiepval ! No, the line suddenly telescopes into a bunch and the bunch scurries to right or left, trying to evade a machine-gun in front, and then with a plunge the first wave, broken now into little groups, vanished amidst the ruined houses. What desperate resistance they encountered in the dark and mysterious passages beneath those ruins, only the men who fought will know, but the other waves swept on up to the slope, till they too were lost amidst the village. Farther to the right, where the barrage had lifted, more brown figures streamed across the open. A black dog ran out of a dug-out to meet them ; a man stooped down and fondled it. When they drew near to a line of chalk heaps I saw black masses emerge and march towards our lines. Prisoners were giving themselves up without a fight. Prisoners were pouring in from all sides, sometimes in black batches, guided by a brown figure and a shining bayonet, sometimes a single Boche would race, hands above head, panic-stricken till he reached our lines. Thiepval was now a closed book, though runners would sometimes emerge and dash stumbling to our trenches. The Boche retaliation was feeble and badly placed. His barrage fell behind all our men, and very few shells had burst among them, and even then never did they cause a man to turn his head or swerve out of place—unless he fell. At this stage a tank crawled on to the scene and crept laboriously, like a great slug, towards Thiepval. It disappeared among the ruins, puffing smoke. Subsequently it caught fire. Thiepval now became as stony, as devoid of life, as it was before the attack. Away to the right, however, a fresh assault was being launched. A new barrage opened, and our men swept forward to another objective, wheeling slightly as the trench in front ran diagonally across their path. Suddenly, as though spirited away, they vanished, sank into the ground. Watching carefully we could distinguish a movement among the long grass and wire, and sometimes a man would leap up, dash forward, or run backward. It seemed they were playing at hide and seek. Probably they were. It is certain they were held up by something, and the bitter fighting which continued the next day for Hessian Trench—the trench in question—made one wonder how they ever got as far as they did. Yet all this time men were streaming backwards and forwards to the Zollern Trench just in the rear. How astounding, this careless movement across the open ! Even during my exploration I had found myself strolling about in places where I could sometimes see Boches running along their trenches. It makes one smile to remember the old Corps Summaries of " peace time " warfare. " Our snipers shot two of the enemy to-day." Slaughter now has become so wholesale that one is careless of the mere individual.

When the light failed, our men were still playing hide and seek. We had taken the Zollern Redoubt, part of the Stiff Redoubt on the right, and part of the Schwaben Redoubt on the left. Above all, Thiepval had fallen. Thiepval, the proud fortress garrisoned by one regiment since September 1914, had at last, after three big attacks, yielded. It was a good conquest, for the slopes of Thiepval are surely as tragic and bloody as any in this war, except, of course, Gallipoli, but the battle of Thiepval was significant, not so much for the actual ground gained, as for the sudden appearance in the conflict of an element hitherto unseen. Not only the battle of Thiepval, but the whole battle of the Somme, must be judged from three points of view :—

1. Strategic progress.
2. Material progress.
3. Moral progress.

Now, strategically, the battle of the Somme is a great British reverse. We had failed to do what we intended to do. The battle was lost on July 1st. The Boche line still held. Moreover, it had taken us months to accomplish what, according to time-table, should have been done in as many hours. Let us not hesitate to confess that strategically the battle was a failure. Of course we are now threatening the communications of Bapaume, Vely and Achiet after *four months*. We had meant to do that in as many hours.

Materially we have turned the battle into a success. We have killed Germans, taken guns, villages and men. Our material progress is as obvious as the map.

Morally we have never obtained complete mastery. The Boche morale remained as hard as his line and as unbreakable. But here we come to Thiepval. For the first time I saw Germans surrendering *in droves* before putting up a fight. For the first time his hitherto faultless military machinery failed to swing reserves where they were wanted. On the 26th September I felt our moral ascendancy. It was as obvious, also, as the map at my elbow or the ground under observation. It was not pronounced, but it was there.

Indeed one can compare, rather fancifully perhaps, our whole offensive to a little boy who sets out to climb a big tree. On failing to reach farther than the first bough he takes out a pocket knife and proceeds to cut it down. That is what we are doing. On 26th the tree, after three months of cutting, was showing a little weakness through loss of sap.

We must push on—on—on without rest and without mercy, even towards ourselves. Our moral ascendancy, however slight, makes one feel like that. It fires one with fresh enthusiasm.

LIEUTENANT ROBERT W. STERLING

Royal Scots Fusiliers

Educated Sedbergh and Pembroke College, Oxford. Joined Army while an undergraduate. Author of *Poems*, published 1915. Killed in action, France, 23 April, 1915, at the age of 21.

[Flanders
[To MACAULAY STEVENSON]   *18 April, 1915*]

. . . I've been longing for some link with the normal universe detached from the storm. It is funny how trivial instances are seized as symbols by the memory ; but I did find such a link about three weeks ago. We were in trenches in wooded country (just S.E. of Ypres). The Germans were about eighty yards away, and between the trenches lay pitiful heaps of dead friends and foes. Such trees as were left standing were little more than stumps, both behind our lines and the enemy's. The enemy had just been shelling our reserve trenches, and a Belgian patrol behind us had been replying, when there fell a few minutes' silence ; and I still crouching expectantly in the trench, suddenly saw a pair of thrushes building a nest in a " bare ruin'd choir " of a tree, only about five yards behind our line. At the same time a lark began to sing in the sky above the German trenches. It seemed almost incredible at the time, but now, whenever I think of those nest-builders and that all but " sightless song," they seem to repeat in some degree the very essence of the Normal and Unchangeable Universe carrying on unhindered and careless amid the corpses and the bullets and the madness. . . . I suppose Kipling meant something when he said that Life runs large on the Long Trail. In a sense I take it, it runs large out here, not only for the reason of which you so eloquently remind me—the inspiration of a Cause, but because Death has become its insistent and intruding neighbour. . . .

MISS BERTHA GAVIN (BETTY) STEVENSON
Y.M.C.A.

Educated St. George's Wood, Haslemere, and Brussels. *Croix de Guerre avec Palme*. Killed in air-raid, France, 30 May, 1918, at the age of 22.

[France]

[TO HER FATHER]   *6th Jan., 1918*

I am going back to my car when I'm fit again, and am coming home in the beginning of February. I shall either ask for indefinite leave, or hand in my permit for a month or two, I'm not quite sure when. I've never really got rid of that silly chill I got, so everyone advises me to have a good big leave, and get braced up for the Summer, so I think I shall....

I'm writing such drivel, but my pen seems to be running away with me, but I don't really feel like it a bit. I feel " mentally unsettled "—what a hideous combination of words, but I can't think of a better. I suppose it's the war really—one feels one is floating about without an anchor—sounding feverishly for something definite to anchor to. " Unsettled " is really the only word I can think of. There is so much here that I see which stamps itself on my mind, and I have to think about it, and can come to no happy or definite conclusion. I long to put all of it down in writing. If only I could !

That's the root of it. There's such a lot inside me which longs to come out in music or writing, and I can hardly bear it when I realise I can't get rid of it anyhow. Perhaps it will get so bad sometime, that I shall be able to write it away,—I only hope so. Everything here seems to mean something to me, to be in inverted commas so to speak, and the most ordinary things seem to excite me in a way which I can't explain, like happiness and sadness mixed. I suppose I've got very fond of everything and yet I often feel homesick. I find myself looking forward absurdly to driving again, and to seeing the things I know—the quayside with all the fishing boats sailing in, and the women clumping across the road, with baskets, to meet them, and

264

take the fish to the market, and yet when they really do these things I get very annoyed, because they get in the way of the car ! This is a funny sort of letter, and I don't know whether I shall ever post it. I've got what I call a " spasm " ; when there's so much I want to write that I can't sort out my ideas, and I can't find words for the impressions I want to give. I think everything here is so elemental—it's like living in a dramatic situation the whole time, and you can't get away from it.

I'm awfully fond of the river here. There is a bridge over it from which you can get the most wonderful view of everything. On one side the river mouth and the sea and the little fishing boats ; the quay and the big sailors' crucifix, where the women pray when there is a storm at sea. The boats anchor quite near, and they look like something hazy and unreal, sitting on a shiny wet river, with every sail and mast and man reflected in the water. I long to put my hand down and stroke them. Behind them are the houses—filthy and ramshackle, but gorgeously picturesque seen from my bridge, with the sun warming their pink, white and grey roofs. Behind the houses again is the camp—the tents crawling up the hill like white snails, and more hills and pine trees behind them. The whole thing is so illogical, boats and fishermen on the one hand, and on the other tents and soldiers and bugle calls. That's one of the fascinations of my bridge—the one side is peace, and the other war. I should love to be able to paint a picture of it,—the boats, and the sea, and heavenly lights in the water. The other side a railway bridge stretching across the river and a train creeping slowly over it. In the distance it looks absurdly unreal and toylike. The train is long, and on the trucks are guns, ammunition waggons and lorries, and men are leaning out of the windows, sitting on the roofs and steps, and crowding round the open doors of goods and horse vans. The little toy train is on the direct line to Amiens. Flat, swampy fields and ditches spread round the river, then come the hills and pine woods and the road to P.—P. I stood on the bridge the other morning and saw all this, and I wanted badly to shout or scream or do something stupid. And then some aeroplanes flew over, and soldiers and ambulances and lorries and trams and bicycles came over the bridge, and it all seemed so futile. I came back feeling I'd over-eaten myself on plain bread and butter and the very richest chocolates, two things totally unlike. Ever since I've been here I've got unhappy over unnecessary things—the gorgeous sunsets behind the hills and at sea. The huge red ball sinks lower and lower, and I try frantically to catch some idea in my mind which I can get hold of, and then the impatient sun dips into the sea, and I'm left feeling silly and small, and wondering what It was I was trying so hard to catch hold of. . . .

I'm horrified at the amount and " quality " of what I have written. I feel better, though. I'm not a bit depressed, as all these ravings might seem to indicate, but sometimes the things I see hurt me so that I nearly rave with the desire to put them all down on paper. To create something out of the colossal amount of material there is waiting to be used. Perhaps I shall be able to some day.

Cutty, darling, I hug you. Don't think I've gone off my head. I've just had a spasm, and I had to write it all. I've done it before and torn it up, but this time I have put it in a letter.

Je t'embrasse de tout mon coeur.

TA BONÇE

A.W.T.S.

LIEUTENANT CHARLES STIEBEL I.M.S.

Educated Clifton and Trinity Hall, Cambridge. Medical missionary in India. Killed in action, Mesopotamia, 2 February, 1917, at the age of 40.

[TO HIS WIFE. *Found in his haversack after his death*]

[Mesopotamia]

Darling Tiny,   *Tuesday, December 5, 1916*

As it seems probable we may recommence fighting before long, I am writing you this letter, which I hope it will be unnecessary to post. You see, dear, if anything should happen to me I would like to send you an aftermessage of love and consolation. . . .

Dear, when I see men around me who are, very likely, in many ways better than myself, going to the devil through that cursed drink, and carelessness of God, and I powerless to help (even though I do pray for them), it makes me so sorry, and the contrast between their lot and ours is so great. Now, dear, seeing that we have such blessings, spiritual largely, which I believe are permanent and everlasting, we cannot expect also on that account to get a greater exemption from physical misfortunes, wounds or death, and it is wrong for us to expect it. . . .

I had meant to ask you to pray for one special blessing for me, but I thought I would not frighten you unnecessarily. It is this which troubles me a little, namely, that if it pleases God that I should go into battle, that I may be—not fearless—but showing no fear. You see, all here know that I try to stand for Him, and I would not like to put Him, or you, or the Babies to shame, but I would like to do you credit as you deserve, you brave, good woman. . . .

I believe that if death should separate us for awhile I should always love you. I think sometimes that in such a case, after the worst of the sorrow was over, it would be good for you to marry again. If there was some one good and true and strong to support you, I should be glad.

Dear, I believe that the love of God and the pure love of one another are one and the same thing. Just as a drop of sea-water is in every way like, and part of, the great big sea, so is a pure soul like, and part of, the great God. I don't believe people can all of them always feel the love to God, nor does He expect it, but we know that it will grow up one day, and then it will be so beautiful that we cannot even imagine it now. Still, I hope, as you do, that we shall keep our individuality.

Dear, whatever you do if we are parted, don't despair. It is the devil's strong weapon which hurls many lives to ruin. If faith fails—that is, the faith of the heart and mind

267

—go on living faithfully—that is good enough for God—
and the other will come. . . .

Now, my darling, give my love to the Babies,

Your own lover and husband,

CHARLIE

" The choicest flowers are watered with tears."

MAJOR BERNARD LEWIS
STRAUSS, M.C.
The Buffs

Educated Winchester and New College, Oxford. Joined Army from
Oxford. Killed in action, France, 1 December, 1917, at the age of 25.

[To V. G.]   *Nov. 20th, 1915*
My Dear Golgotha,   Same Address [Flanders]

Your letter was an inspiration, and a revelation—a revelation (if such were needed) of your nobility of character, and
of the real worth and meaning of our friendship—and it
will be an inspiration to me in the long winter months which
lie before me. Altho' I have forgotten exactly what I wired
on the impulse of the moment, it was never a Goodbye to
Liberalism. I think it ran Goodbye. Liberalism for ever !
a flaming watchword ; no farewell cry of departure. Indeed, as you say, I could not say Goodbye, even if I wished
to—for by Liberalism I understand everything worth living
and dying for—that is why years ago I once said that you
and I were the only two real Liberals in Oxford : to us it
was a passionate religion embracing all life's activities, not
merely a hotchpotch of political views—γνῶσις not δόξα—
it still is. With you I share the conviction that nothing dies,
except what is evil.—That is why the thought of Death
has no terrors for me : and if I fall, it will be cheerfully and
with a good conscience, and with the passionate hope that
the sacrifice will not have been in vain—indeed it will not
have been.

Excuse these wandering cries : the mud of Flanders has clogged the mind and pen of one who was once a ready writer. Mud is the keynote of our life : mud, mud, mud, inches deep : on one's feet, clothes, and in one's food : mud everywhere : what a country : I cynically suggested the other day that we should offer it to Greece, as a compensation, instead of Cyprus ! I keep fit and cheerful notwithstanding it is getting extremely cold now, and it looks like a severe winter : the rain and the cold combine in this country to make life difficult : usually in other lands they are rarely on speaking terms. We are out of the trenches now for a rest in a deserted chateau ; oh ! the joy of being warmly within four walls again, even if Monsieur Le Comte, who I believe was a German, has not left behind him many of the appanages of civilized life : still there are fires, and good food to be consumed—and a real lavatory with a real plug.

It is strange being a 2 /Lt. in a Regular Battalion (I have been transferred to the Regulars for the war) : it is like being a new boy at school again : in the 9th I was always one of τὰ ἐν τελεῖ : now I am a very unimportant and insignificant person, who tries to be as active and serviceable as active service conditions will allow him to be—still they are good fellows, my brother officers : and I get on well enough with them. I am not going to harrow you with accounts of life in the trenches : enough to say that it is extremely dangerous (for the enemy is still hostile), dirty and unpleasant ; boring, and dramatic at the same time : quite tolerable, provided one possesses good boots and a good heart : I have only been really miserable for 3 days, when my stomach was out of order : and the world seemed very grey.

Necessity is the Mother of Indigestion : quite original ! I had a very narrow escape from αἰπὺν ὄλεθρον the other day, a bullet grazing my coat, as I was going up by night into the front line. θειᾷ τίνι τυχῇ I have spent many hours with my brother Eric, monocle and all—he is in the same division, and now on leave ; you can imagine the joy of our meeting ; for we are devoted to one another : he is a remarkable person with an extraordinarily eerie and attractive personality : I believe he has done very well out here and is very popular among his fellow officers. . . .

I don't know what is happening, and if I did, I should be overpowered by the knowledge. Things *must* turn out all right some day : that is how I feel : not even Hindenburg can call men from the grave : and sooner or later Germany will have used up her human reservoirs ; do you agree ? I really can't think about it all : I am overpowered by the magnitude. Still, even when ' *fractus illabitur orbis,*' I can appreciate Churchill's splendid defence of his policy in the Commons : I read it to the booming of the heavy guns. A great man ! he will return to his own one day. Carson's resignation left me unmoved. I can't forget Ulster. Do I lack mental proportion ? . . .

Goodnight. Your ever affectionate

BERNARD

LIEUTENANT CLEMENT AUBREY SYMONS

Gloucestershire Regiment

Educated King Edward VI. School, Bath. Schoolmaster. Killed in action, France, 25 September, 1915, at the age of 22.

Somewhere near France

[TO HIS MOTHER] *Sept. 3rd, 1915*

For the first time as long as I can remember I am writing birthday letters on my birthday. Thank you very much indeed for the Pears and the periscope ; it seemed quite like an ordinary birthday yesterday when I got four letters and two parcels, but how different it is really—no picnic, as it always used to be when we were at the sea. How vividly the 3rd always stands out for me—those days up to about two years ago were always so sordidly happy—a good stomach-filling picnic, expectation of presents—the speculation as to how much money I should be sent. Still there is no regret that those days have gone—isn't it curious how one's ideas of being contented and happy change ? I should have been very miserable in the old days if the birthday " treat " had not come up to expectation ; but to-day I am not sure whether it is the 3rd or only the 2nd (I asked several people, and no one is sure, but just " think " it is the 3rd). . . . We had a very easy time from the time of leaving the trenches until we moved off from our rest town —a period of about 8 days. . . . The rest town was crowded with Scotch troops of all sorts, and we were one of the few line regiments there. On the 31st August at 2 P.M. we marched to this place (about 13 miles back from the firing line) with a Divisional Rest ! ! Camp. . . . Talk about 'rest' camp—it's ghastly—one small village which itself is never at rest (dirt and fleas) and about 6000 men billeted there —the H_2O is bad of course, and we have gone back to the ordinary Codford–Cheltenham–Sutton–Vevey–Longridge–Deverill training. Thank goodness we are going back to the trenches. You mustn't think because I talk of the stomach feeling and the ' jumps ' that the trenches frighten me, or that the nerve-strain is anything worse than the nerve-strain of a door banging, because I feel perfectly happy in the trenches, and only object to them at night because of the noise disturbing my sleep. No one is, possibly, fond of the trenches and all long to get out of them, as it's not human nature to us to stand still and do nothing while being bombarded day after day and go on doing nothing. We had a very hard march—at the rate of $3\frac{1}{2}$ m.p.h. As we (the brigade) passed through the various towns and villages, the people thronged out to see us—thinking that we were retreating they looked frightened and asked us repeatedly if we had come from the trenches—our men looked very fatigued, my platoon was the only one in the battalion that lost no men on the march, and No. 2 Coy. lost only 4 to the other Companies' 15's and 20's. I don't know why it should be so, but we seem to have a better stamp of man—either by nature or our training—than the other companies.

We got in at 7 p.m. and found squashed billets waiting for us, flea-ey and no more than 6 sq. ft. for each officer. We are in a coal-mining district, and all the men are long thin and big faced fellows, who are ' ill ' every other day from the effects of cognac. Why we were sent here I can't think, as there isn't room for two battalions, let alone about 10. You mustn't take this grumbling as " unhappiness," as we make ourselves as comfortable as possible under the circs, and manage fairly well, but it *would* be awful if we were hated by the inhabitants.

Well, M., I am spending as happy a birthday as it is possible to do and don't wish for anything more at present, thank you. . . .

The periscope is not a musical instrument (did you really think it was ?) but is very compact and handy—its " harmony " means harmony of mind for the user, I imagine. Good-bye and thanks for the white heather—it will be stored along with my other ' sort of keep-sakes.' Love to all and t'owd man.

―――――

[To His Brother]   [France]

. . . Bombs dropped from aeroplanes do great damage. . . . One was dropped 30 yds. from our Headquarters. Two fellows near by saw the plane coming, and one said to the other : " Wouldn't it be a blighter if they dropped a bomb here ! " Drop it did, and he had his left leg blown off. I saw it hanging across his chest—it looked like a leg of beef —awful ! All he said was " Dear me ! dear me ! " about 100 times, and said the Lord's Prayer over and over. He died in the night. It was the first thing I had seen of the kind, and it upset me badly and it then dawned on me what war was. That was on 15th August : since then―― !

―――――

LIEUTENANT GILBERT WALTER LYTTELTON TALBOT

The Rifle Brigade

Educated Winchester and Christ Church, Oxford. President of the Oxford Union. Killed in action, Flanders, 30 July, 1915, at the age of 24.

[Flanders]

[TO HIS PARENTS] *June [1915]*

. . . In the afternoon, about 5, of June 17, I met Harry Altham (who, as you know, is Staff Captain to our Brigade). He asked me to go with him to see the ruins of the town and of the famous Cloth Hall and Cathedral, which had been visible all the time from our railway embankment about $\frac{1}{2}$ a mile away. I naturally went.

I find it very hard to give you any account of this expedition which fairly describes it, or to avoid writing mere journalese. It was, to start with, intensely moving. One visited the spot which since October has been held by British arms in spite of attacks more violent and persistent than had been dreamt of, and near to which so many thousands of our finest men fell and are now buried. Everybody almost connects the place with some separate individual. It's a quiet little provincial town, partly industrious, and partly just beautiful with its Cathedral and Cloth Hall. The trenches were drawn in a close circle round it, and perhaps never have efforts so great been made to effect anything than the German efforts to burst these few miles. One is partly moved therefore and partly amazed. I despair of telling you what the place looks like. It beggars description. The suburbs of the town are comparatively intact, though most houses there have been shelled. But the whole inside is simply a desolation. You cannot imagine it being rebuilt. We walked through the streets and found not one house which was not a mere mass of ruins or just a big heap of bricks. Of course there are fragments that remain, some with odd familiar advertisements—I saw one of Singer's Sewing Machines. Odder than anything is to go into any

SE 273

of the ruined houses. They nearly all show signs of being abandoned in panic, without their owners waiting so much as to pick up anything : half eaten meals are on the tables : clothes lie in confusion on the floors. Most people take away tiny little bits of loot : I put a few little lace bobbins in my pocket. And then we came into the famous *Place*. The Cloth Hall, roofless and ruined, lies all the way down one side, and the Cathedral is just beyond it. The whole square is covered with loose stones and rubble. As everywhere else in the town, there's not a living soul to be seen, except passing British soldiers. We wandered through the Cloth Hall and saw the fragments of the famous frescoes, and oddly came upon two hearses—pushed inside there by some chance. I didn't go into the Cathedral till the next day. It's not quite as big as Southwark and must have been very lovely. Now it's got no roof and there are huge holes in the walls, and the aisles are heaped high with fallen masonry. I saw two shell holes which made one gape, one by the Cloth Hall, one at the East end of the Cathedral, the last the biggest, 16 yards across and 50 yards round : we measured it.

Nothing has brought the war home to me as has this town. Its people had no connection with the war, no interest in the war, and their lovely home has been gutted until it's unrecognizable. I wish everybody in England could see it. Harry and I remembered that the last expedition we made together was to Oxford. I tried to think of the peace and loveliness of Magdalen and Christchurch on that May evening and to contrast it with the blackened ruins we were now seeing. And we thought what Prussian Militarism would do for Oxford if it could. . . .

CAPTAIN CLAUDE TEMPLER

Gloucestershire Regiment

Educated Wellington and Sandhurst. Regular Army. Wounded and
Prisoner of War, December, 1914. Escaped from Germany, 1917, and
killed in action, France, 4 June, 1918, at the age of 23.

April, 1918
B.E.F., France.

When I was locked up in Germany I used to pray for this
moment ; I used to dream of the romance of war, its wild
strange poetry crept into my soul ; I used to think that the
glory of going back to the beautiful adventure was worth any
price. And now it's all come true, just like things happen in
fairy tales. I go into my dream country like a baby, eyes
wide with wonder, ears strained to catch every note of the
magic music I hear there. In my dream country is a piper
like Hamelin's piper and I follow him. I follow into his
cavern a spell bound child, and I come out at the other end
a warrior fully armed, longing for the day that my mettle
shall be proved. And often I fail and then I must cross over
to the dream country and I must drink romance from the
music of the magic piper. And when I come out of the
cavern again perhaps this time *I win*. The romance of war
and love. That is what the music tells me. And I resolve to
be a worthy warrior. To fight to the finish, to love to the
finish, to sacrifice everything but never honour. And to do
all this with no hope of payment, but as a volunteer, just for
the beautiful poetry of it all.

LIEUTENANT THE HON. EDWARD WYNDHAM TENNANT

Grenadier Guards

Educated Winchester. Joined Army from school. Killed in action, France, 22 September, 1916, at the age of 19.

[TO HIS MOTHER. *He was killed two days later*]

[France]
20th September, 1916

. . . To-night we go up to the last trenches we were in, and to-morrow we go over the top. Our Brigade has suffered less than either of the other two Brigades in Friday's biff (15th), so we shall be in the forefront of the battle. I am full of hope and trust, and pray that I may be worthy of my fighting ancestors. The one I know best is Sir Henry Wyndham, whose bust is in the hall at 44 Belgrave Square, and there is a picture of him on the stairs at 34 Queen Anne's Gate. We shall probably attack over about 1,200 yards, but we shall have such artillery support as will properly smash the Boche line we are going for. And even (which is unlikely) if the artillery doesn't come up to our hopes, the spirit of the Brigade of Guards will carry all resistance before it. The pride of being in such a regiment ! The thought that all the old men, ' late Grenadier Guards,' who sit in the London Clubs, are thinking and hoping about what we are doing here ! I have never been prouder of anything, except your love for me, than I am of being a Grenadier. To-day is a great day for me. That line of Harry's rings through my mind, ' High heart, high speech, high deeds, 'mid honouring eyes.' I went to a service on the side of a hill this morning, and took the Holy Communion afterwards, which always seems to help one along, doesn't it ? I slept like a top last night, and dreamed that someone I know very well (but I can't remember who it was) came to me and told me how much I had grown. Three or four of my brother officers read my poems yesterday, and they all liked them very much, which pleased me enormously.

I feel rather like saying ' If it be possible let this cup pass from me,' but the triumphant finish ' nevertheless not what I will but what Thou willest,' steels my heart and sends me into this battle with a heart of triple bronze.

I always carry four photies of you when we go into action, one is in my pocket-book, two in that little leather book, and one round my neck, and I have kept my little medal of the Blessed Virgin. Your love for me and my love for you have made my whole life one of the happiest there has ever been ; Brutus' farewell to Cassius sounds in my heart : ' If not farewell ; and if we meet again, we shall smile.' Now all my blessings go with you, and with all we love. God bless you, and give you peace.

Eternal Love,

from BIM

SECOND LIEUTENANT ERIC LEVER TOWNSEND
15th London Regiment

Educated City of London School. Killed in action, France, 15 September, 1916, at the age of 20.

[To HIS PARENTS. *Enclosed in his will, to be opened in the event of his death. He was killed a week later*]

Dearest Mother and Father, *September 8, 1916*

You are reading this letter because I have gone under.

Of course I know you will be terribly cut up, and that it will be a long time before you get over it, but get over it you must. You must be imbued with the spirit of the Navy and the Army to " carry on." You will still have dear little D——, who is safe at any rate for some while. If he should ever have to go on active service again I somehow feel that his invariable good luck will bring him through.

You must console yourselves with the thought that I am happy, whereas if I had lived—who knows ?

Remember this saying attributed to Solon, " Call no man happy till he is dead." Thanks to your self-sacrificing love and devotion I have had a happy time all my life. Death will have delivered me from experiencing unhappiness.

It has always seemed to me a very pitiful thing what little difference the disappearance of a man makes to any institution, even though he may have played a very important rôle. A moment's regret, a moment's pause for readjustment, and another man steps forward to carry on, and the machine clanks onward with scarce a check. The death of a leader of the nation is less even than a seven days' wonder. To a very small number it is given to live in history ; their number is scarcely one in ten millions. To the rest it is only granted to live in their united achievements.

But for this war I and all the others would have passed into oblivion like the countless myriads before us. We should have gone about our trifling business, eating, drinking, sleeping, hoping, marrying, giving in marriage, and finally dying with no more achieved than when we were born, with the world no different for our lives. Even the cattle in the field fare no worse than this. They too, eat, drink, sleep, bring forth young, and die leaving the world no different from what they found it.

But we shall live for ever in the results of our efforts.

We shall live as those who by their sacrifice won the Great War. Our spirits and our memories shall endure in the proud position Britain shall hold in the future. The measure of life is not its span but the use made of it. I did not make much use of my life before the war, but I think I have done so now.

One sometimes hears people say, when a young man is killed, " Poor fellow, cut off so early, without ever having had a chance of knowing and enjoying life." But for myself, thanks to all that both of you have done, I have crowded into twenty years enough pleasures, sensations, and experiences for an ordinary lifetime. Never brilliant ; sometimes almost a failure in anything I undertook ; my sympathies and my interests somehow or other—why, I cannot tell— were so wide that there was scarcely an amusement, an occupation, a feeling which I could not appreciate. And as I have said, of most of these I had tasted. I don't suppose I ever met anybody who was not my superior in knowledge or achievement in one particular subject ; but there his knowledge and his interest ended, whereas my interests comprised nearly the whole field of human affairs and activities. And that is why it is no hardship for me to leave the world so young.

Well, I have talked a lot of rot which must have given you great pain to read and which will not bring you much comfort. I had intended to try and say words of comfort, but that scarcely being possible, it has drifted into a sort of confession of faith.

To me has been given the easier task ; to you is given the more difficult—that of living in sorrow. Be of good courage, that at the end you may give a good account.

Kiss D—— for me.

Adieu, best of parents.

Your ever loving son,

ERIC

———

CAPTAIN EDWIN GERALD VENNING

Royal Sussex Regiment

Educated Clergy Orphan School. Actor. Killed in action, France, 6 August, 1915, at the age of 32.

[France,

[TO HIS SISTER]   *May, 1915*]

I am resting now after some fairly strenuous work. Somebody told the powers that I should probably crock up if I were left in position much longer, so they sent up and relieved me. Now I am in a nice little wood, the shells pass over, and fall short, but they don't touch us here, and I'm supremely contented. I've had my clothes off and caught all intruders ; it only remains to get a bath, but that is a great luxury to hope for. A man is actually coming from a far town to cut my hair this afternoon. I've had rather phenomenal luck out here ; twice I've found myself the only officer left. I can tell you no news owing to the Censor's vigilance, or rather to the fact that we are on our honour to impart nothing ; but I can tell you the happenings of weeks, nearly months, ago at Ypres (the regiment has long left there and I can tell you nothing of where we are now). I had rather a ghastly time then. I remember a certain two days during which we attacked incessantly in the open, and I had to lead two bayonet charges. You can't really gather what that means, and I can scarcely tell you. There was an open field between ourselves and the Germans, and I got my men to the edge of it (having lost Lord knows how many from shell fire), and we started a fire fight with rifles and machine-guns at about 5 yards. After some time of this I saw the right move, and gave my orders accordingly ; it was my first charge, my first real big fight. We tried to spring across that field, but the fire was one solid block of lead. Literally I could see no chance for a fly in it, and a high staff personage told me it was the heaviest he had ever heard in that district (the worst on the line). We struggled along some of us. I remember falling about 10 yards ahead of my Company with a slight shrap hit in the back, that didn't even draw blood, and the shock of the revolver at my waist being broken by a bullet ; then I heard my sergeant-major's voice (he's one of the finest men I know) saying, " Where are you, sir ? " He said, " That's right, sir, I'm with you when we get up again." Well, we did get up again, and I had to drop back owing to difficulty in getting my remaining men on. I had a shot at one, and missed him, but it settled the rest, a man by me shouting, but he had his head and shoulders taken off ; they sagged back from him, you know, riddled in a line, and I fell behind the rest of his body just in time. Then my men broke, and I remember standing somewhere in front of the German trenches, with a wounded pal's revolver, that he slipped into my hand, yelling at my men some of the filthiest language ever heard. They were appalled, and I rallied a dozen or so ; as it happened, they were all killed almost at once, and I was left, so far as I could see, alone. Then I ran off the field faster than I have ever run in my life, dodging, taking cover behind dead men, and in shell holes ; at the edge of the field I pulled myself together. Why they didn't get me on the skyline I have no idea. I disguise none of my clothes, and am palpably an officer, revolver and all, including a dead cigarette. I had another talk to the men below, and tried to get them back, but in the middle of it I heard my C.O.'s voice. He said, " It's all right, old man, I ordered them to fall back here." I had heard no order at all, and lost a good many lives rallying. Of course, when I heard it was an order, I dropped on my head off the field into a ditch and lay there. Lord, it was good to be under cover. The rest of it was a rotten affair ; we were surrounded and retired. I was too sick and tired to move, and just lay among the wounded, smoking innumerable cigarettes ; in two or three hours came the order for another attack in a different place, that was worse. We attacked at dawn ; the poor old C.O. was killed among many others. At the end of it I came near to blowing my own head off with my revolver, but a wounded Northumberland officer saved me, and I carried him off the field in a coat. It was a beastly business. Since that time I have had some queer goes and weird escapes. A day or two ago I was sniping a sniper ; he sent one across that burst the sand-bag in front of my head ; the bullet came clean through the bag, but there was just enough sand to turn it a little sideways, and the heat and whirr of it all I felt. That happens so often, though, that one takes no count of it. It's a queer thing, but my impression of all this mighty business is the utter smallness of it all, the infinite smallness ; the meaningless orders, obeyed by brainless heads, all willing to do their little best, until some tiny men cart them off to a little grave behind one of the small houses one uses for headquarters. I can't explain what I mean, but quite literally it all seems far smaller to me than prize-giving, or sports day at school. The Magnificats of journalism serve to show it smaller still. I think in all the world the smallest must be government, but certainly war is scarcely less small. I'm surprised to find my former views so true ; the individual counts, and this aggressive herding is almost too mean to notice at all. I was never more disappointed. Where I looked for grandeur, I find a pettiness lost sight of almost since my school-days. I'm writing acres ; I really must stop and do some work ; there's plenty of it here.

Oh, I'm so pleased ; my Q.M. Sergeant was asked to go for promotion yesterday and be made a S.M., but he heard it meant leaving me for another Company and refused to take it. My servant also refused because he would not be able to look after me. So evidently my love of men is not wasted here. I think I know the ways and peculiarities of every man of mine ; it surprises them, and they like it and work well for it. I must go. Yours,

G.

[France
[To His Sister]   June 20, 1915]

I am still stuck in this trench, and so far as I know not likely to be relieved for some days, as I've had a week of it, and the regulation dose is four days. You can imagine that my nerves are not exactly what they should be for the moment. I haven't washed or had my clothes off at all, and my average of sleep has been $2\frac{1}{2}$ hours in the twenty-four. I don't think I've started to crawl yet, but I don't suppose I should notice if I had ; it is a matter of such small import-ance. My particular desire just now, apart from running this concern to the best advantage, is to get home. My men are awfully cheery; they are the best souls in the world, bless them, although I've lost a good many lately. It's been rather harrowing these last two days, especially for one who, if you remember, was up to quite a mature age, afraid in the dark. But there are points in the life that appeal to me vastly, the contrast for instance : The long, lazy, hot days, when no work is done, and any part of the body that protrudes about the trench is most swiftly blown off; the uncanny, shrieking, hard-fought nights with their bizarre and beastly experiences, their constant crack and thunder, their stealthy seeking for advantage, and regardless seizure of it, and in the middle of it all perhaps a song sung round a brazier, a joke or two yelled against the noise of shells and rifles until the sentries warning. I stay as little as possible at headquarters, and spend almost all the night with my men, taking a rifle, sometimes even sharing a guard with them, and we are all fast pals. It's a great life for some things, but it's a dirty repulsive and utterly foolish game, and I feel sick for words to think that war and international attainment is nothing more than this—this infantile, puerile, heedless rubbish. Good Lord, my dear, there'll be people so glad when it is all over that some, I think, may drop dead from sheer joy and others from heart-break with the despondency of what has been. Surely it is not good that we should explode the human body and mind into all twists and writhes and leave it to work out its own death, as best it has strength. Yet I have seen roads and railroads lined with unrecognizable creatures, living, cursing, dead, and utterly forsaken, all struggling and trying to turn their blind efforts at what we call patriotism to some kind of individual peace. Happily one has no chance to think. The "Why?" and "What is it all about?" trouble only the few. Well, my dear, I've been thoroughly depressing without in the least meaning to, but you must understand that every night here is an age of nerve-wracking tenseness, and one may be safe and well and yet overstrung. You understand, dear, I'm awfully fit, eat like a pig, and show no more sign of wear than my neighbour, that I am about as

safe now as a man reasonably can be, and do not worry at
all (I have no time to). But I felt like talking to someone,
so I have talked to you. Well, I'm going to have a short
sleep now. My very, very best love to all of you, dear ! I
do so want to see you all. Love.

G.

I'm thinking this letter makes me look a bit of a fool.
Well, I am in a way—you know just how much of a fool, so
what does it matter ? But you mustn't worry about me ; I'm
getting on a treat, and I've never been better. You wait till
you see me. Bye-bye, kid.

SECOND LIEUTENANT ROBERT
ERNEST VERNÈDE
The Rifle Brigade

Educated St. Paul's and St. John's College, Oxford. Writer ; author of
The Pursuit of Mr. Faviel. Died of wounds, France, 9 April, 1917, at the
age of 41.

[France]
[To His Wife]   *Sunday, February 6 [1916]*

I am very well and fit but I suppose I have just found out
what it can be like. We have been heavily shelled for about
two hours, and one sat there with intervals of seconds, it
seemed, not knowing where the next would come. The
Boches have just left off for the day, I hope, as, though the
casualties were not heavy, it was enough for everybody's
nerves. Several men are suffering from shock—shivering
and quaking and having to be carried off on stretchers. I'm
sitting beside a bad case now—he can't even move. The
marvel is that he came out alive—he was one of four in a
dug-out, and was pulled out uninjured, the rest being
killed. I don't want to meet any one who's had a ripping
time out here. . . .

T. is splendid under this sort of thing. I wasn't as bad as I expected. I was in our dug-out to begin with with two Buff officers and got a stone pretty hard on my tin hat, after which I proposed we should move out, which we did, and the dug-out was knocked in a little later. Sat behind the parapet with the Buffs trying to find a safe place, but there wasn't any available. Found a man horribly injured in the face, with the C.S.M. who had just escaped. Tried to give him morphia, but couldn't manage it, so went for stretcher-bearers, who attended to him.

Boches have just begun shelling again—confound them —after half an hour's interval. Will send this off if we get out safely. We move in about three hours—none too soon.

Monday. Arrived here safe and sound in support trenches about 3.30 a.m. after the most unpleasant day—very nearly —that I've had. I still think it's right that war should be damnable, but I wish everybody could have an idea of how beastly it can be.

The Boches shelled us twice yesterday after I wrote, but only for a little, I'm glad to say, as everybody had had enough, I think, and several of the oldest hands said it was the worst shelling they had ever been through. Our casualties were remarkably small considering that whenever you crouched two or three shells seemed to split over your head every second. We had only five killed and about a dozen injured. T. sat most of the time with a wounded man across his knees, and the man said he knew it would be all right when the captain came along : which I thought was rather nice. One of our best sergeants was killed—a very nice man who was rather a friend of mine, though not in my platoon. I think the men are wonderful and awfully good to one another. The C.S.M. was knocked senseless by the same shell that injured the man I mentioned, and when he came to, dragged him into the dug-out, to which I traced them by a pool of blood. Even the chef, when I went for the stretcher-bearers, dashed out and leapt an open part of the trench where it had been crumped in to go and help, which I'm afraid will render me weak-minded towards his cookery in future ; the shells flying as hard as ever. It's an extraordinary sensation—every portion of the trenches seemed to have shells exploding over them and you were nearly deafened by the near ones. I really was in a great state of funk, but I'm not sure that it's avoidable. The least sensitive of the men, I fancy, are strung up to the last pitch, and I doubt if even T. was as cool as he looked, though looking it is all the battle under the circumstances.

C. was our only other officer there and he was very cool, and pulled the living man out of the smashed dug-out, which was a terrible sight. I would like all praisers of war to be under that sort of fire for a day, and if any remained, they would have less to say for it. The Buff youths were young and quite cheery, though they would ask me where to go, which I wasn't at all competent to tell them, and had to make them try several places without finding any that was really of use. At the end of it—about 5 o'clock—T., C. and I ate cake without tea and waited for the regiment that was due to relieve us. The latter arrived about two or three hours after time—a thing that can be singularly annoying under those circumstances, as the Boches began shelling again after we should have been well away, and I thought it was all going to recommence for another three hours. Luckily it didn't and I got off with my party about 11.30 p.m. for a five mile walk in thigh gum-boots and all our packs and things. I don't know when I have been more hot and exhausted. Rather over halfway luckily we came to the place where we hand in the gum-boots—an enormous dark building where they gave us hot soup (it tasted of tea and oxo mixed—in muddy cups !), grateful and comforting nevertheless. During the last half of the way we passed a man who'd gone lame from another platoon and I dropped behind to give him directions, but couldn't find him in the dark, so went on by myself. Rather eerie in the dark in unknown country with the sound of the guns in the distance.

I was very glad to get in at 3.30 a.m. and find hot tea and a bed. Have washed this morning—first time for four days !

Outside there is the most peaceful scene I have seen for weeks—green fields and unstruck trees, though the brutes put a few shells over here even, yesterday.

I couldn't get this off yesterday as there was no posting during the shells, but it will go this afternoon.

I feel rather doubtful as to whether I should tell you quite the unpleasantest side like this ; but I think it's rather good that nowadays, when women have so much influence, they should not be fooled with the rosy side of things only. I don't think I'm using my imagination. At any rate I'm willing to bet that not one of the men but would have given a good deal to be out of it.

———

LIEUTENANT ALGERNON HYDE VILLIERS
Machine-Gun Corps

Educated Wellington and Magdalen College, Oxford. Stockbroker. Killed in action, France, 23 November, 1917, at the age of 31.

Abbassia.
October 25th [1914]

One of the many miseries of war is the confusion it brings. I remember French stories about '70 which made one feel the desolation brought by the destruction of the many little certainties on which we commonly depend. It is just when by the war we need them most that these things go, isn't it ? and that suggests the only grain of comfort which one can get from this hideous state of things—that the true values of life emerge with irresistible clearness. There is a moral value in the great upheaval and the testing which all are going through, but I remember of old that I used to argue against Johnner that the destruction and ruin lasting on for generations, after the moral élan of a warlike effort was spent, more than outweighed the value of the latter. I am of the same opinion still. If one could really believe that a different world would come out of this struggle, one could be more hopeful. But I don't now see any good reason for the feeling one had in the first excitement that the old order was changing. Not by such means are the changes brought which matter. We shall go back to the same world with more antagonisms and a huge legacy of broken lives, broken homes and broken resources. Poverty will be greater and the hope of alleviating it dimmer. Still, there is for me at least a strong sense of the other side of the medal. . . .

I will try and set down after a month's trial what seem to be the really good things which this life is teaching me to recognise. I speak with full consciousness of the shortness of the trial, and therefore very " provisionally," and of the difficulty of making such things clear to oneself, still more to anybody else. First there is the delight of having quite definite new things to master. In every life one is always learning about new things. Here, however, they are gloriously defined—to ride and groom, to drill and shoot. Then there is the health of these simple things and the satisfaction of doing them. . . . One feels one's successes so keenly too—a horse under good control—a horse nicely groomed—a good bit of drill, and without doubt in time a straight shot—these are very *savoureux* things. The long and short of it all is, this is a man's life, and it does look as if by the sweat of his brow a man should live.

CAPTAIN ARTHUR GRAEME WEST
Oxford and Bucks Light Infantry

Educated Blundell's and Balliol College, Oxford. Post-graduate student at Oxford. Killed in action, France, 3 April, 1917, at the age of 26.

[TO A FRIEND]   An Estaminet [France]
Dear Lad,   *Saturday, Feb. 12th, 1916*

I had your letter this afternoon and set myself to answer it at once. We have had rather a bloody—literally—time of it. The Tab I had met early at Woldingham was shot in the head and killed instantly one night standing next to me, and you may have observed that we lost several officers. We had an extraordinarily heavy bombardment. Also I had rather an exciting time myself with two other men on a patrol in the " no man's land " between the lines. A dangerous business, and most repulsive on account of the smells and appearance of the heaps of dead men that lie unburied there as they fell, on some attack or other, about four months ago. I found myself much as I had expected in the face of these happenings : more interested than afraid, but more careful for my own life than anxious to approve any new martial ardour. I become, I assure you, more and more cautious, though more accustomed and easy in face of the Hun.

For the moment, thank God, we are back resting, and the certain knowledge that I shan't be killed anyhow for a day or two is most invigorating.

The spring is manifest here, in young corn, and the very air and strong winds : and even here I react to it, and find myself chanting verses of " *Love in the Valley* " as I did last year in Surrey. I have an odd feeling, though very insistent and uplifting to me, a feeling which I probably vainly unfold to you, of being so integrally a part of, and so thoroughly approved and intimately associated with all these evidences of spring, that Nature herself will not suffer me to be killed, but will preserve unharmed a lover so loyal and keen-sighted as myself. We shall see. . . .

It is bruited about that the Battalion starts leave in a day or two. My God ! What heaven it will be while it lasts, and what awful hell going back !

However, I live so utterly in the moment that I can easily shelve the last few hours till they come. I hope it arrives when the spring is farther on. I will bear witness to all I can to keep you out of the Army ; I am so intensely pleased that you've not got forced in yet, and I hope you will still escape. How bloody people seem to be in England about peace and peace meetings. I suppose they are getting rather Prussian in the country, but are all peace meetings always broken up by soldiers (who've probably never been here at all) ?

I have contracted hatred and enmity for nobody out here, save soldiers generally and a few N.C.O.'s in particular. For the Hun I feel nothing but a spirit of amiable fraternity that the poor man has to sit just like us and do all the horrible and useless things that we do, when he might be at home with his wife or his books, as he preferred. Well, well ; who is going to have the sense to begin talking of peace ? We're stuck here until our respective Governments have the sense to do it. . . .

I must really stop, dear lad.

A. G. W.

————

LIEUTENANT MALCOLM GRAHAM WHITE
The Rifle Brigade

Educated Birkenhead School and King's College, Cambridge. Assistant Master, Shrewsbury. Killed in action, France, 1 July, 1916, at the age of 29.

1st Bn. The Rifle Brigade—
B.E.F.

[TO MRS. HOWSON]   *May 27, 1916*

I have been very busy lately, in temporary command of my Company, and always shadowed by the knowledge that, if I did a thing well, it would be taken for granted, and if I did anything wrong, or if anybody in my Company did anything wrong (which is the same thing), I should most certainly be blamed. All this, at a time when this country has been almost as beautiful as England, gave me much sympathy with the Scout in *Punch*, who was sent out to find the enemy, and returned breathless, saying ' The lilacs are out.' As indeed they are.

I never know what to think about democracy, except that it seems to me the most ideal kind of government, and the only really justifiable one. It is the only system which does ultimately and theoretically lead to freedom. I always feel that it is a system which has never gone right yet, but which it is a duty to make to go right. It produces bad results, but it has got to be made to produce good results, simply because in the world of ideal, and not in the world of fact, it is the right system. I do agree with you most heartily as to the hopelessness of democracy without education. It is terribly unfortunate that the hour-hand of Power should be so far ahead of the minute-hand of Education. But I don't think we can help that, except by putting forward the minute-hand of Education. And, by the way, it is comforting to remember that, with most clocks, the minute-hand also works the hour-hand. At present we seem to be letting Education suffer by the War equally with other things. The saying that ' We don't care about Education in England ' seems to be quite true.

But all this does not prove the badness of democracy as an ideal ; it only proves its impracticability. And I think the answer to that is that we must make democracy ' work ' because it is the right ideal. If democracy without education is hopeless, then we must educate, not give up democracy. There is no ideal in the world that has ' worked ' yet. Christianity is still only an ideal, because we don't believe in it enough to make it a fact. Justice and honesty don't really ' pay,' because there are not enough people who practise them. There is very little idealism in the world so far. So far, the only thing which really produces idealism is, unfortunately, war, and the thing called patriotism. When a war breaks out, thousands of leisured young men, who have hitherto thought of little but of how to enjoy themselves, who have hitherto turned their backs on all that was unpleasant and all that provoked thought, suddenly discover that, though it was not ' up to them ' to live for their country in peace time, yet it is absolutely their duty to die for it in war time, and fling away their lives with heroism. It is, apparently, easier to fight for one's country than to devote one's leisure to social problems. That is to me the most amazing thing.

So far, with all our civilisation, we have not yet discovered any other way of expressing our idealism than by war. Even the poets, who ought to know better, haven't got much farther. Wordsworth says : ' How ennobling thoughts depart, When men change swords for ledgers ' ; and Rupert Brooke, in his 1914 sonnets, seemed to welcome the War as a release from materialism. The arts are inspired by war, and in the pulpit it is able to be reconciled with Christianity, because of the great unselfish, non-utilitarian virtues which it produces. But when the world is really democratic, perhaps peace will inspire us in the same way. . . .

We are not actually in the trenches at present, but we make frequent tedious visits to them to work by day and night, and return to a village and listen to the guns from a respectful distance. It is not so lovely a place as some that I have lately seen, and the inhabitants rather hate us. In fact, the lady of this house wanted to turn us away the first night we arrived, very late after a long march. The good woman still brings us absurd little complaints daily, and my servant, generally the culprit, stands gravely to attention in the doorway, while she delivers them. All of which pleases me hugely, because it reminds me that the English are not the only selfish people.

———

[France]
[TO A. E. KITCHIN]   *Whit-Sunday, June 11, 1916*

I am reviving my interest again in the European problem. Do you know, I believe that, if we win, the best solution will be almost the status quo, because it would only be the status quo materially, not spiritually. For the Germans would not be humiliated, and the large better element among them (I don't believe it doesn't exist) would probably ' rapproche ' with the good elements among the Allies, and that would be the basis for a European understanding and a determination on all our parts to behave better in future, seeing how little the War would have brought to all of us. The greatest victory that could be won in this War would be, not the particular gain of one or a few nations, but the tragic realisation by all nations that nobody has gained anything ; statement ! As for ' The War after the War,' and Mr. Hughes, and all that disastrous sort of idea—-what *are* we to do about it ? . . .

I am longing for more news from Shrewsbury.

SECOND LIEUTENANT ALFRED RICHARD WILLIAMS
Machine Gun Corps
Journalist. Killed in action, France, 16 August, 1917, at the age of 23.

[France]
Oct. 16th, 1916

You will know by this that we have had another pleasant sojourn out of the trenches. When we return, which we are likely to do shortly, it will be to something more satisfying to some of us than the stagnant wearing unproductive sort of existence that we have led in recent weeks. It is the physical, and not so much the mental strain that tells now. A year ago it was just otherwise. It is remarkable to what conditions the mind becomes accustomed, irrespective of nervous wear and tear.

I am glad Father is so optimistic about the prospect. I fear he expects too much. I quite agree that events have been for the best so far. Had my commission come through in March I should have gone home without some experiences, which, however coarsening and destructive of the finer instincts in human nature, have an emotional and intellectual value in framing one's outlook on war.

So much is written about the war now-a-days, and in proportion so little of it strikes a right and wholesome note, —and yet it is so clear. It is nothing but an intimately personal tragedy to every British (and German) soldier concerned in the *fighting* part of it. Also it is quite the exception to note any ill feeling towards the individual German. I saw to-day a sentry pointing out our Lewis Gun with animation to a prisoner working by the road side, expatiating on its qualities, to all appearance to an interested listener. In many cases it is impossible not to feel pity. The belief at home that the individual enemy is an incurable barbarian is simply wrong, however black his record has been in the war organisation. I confess to some distrust (and here you may differ from me) of the attitude which consents to, and even demands, a permanent European estrangement. Germany has got to be beaten, and, in that way, since it is the only way, shown the error of her ways. *Then*, we must not only tolerate the return of the whipped child into the family circle again, but, if we sincerely want peace, not merely for our own advantage but for the sake of peace itself, we must even be prepared to lend a helping hand.

But I am rambling rather stupidly, and the noise of the " whipping " is never far distant. . . .

———

CAPTAIN THEODORE PERCIVAL CAMERON WILSON

Sherwood Foresters

Educated Oxford. Schoolmaster and writer. Killed in action, France, 23 March, 1918, at the age of 29.

10th Sher. For.
17th Div.
B.E.F.
France.

[To His Mother] *1/3/16*

. . . I saw about 50 German prisoners marched through the village. Three officers were in front—white, broken, muddy, and one of them wounded. Most of the men were very boyish and intelligent looking, but one officer, who looked about 20, was one of the noblest looking men I have ever seen. He held his head up and looked so proud that I could have wept. War is indescribably disgusting. Any man who has seen it and praises it is degenerate. I had a long time to think, by myself, on that fatigue job—under the stars, and please God I'll live to put some of it in print, one day, but I can't write it in a letter. The rats interrupted me. They are fat and grey and bold. One came and looked at me and squealed at about 3 o'clock in the morning when I could see no prospect of going to bed ever, and so infuriated me that I slashed at him with my stick and splashed my whole face so with mud that I had to spend the next hour or so trying to get a lump of it out of my eye. I missed the rat, and imagined him with a paw to his horrible nose laughing at me. There's a subject for Charlie's pencil. Well that's all the news, darling. As to my own feelings under fire, I was *horribly* afraid—*sick* with fear—not of being hit, but of seeing other people torn, in the way that high explosive tears. It is simply hellish. But thank God I didn't show any funk. That's all a man dare ask, I think. I don't care a flip whether I'm killed or not—though I don't think I shall be—the chances are about 100 to 1. Out here you must trust yourself to a bigger Power and leave it at that. You can't *face* death (I've used the phrase myself about this war). There's no facing it. It's everywhere. You have to walk through it, and under it and over it and past it. Without the sense of God taking up the souls out of those poor torn bodies—even though they've died cursing Him —I think one would go mad. . . .

----

10 Sherwood Foresters.

B.E.F.

27.4.16

[To His Aunt]

Thank you so much for your two cheery letters and your offer of things for the men, which I have accepted gratefully by asking Mother for cigarettes. Someday I'm going to write a ' paper ' on the ' psychology of the cigarette ' ! It fills the place in a man's life, out here, which the snuff box held with the old French aristocrat. It helps a man to go to his death with a brave hypocrisy of carelessness, just as it helped the aristocrat to go daintily to the guillotine. But I can't enlarge on it here. I'm writing in a trench not very far from the Germans and I've just heard the first cuckoo ! It's blazing sunlight. Behind, there is a French town—quivering in the heat—chimneys and roofs apparently intact from here, though the whole place in reality is a mere *husk* of a town. Nearer, between the town and us, is a village, which is quite a ruin—its church spire a broken stump, its house walls honeycombed with shell fire. Then comes a great blazing belt of yellow flowers—a sort of mustard or sharlock—smelling to heaven like incense, in the sun—and above it all are larks. Then a bare field strewn with barbed wire—rusted to a sort of Titian red—out of which a hare came just now, and sat up with fear in his eyes and the sun shining red through his ears. Then the trench. An indescribable mingling of the artificial with the natural. Piled earth with groundsel and great flaming dandelions, and chickweed, and pimpernels, running riot over it. Decayed sandbags, new sandbags, boards, dropped ammunition, empty tins, corrugated iron, a smell of boots, and stagnant water and burnt powder and oil and men, the occasional bang of a rifle, and the click of a bolt, the occasional crack of a bullet coming over, or the wailing diminuendo of a ricochet. And over everything the larks and a blessed bee or two. And far more often, very high up in the blue—a little resolute whitish-yellow fly of an aeroplane—watching, watching—speaking, probably, by wireless to the hidden stations behind the lines ; dropping, when he thinks fit, a sort of thunderous death on to the green earth under him ; moving with a sort of triumphant calm through the tiny snow-white puffs of shrapnel round him. And on the other side, nothing but a mud wall, with a few dandelions against the sky, until you look over the top, or through a periscope, and then you see barbed wire and more barbed wire, and then fields with larks over them, and then barbed wire again—German wire this time—and a long wavy line of mud and sandbags—the German line —which is being watched all day from end to end with eyes which hardly wink. The slightest movement on it— the mere adjusting of sandbag from below—is met with fire. The same goes on of course with our line. Look over the top for longer than two seconds and you are lucky to step down without a bullet through your brain. By day it's very quiet. Some twenty shells or so have come over this morning from the German side. You hear a sound rather like a circular saw cutting through thin wood and moving towards you at the same time with terrific speed straight for your middle it seems, till you get used to it ! It ends in a terrific burst—a shower of earth or bricks or metal, a quiet cloud of smoke—and sometimes a torn man to be put out of sight, or hurried down to the dressing station. Sometimes, but astonishingly seldom with this desultory shelling. Of course a real bombardment where the sky is one screaming sheet of metal, is hell indescribable. This place is very quiet, on the whole. But even the beauty of

Spring has something of purgatory in it—the sort of purgatory a madman may know who sees all beautiful things through a veil of obscenity. Whatever war journalists may say, or poets either, blood and entrails and spilled brains *are* obscene. I read a critique of Le Gallienne's out here, in which he takes Rupert Brooke to task for talking of war as ' cleanness.' Le Gallienne is right. War is about the most unclean thing on earth. There are certain big clean virtues about it—comradeship and a whittling away of non-essentials, and sheer stark triumphs of spirit over shrinking nerves, but it's the calculated death, the deliberate tearing of fine young bodies—if you've once seen a bright-eyed fellow suddenly turned to a goggling idiot, with his own brains trickling down into his eyes from under his cap—as I've done, you're either a peace-maker or a degenerate. . . . God help us all ! I pray, when I fire a rifle myself into the unknown, that if that little singing splinter of metal must kill someone it will a man who loves killing. But I wonder does it ? It may take the life of some Saxon boy who thinks the Kaiser a god, and who has a girl waiting for him at home. All this is what Bismarck would call weakness. . . . Well, all this is perhaps a little florid. One lives a life of continuous strain and reaction, strain and reaction, and it's difficult to write or think quite quietly. We are a very cheerful crowd, needless to tell *you*, who saw the wounded Tommies in ' Blighty.' They are very wonderful people.

Much love to you, and many thanks

from

JIMMY

———

[France]

[TO MRS. ORPEN]   *3.5.16*

. . . We've just had a very trying day, as the Hun has bombarded us rather violently and smashed up one or two men badly. That is a rare thing just here, as we are so quiet that they call it a rest cure ! Machine guns and rifle fire are, as a rule, all we have to suffer, though they are bad enough in all conscience. I wish I could see you, and tell you a little of what I think of war. It is utterly peaceful now. Evening, with birds singing their hearts out, larks over the fields, lilac in the gardens of the poor ruined farms round us, a wonderful sea of brilliant yellow turnip-flower which smells like meadow-sweet, swallows flying high and happy —and, higher still, a little resolute yellow-white fly of an aeroplane, watching, watching, and moving with a sort of calm certainty through the shrapnel which is bursting round it. That is very far and unreal. The shells burst silently, in snow-white puffs of smoke, which remain for ten minutes or so unchanged by wind or rain in those still places. It is as though some huge hand dabbed the blue canvas with little fanciful flakes of white. Then, many seconds later, you hear the bang of the shell, and the whine of the fragments through the air—very faint and elfin. It is as I say, unreal, and not terrible, somehow, to us on the green earth here. But every now and then there comes a sound like a steam-saw cutting through thin wood and moving towards you with great speed. It ends suddenly, far off, in thunder. At any minute it may end in thunder close at hand. It is merely an interesting phenomenon to those new comers who haven't yet seen the work a shell can do. To the rest who *have* seen, it is a terrible and fiendish thing, which one must keep so to speak, masked—which one mustn't talk too much of ! I saw a man to-day, for instance —No. One can't describe it. Only the memory of things like it makes one see this Spring evening's beauty through a sort of veil of obscenity, as a madman may see beauty. For mangled bodies are obscene whatever war-journalists may say. *War* is an obscenity. Thank God we are fighting this to stop war. Otherwise very few of us could go on. Do teach your dear kids the horror of responsibility which rests on the war-maker. I want so much to get at children about it. We've been wrong in the past. We have *taught* schoolboys " war " as a romantic subject. We've made them learn the story of Waterloo as a sort of exciting story in fiction. And everyone has grown up soaked in the poetry of war—which exists, because there is poetry in everything, but which is only a tiny part of the great dirty tragedy. All those picturesque phrases of war writers—such as " he flung the remnants of his Guard against the enemy," " a magnificent charge won the day and the victorious troops, etc. etc.," are dangerous because they show nothing of the *individual* horror, nothing of the fine personalities smashed suddenly into red beastliness, nothing of the sick fear that is tearing at the hearts of brave boys who ought to be laughing at home—a thing infinitely more terrible than physical agony. I can't explain it all without getting into a sort of confounded journalese swing of words, but you'll understand. It isn't death we fear so much as the long-drawn expectation of it—the sight of other fine fellows ripped horribly out of existence by " reeking shard," as a great War-journalist says who spoke (God forgive him) of " a fine killing " in some battle or other.

Meanwhile there are the compensations of a new sort of comradeship, of new lights on life, of many many new beauties in humanity. I hope I shall come through it alive, though it's doubtful. I hope I shall be a much, much better sort of person for it all though that is a selfish sort of aspect of a huge drama like this. Anyhow I suppose one's friendships don't end here ?

Strangely enough, or is it naturally enough, I have found myself growing reluctantly *materialistic* out here—I don't think that is quite the word, but I find myself—my *reason*— doubting so much, such as the survival of personal identity —the whole idea of personality or individuality is so very difficult to keep, before what one sees of man's mortality. Anyhow there is always God. That stays firm. And if He *is Love*, it must all be working out somehow, but how sad He must be sometimes, when even a little little heart like one's own nearly bursts with pity. Don't think me overwrought or sentimental—unduly so at any rate—I am sticking things very well really. Only to you who understand so well, it is a relief to pour out a little of all one feels.

B.E.F.

[TO HAROLD MONRO]   *1.6.16*

I wish you were here, with your sympathy and your power of laughing at the same things as the man you're with—laughing and weeping, almost, it would be here. Here's a thing that happened. When I first " joined " out here I noticed a man—a boy, really, his age was just 19— who had those very calm blue eyes one sees in sailors sometimes, and a skin burnt to a sort of golden brown. I said to him, " When did you leave the Navy?" and he regarded this as the most exquisite joke ! Every time I met him he used to show his very white teeth in a huge smile of amusement, and we got very pally when it came to real bullets— as men do get pally, the elect, at any rate. Well, the other day there was a wiring party out in front of our parapet— putting up barbed wire (rusted to a sort of Titian red). It is wonderful going out into ' No Man's Land.' I'll tell you about it one day—stars and wet grass, and nothing between you and the enemy, and every now and then a very soft and beautiful blue-white light from a Very pistol— bright as day, yet extraordinarily unreal. You have to keep still as a statue in whatever position you happen to be in, till it dies down, as movement gives you away. Well, that night they turned a machine gun on the wiring party, and the ' sailor boy ' got seven bullets, and died almost at once. All his poor body was riddled with them, and one went through his brown throat.

When I went over his papers I found a post-card addressed to his mother. It was an embroidered affair, on white silk. They buy them out here for 40 centimes each, and it had simply " remember me " on it. And they say " don't get sentimental ! " I wanted you then, to—oh ! just to be human.

We had to collect what had been a man the other day and put it into a sandbag and bury it, and less than two minutes before he had been laughing and talking and *thinking.* . . .

We are much happier now. Out of the "strafe" and in a quiet village, from which visits to the trenches are simply a rather exciting little jaunt instead of a dangerous duty!

And now for my most exciting bit of news. I was sitting yesterday at my table—where I am writing this—when the door opened and in walked Sir Douglas Haig—the C. in C!! The room was full of officers all discussing high tactics or swearing at the weather, or telephoning or consulting maps, and an "awful hush" fell. Our General was with him and they walked round, talking to each officer in the room. They were all Staff Majors and Colonels and I was the only New Army man in the room and the only subaltern at that, and I had a hole in the knee of my breeches! I tried to slip out (my table is near the door) but everyone was standing motionless to attention and the Colonel—my Colonel—frowned at me to stand still, which I did, feeling awful.

When the C. in C. came opposite me, the General said "This is Wilson, sir, who is helping us with staff work." The C. in C., to my great confusion, put out his hand and we shook hands. (Historic moment! Licks Nelson and Wellington hollow, doesn't it?)

The C. in C. is a wonderful looking man with a very firm chin, and dark blue eyes (or slate coloured). He is rather short but very broad and strong looking. He looks at everything so directly and deliberately that you would almost think he was doing something difficult in just seeing—if you know what I mean. He never takes his eyes off the eyes of the man he is talking to.

He said "What's your regiment?" I said "The Sherwood Foresters."

C. in C. "What battalion?"

I. "10th, Sir."

C. in C. "Oh! are you a New Army officer?"

I. "Yes, Sir."

C. in C. "You weren't a soldier before the war?"

" No, Sir."

Our General. "Wilson enlisted in the ranks in August 1914, Sir."

C. in C. " *Did* you ? *Did* you ? "

He asked about 6 questions, said something very complimentary, and as he turned to the door, said " Good luck ! " leaving me red to the roots of my hair, feeling an awful fraud and a silly ass, and ready to cut my hand off for him if he asked me. Wasn't it splendid of him, though, to talk like that to a mere New Army Sub. in the midst of countless be-ribboned red-hats to whom he only said a few words. I have had my leg pulled horribly about it here —as they all say I had bribed the General to put in a good word for me, and that I was the only man " Sir Douglas " wished " good luck " to, and that he only stood in front of me for so long because he had never seen anything so odd to look at before in his life, and wanted a good stare while he was about it ! They also say that I was polishing my hand on the back of my breeches before I shook hands and that I called him " Duggie, old boy " and asked after " Mrs. Duggie ! . . ." Everyone rags all day here. They are a most jolly crowd. Out of work hours we hardly ever stop laughing. . . .

Well, good luck.

Yours very sincerely,

T. P. C. W.

CAPTAIN WILLIAM SCOTT BRANKS WILSON
The Cameronians

Educated Hamilton Academy and Glasgow University. Lawyer. Killed in action, France, 19 September, 1918, at the age of 39.

[France]

[To His Wife]   *15.9.18*

I think, to pass the time, I'll write you a little sketch of one day in the great stunt. At two o'clock in the afternoon a chit comes round, as we are in a sunken roadway in fairly good dugouts and huts. " Company will move to sunken roads leading south from cross-roads at U25, 6.45 " (or some such thing) " in support of the . . . Brigade. Move to be completed by 5.45 p.m., and notified by code word ' Bananas.' Company Commanders will reconnoitre the roads forthwith. . . ."

Up I get, rather ill-natured, and walk with a perspiring runner down the trench, and have a look at the place—no dugouts, no anything. Two platoons put in road to cut niches for themselves, and put a sheet of corrugated iron on top. Two platoons in trenches, Company H.Q. in field behind. I, as a man of luxurious habits and somewhat refined tastes take a disused and partly roofless stable as my spot. Go round and see all O.K., arrange as to rations and water, and exchange reports with H.Q. as to my place. Back come the wounded of the . . . Brigade through my lines, walking cases first, some cheerful, some wind up, and later stretcher cases, some also cheerful, some fed up, some ominously quiet. Then we try to cook a little tea, dinner, and supper combined but have to put out our fire four times, because a bombing Taube, with its ominous drone, comes over, looking for a place to lay its eggs.

A walk round to see all is quiet, then back to my stable, too cold to sleep, so huddle up, smoke a cigarette or two, then at midnight, just as I am beginning to doze off, up comes a runner. " Company Commanders will report at Battalion Headquarters immediately, with maps." Turn to my sub. and say, " Well, we're for it to-morrow morning ; it is a case of ' Over you go and the best of luck.' " Off to Battalion H.Q. I go. " Come in. Have some coffee ? Are we all here ? " And so to detail, objective, routes, and the task. Zero hour is confirmed, and watches checked. Nothing to be done till the word " Move " comes, and then all companies to be at jumping-off trench before 4.30 a.m. Back, and go over position with my platoon commanders, and, just as we are finished, in comes order, " Move." Send runner round platoons, etc., all to be at sunken road facing north at 3.15 a.m. Then we have a cup of tea, and don't stop for Taubes. After all, if you go over the top at 5.30 an aeroplane at three doesn't matter a cuss.

At 3.30 the road is full of struggling figures, and up you go the head of the column. " Everybody here, Sergeant Major ? " No. 13 Platoon not up yet. Fussing and annoyance. At last reported all up, and we march off. Half a mile, and we get to what the map calls a village, but no signs of anything except long grass and desolation. Then we come to four cross-roads, and down to a corner where with a match I look at the map. Yes, it should be the centre one. Then on below camouflage strips and behind trees. The road gets worse and worse, and shell-holes thicker. The place gets more desolate till we are quite sure we have lost the way. However, up pops the head of the Battalion Scout Officer, who says, " What company is that ? " " D Company." " Oh, have you seen A and C ? " " No." " Well lead on 500 yards, and to the right, and you'll get your trench." We were flanking on the right side, and the attacking companies were not up till dawn, 5.30.

At six o'clock, just as a pale yellow and blue, or what poets call saffron, was showing in the east, there is a dead silence, and at three minutes past there is a sudden crash as our guns open ; 2,000 yards away is the enemy line, and we watch the bursts, half shrapnel, half H.E., and one in six of the latter smoke. It is not our barrage, and it lasts forty-five minutes, one continual war crash and bang. It did a lot of damage, as some hours afterward, when we went over we found a lot of dead and smashed Boches in the trench. At 7.45 we got word to go over in three minutes and wait 1,000 yards in front of our barrage, so, lighting a cigarette, off we went, and on till we got down to the Boche trench, less some twenty men, two only killed ; and then we did have a great time. We were on one side of a valley 500 yards wide, and on the other side the Boche was still moving, so eight Lewis guns and two machine-guns opened fire, and for an hour and a half bowled them over like rabbits. We were being avenged for our machine-gun casualties. Then a patrol pushed out with gunners behind us looking over their sights ready to wither up any resistance, but nobody was left to bar progress, so we let others come through us and settled down in shell-holes and ruts, to make tea and get a scrap of rest.

As for the Company Commander, he goes to Battalion H.Q., makes his progress reports, casualties, etc, also makes all arrangements as to rations and water, gets back at eleven, hungry and tired, and meets a message that he is to alter his posts to conform to another Company and Battalion, and so on until at 2.30 everybody is at peace except the ration party, and at three I get to sleep. . . .

PRIVATE A. J. WOOD
Australian Imperial Force

Enlisted in Australia, February, 1917. Killed in action, France, 6 November, 1917, at the age of 34.

[To His Wife. *Found in his wallet after his death*]

[France,
1917]

My dearest and best of Wives.

If ever you read this letter I shall have been laid to rest in a land that is enriched by the blood of Australia's noblest sons.

Grieve not for me, my darling, but rather for our homeland. When one knows all that our Boys have gone through, the conditions that they are living under, and the unconquerable spirit which enables them to make light of their trials and dangerous undertakings, one's heart aches to think of the inestimable loss to the Nation of all those precious lives.

I feel privileged to share their sorrows and loss, and if need be to die with them.

If we only had a few millions to throw in now, what numbers of lives would be saved.

God grant that Britain and her Allies may emerge victorious & strong to protect her Dominions through centuries of Peace and prosperity.

Heaven strengthen you dear, A——, to bear your trials and watch over your earthly needs and our children. May a just and kind Providence prosper you and provide for your earthly needs.

Though we are thousands of miles apart I am always with you in spirit and if the spirits of the departed have any influence over the lives of the living, mine will surely watch over you and our children and work for your good.

Good-bye my true wife. The long and sad good-bye. Kiss our babies for me and tell them my last thoughts were of you and them. May they all be spared to live long, honourable and peaceful lives under the good old Flag that so many have died to uphold nor deem the sacrifice too great.

May our boys and girls grow up to be a comfort to you, dear, and may we all meet again in that land beyond where there is no war or strife.

Good-bye, my sweet and true. My sweet sad love. With the love that is stronger than death. And God bless Australia and keep her for our children's children.

Your soldier husband
A. J. W.

———

SECOND LIEUTENANT EDWIN LEONARD WOOD

Royal Scots Fusiliers

Cartographer and naturalist. Killed in action, Flanders, 27 September, 1917, at the age of 25.

[TO HIS BROTHER. *He was killed six days later*]

B.E.F.

Dear Bert, *21.9.17*

Very many thanks for your letter, which has reached me in good time, at a place you have not long left. I guess you will be knowing more about us by the time you read this.

Of course I'm sorry you are coming back, tho' I've no great fears for you Bert—it is chiefly the anxiety of oor ain folk ! I can quite comprehend your feelings about lost chums—who has not the same ?—and for us, this is *the* country. However, while Johnnie is standing up, it is up to us to hit him hard. We can but trust that our folk will stand the strain.

Jolly square of you to reassure me about D—— and P——. Although it was not so much their actual wants I meant (I knew that would be looked to), I am the happier that you mentioned it. What just concerned me was the crash, if it comes. Rather I want you to lend them some of the far sighted philosophy that must be yours by now— a little insight into the beyond to tide them over the loss. I've always striven hard to keep them all up to a high mark of cheerfulness—I have never been happier myself, and I hate that my state should be better than theirs. So I leave it with you.

We are really having " some " time out here. Every man is just ready for the scrap—we play soccer, eat, drink and sing our songs to death—living healthily every moment, drinking greedily each drop of sunlight. In experience like yours—of continual offensive work—you will hardly realize the fascination of working up to a big show. The strange paradox is that the human temperament increases in depth and quality as the show approaches.

Don't be too serious about me, laddie. When I am an old hand, a hardened killer of men like my brother, you will think less of my little affairs. This is the first, and it will be the best. It is an inspiration to be under the old church spire that you know so well—or ought to since you mention the town in your letter. It is indeed a privilege to live in these places, to mix with the men whose eyes—for all their smiling carelessness, despite all the wild desire to appear what they are not, pessimists, thoughtless of the cause they represent—are set only on the one goal, which is a clean finish to a bitter game. I like to be one amongst the rough masons of the world's future, and my prayer is but one,

> *Gift this guerdon and grant this grace,*
> *That I bid good e'en—*
> *The sword in my hand and my foot to the race,*
> *The wind in my teeth and the rain in my face. . . .*

It is an old song, and gets near to the heart of a sportsman. There is difficulty in writing one's mind, even to a wife who is a right chum, or a brother who is a sterling friend ; somehow the more actively I live, the more clumsily and unconfessedly I write. One day we'll tell the tale together —what do you say to a log fire in a wee cottage in the lee of a Theddlethorpe dune, after a wild night's " flighting," and the snow still on our shoulders and caps ? Ye gods, Bert, we must have a long vacation longshore when this is over. I can hear the wild duck now—remember the flight you missed ? Or the godwit you shot ?

Cheerio laddie. I'm getting off the mark. Write when you get out, and we are sure to meet—your people will tell you where we are. . . .

Yours,
TED

SECOND LIEUTENANT ARTHUR
CONWAY YOUNG
Royal Irish Fusiliers

Educated City of London School. On staff of *Japan Chronicle*, Kobe, Japan. Killed in action, Flanders, 16 August, 1917, at the age of 27.

R. Irish Fusiliers.
B.E.F.

[TO HIS AUNT]   France.
My dear Auntie Maggie.   *Sept. 16, 1916*

As I told you in my last brief note, I took part in the battle of Ginchy, and I promised you when I had time that I would give you an account of it. . . .

Try and picture in your mind's eye a fairly broad valley running more or less north and south. You must imagine that the Germans are somewhere over the further, or eastern, crest. You are looking across the valley from the ruins of Guillemont. About half-right the further crest rises to a height crowned by a mass of wreckage and tangled trees. Well, that is Ginchy. . . . It was like being near the foot of Parliament Hill, with the village on top. Our right flank was down near the bottom of the valley ; our left extended up to the higher ground towards the ruins of Waterlot Farm. The trench was very shallow in places, where it had been knocked in by shell-fire. I had chosen it as the only one suitable in the neighbourhood, but it was a horrible place. British dead were lying round everywhere. Our men had to give up digging in some places, because they came down to bodies which were lying in the bottom, having been buried there when the parapet blew in. The smell turned us sick. At last, in desperation I went out to look for another trench, for I felt sure the Germans must have the range of the trench we were in, and that they would give us hell when dawn broke. To my joy I found that a very deep trench some distance back had just been vacated by another regiment, so we went in there.

The night was bitterly cold. I have felt hunger and thirst and fatigue out here to a degree I have never experienced them before, but those are torments I can endure far better than I thought I could. But the cold—my word ! it is dreadful. . . .

However, dawn broke at last. It was very misty. All night we had been trying to get into touch with the unit on our left, but without success. So the Captain sent me out with an orderly to see whether I could manage it. We two stumbled along, but the mist was so dense we could see nothing. We came to one trench after another, but not a living thing could we see—nothing but dead, British and German, some of them mangled beyond recognition. Bombs and rifles and equipment were lying all over the place, with here and there a greatcoat, khaki or grey according to the

310

nationality of their one-time owners, but of living beings we could see no sign whatsoever. There was a *horrible* stench in places which nearly turned our stomachs. To make matters more wretched we could not make sure of our direction, and were afraid of running into a German patrol, or even into a German trench, for such accidents are by no means uncommon in this region. However, we managed to find our way back, and report that up to such and such a point on the map (approximately) there was no-one on our left. The Captain was not content with this, so I went out again, this time with another officer. Having a compass on this second occasion I felt far more self-confidence, and to our mutual satisfaction we discovered that the unit on our left was the right flank of an English Division. Captain Edwards was very bucked when we brought back this information. As the mist continued for some time afterwards we were able to light fires and make breakfast. . . .

It was about 4 o'clock in the afternoon when we first learned that we should have to take part in the attack on Ginchy. Now, Auntie, you expect me to say at this point in my narrative that my heart leapt with joy at the news and that the men gave three rousing cheers, for that's the sort of thing you read in the papers. Well, even at the risk of making you feel ashamed of me, I will tell you the whole truth and confess that my heart sank within me when I heard the news. I had been over the top once already that week, and knew what it was to see men dropping dead all round me, to see men blown to bits, to see men writhing in pain, to see men running round and round gibbering, raving mad. Can you wonder therefore that I felt a sort of sickening dread of the horrors which I knew we should all have to go through? Frankly, I was dismayed. But, Auntie, I know you will think the more of me when I tell you, on my conscience, that I went into action that afternoon, not with any hope of glory, but with the absolute certainty of death. How the others felt I don't exactly know, but I don't think I am far wrong when I say that their emotions were not far different from mine. You read no end of twaddle in the papers at home about the spirit in which men go into action. You might almost think they revelled in the horror and the agony of it all. I saw one account of the battle of Ginchy, in which the correspondent spoke of the men of a certain regiment in reserve as almost crying with rage because they couldn't take part in the show. All I can say is that I should like to see such super-human beings. It is rubbish like this which makes thousands of people in England think that war is great sport. As a famous Yankee general said, " War is Hell," and you have only got to be in the Somme one single day to know it. . . .

But to get on with the story. We were ordered to move up into the front line to reinforce the Royal Irish Rifles. . . . The bombardment was now intense. Our shells bursting in the village of Ginchy made it belch forth smoke like a volcano. The Hun shells were bursting on the slope in front of us. The noise was deafening. I turned to my servant O'Brien, who has always been a cheery, optimistic soul, and said, " Well, O'Brien, how do you think we'll fare ? " and his answer was for once not encouraging. " We'll never come out alive sir ! " was his answer. Happily we both came out alive, but I never thought we should at the time.

It was at this moment, just as we were debouching on to the scragged front line of trench, that we beheld a scene which stirred and thrilled us to the bottommost depths of our souls. The great charge of the Irish Division had begun, and we had come up in the nick of time. . . . Between the outer fringe of Ginchy and the front line of our own trenches is No Man's Land—a wilderness of pits, so close together that you could ride astradle the partitions between any two of them. As you look half-right, obliquely along No Man's Land, you behold a great host of yellow-coated men rise out of the earth and surge forward and upward in a torrent—not in extended order, as you might expect, but in one mass,—I almost said a compact mass. The only way I can describe the scene is to ask you to picture five or six columns of men marching uphill in fours, with about a hundred yards between each column. Now conceive those columns being gradually disorganised, some men going off to the right, and others to the left to avoid shell-holes. There seems to be no end to them. Just when you think the flood is subsiding, another wave comes surging up the beach towards Ginchy. We joined in on the left. There was no time for us any more than the others to get into extended order. We formed another stream, converging on the others at the summit. By this time we were all wildly excited. Our shouts and yells alone must have struck terror into the Huns, who were firing their machine-guns down the slope. But there was no wavering in the Irish host. We couldn't run. We advanced at a steady walking pace, stumbling here and there, but going ever onward and upward. That numbing dread had now left me completely. Like the others, I was intoxicated with the glory of it all. I can remember shouting and bawling to the men of my platoon, who were only too eager to go on. The Hun barrage had now been opened in earnest, and shells were falling here, there, and everywhere in No Man's Land. They were mostly dropping on our right, but they were coming nearer and nearer, as if a screen were being drawn across our front. I knew that it was a case of " now or never " and stumbled on feverishly. We managed to get through the barrage in the nick of time, for it closed behind us, and after that we had no shells to fear in front of us. I mention, merely as an interesting fact in psychology, how in a crisis of this sort one's mental faculties are sharpened. Instinct told us, when the shells were coming gradually closer, to crouch down in the holes until they had passed. Acquired knowledge on the other hand—the knowledge instilled into one by lectures and books (of which I have only read one, namely Haking's " *Company Training* ")— told us that it was safer in the long run to push ahead before the enemy got our range, and it was acquired knowledge that won. And here's another observation I should like to make by the way. . . . The din must have been deafening (I learned afterwards that it could be heard miles away)

313

yet I have only a confused remembrance of it. Shells which at any other time would have scared me out of my wits, I never so much as heard and not even when they were bursting quite close to me. One landed in the midst of a bunch of men about seventy yards away on my right : I have a most vivid recollection of seeing a tremendous burst of clay and earth go shooting up into the air—yes, and even parts of human bodies—and that when the smoke cleared away there was nothing left. I shall never forget that horrifying spectacle as long as I live, but I shall remember it as a sight only, for I can associate no sound with it. . . .

We were now well up to the Boche. We had to clamber over all manner of obstacles—fallen trees, beams, great mounds of brick and rubble,—in fact over the ruins of Ginchy. It seems like a nightmare to me now. I remember seeing comrades falling round me. My sense of hearing returned to me for I became conscious of a new sound ; namely the continuous crackling of rifle-fire. I remember men lying in shell-holes holding out their arms and beseeching water. I remember men crawling about and coughing up blood, as they searched round for some place in which they could shelter until help could reach them. By this time all units were mixed up : but they were all Irishmen. They were cheering and cheering and cheering like mad. It was Hell let loose. There was a machine-gun playing on us near-by, and we all made for it. At this moment we caught our first sight of the Huns. They were in a trench of sorts, which ran in and out among the ruins. Some of them had their hands up. Others were kneeling and holding their arms out to us. Still others were running up and down the trench distractedly as if they didn't know which way to go, but as we got closer they went down on their knees too. To the everlasting good name of the Irish soldiery, not one of these Huns, some of whom had been engaged in slaughtering our men up to the very last moment, was killed. I did not see a single instance of a prisoner being shot or bayoneted. When you remember that our men were now worked up to a frenzy of excitement, this

314

crowning act of mercy to their foes is surely to their eternal credit. They could feel pity even in their rage.

By this time we had penetrated the German front line, and were on the flat ground where the village once stood surrounded by a wood of fairly high trees. . . . As I was clambering out of the front trench, I felt a sudden stab in my right thigh : I thought I had got a " Blighty " but found it was only a graze from a bullet, and so went on. . . . McGarry and I were the only two officers left in the company, so it was up to us to take charge. We could see the Huns hopping over the distant ridge like rabbits, and we had some difficulty in preventing our men from chasing them, for we had orders not to go too far. We got them—Irish Fusiliers, Inniskillings and Dublins—to dig in by linking up the shell-craters, and though the men were tired (some wanted to smoke and others to make tea) they worked with a will, and before long we had got a pretty decent trench outlined.

While we were at work, a number of Huns who had stopped behind and were hiding in shell-holes commenced a bombing attack on our right. But they did not keep it up for long, for they hoisted a white flag (a handkerchief tied to a rifle) as a sign of surrender. I should think we must have made about twenty prisoners. They were very frightened. Some of them bunked into a sunken road or cutting which ran straight out from the wood in an easterly direction, and huddled together with hands upraised. They began to empty their pockets and hand out souvenirs—watches, compasses, cigars, penknives —to their captors, and even wanted to shake hands with us ! There was no other officer about at the moment so I had to find an escort to take the prisoners down. Among the prisoners was a tall, distinguished looking man, and I asked him in my broken German whether he was an officer " *Ja ! Mein Herr !* " was the answer I got. " *Sprechen Sie English ?* " " *Ja !* " " Good," I said, thankful that I didn't have to rack my brains for any more German words. " Please tell your men that no harm will come to them if they follow you quietly." He turned round and addressed his men, who seemed to be very gratified that we were not going to kill them. I must say the officer behaved with real soldierly dignity, and not to be outdone in politeness by a Hun I treated him with the same respect that he showed me. I gave him an escort for himself and told off three or four men for the remainder. I could not but rather admire his bearing, for he did not show anything like the terror that his men did. I heard afterwards that when Captain O'Donnell's company rushed a trench more to our right, round the corner of the wood, a German officer surrendered in great style. He stood to attention, gave a clinking salute, and said in perfect English, " Sir, myself, this other officer, and ten men are your prisoners." Captain O'Donnell said " Right you are, old chap ! " and they shook hands, the prisoners being led away immediately. . . .

There were a great many German dead and wounded in the sunken road. One of them was an officer. He was lying at the entrance to the dug-out. He was waving his arms about. I went over and spoke to him. He could talk a little English. All he could say was, " Comrade, I die, I die." I asked him where he was hit and he said in the stomach. It was impossible to move him, for our stretcher bearers had not yet come up, so I got my servant to look for an overcoat to throw over him, as he was suffering terribly from the cold. Whether or not he survived the night I don't know. . . .

After the counter-attack had subsided I was ordered to take my men and join up with the rest of the battalion on our right. There we spent the night in a trench. We must have been facing south. It was a miserable night we passed, for we were all very cold and thirsty. We had to keep digging. When morning broke it was very misty. We expected to be relieved at 2 in the morning, but the relief did not come till noon. Never shall I forget these hours of suspense. We were all hungry. The only food we could get was Hun black bread, which we picked up all over the place ; also Hun tinned sausages and bully beef. We had to lift up some of the dead to get at these things. Some of them had water-bottles full of cold coffee, which we drank. We all craved a smoke. Fortunately, the Hun haversacks were pretty well stocked with cigarettes and cigars. I got a handful of cigars off a dead Boche, and smoked them all morning. Also a tin of cigarettes. His chocolates also came in handy. Poor devil, he must have been a cheery soul when living, for he had a photograph of himself in his pocket, in a group with his wife and two children, and the picture made him look a jolly old sport, and here he was, dead, with both legs missing ! The trench (between ours and the wood) was stacked with dead. It was full of debris—bombs, shovels, and whatnot—and torn books, magazines, and newspapers. I came across a copy of Schiller's " *Wallenstein*."

Hearing moans as I went along the trench, I looked into a shelter or hole dug in the side and found a young German. He could not move as his legs were broken. He begged me to get him some water, so I hunted round and found a flask of cold coffee which I held to his lips. He kept saying " *Danke, Kamerad, danke, danke*." However much you may hate the Huns when you are fighting them, you can only feel pity for them when you see them lying helpless and wounded on the ground. I saw this man afterwards on his way to the dressing station. About ten yards further on was another German, minus a leg. He too craved water, but I could get him none, though I looked everywhere. Our men were very good to the German wounded. An Irishman's heart melts very soon. In fact, kindness and compassion for the wounded, our own and the enemy's, is about the only decent thing I have seen in war. It is not at all uncommon to see a British and German soldier side by side in the same shell-hole nursing each other as best they can and placidly smoking cigarettes. A poor wounded Hun who hobbled into our trench in the morning, his face badly mutilated by a bullet,—he whimpered and moaned piteously as a child—was bound up by one of our officers, who took off his coat and set to work in earnest. Another Boche, whose legs were hit, was carried in by our men and put into a shell hole for safety, where he lay awaiting the stretcher-bearers when we left. It is with a sense of pride that I can write this of our soldiers. . . .

Well now, that's the story of the great Irish charge at Ginchy so far as I can tell it. I suppose by this time the great event has been forgotten by the English public. But it will never be forgotten by those who took part in it, for it is an event we shall remember with pride to the end of our days. Need I tell you how proud we officers and men are of the Royal Irish Fusiliers, who played as big a part as any in the storming of that stronghold, and who went into action shouting their old battle cry of " Faugh-a-Ballagh," which means " Clear the way ! "

Will write again soon.

With fondest love,

Ever your affectionate nephew,

ARTHUR